CHINESE WHISPERS

CHINESE WHISPERS

WHY EVERTHING YOU'VE HEARD ABOUT CHINA IS WRONG

BEN CHU

Weidenfeld & Nicolson
LONDON

First published in Great Britain in 2013
by Weidenfeld & Nicolson

1 3 5 7 9 10 8 6 4 2

A CIP catalogue record for this book
is available from the British Library.

ISBN (hardback): 978 0 2978 6844 6
ISBN (paperback): 978 0 2978 6845 3

Typeset by Input Data Services Ltd, Bridgwater, Somerset

Printed and bound by CPI Group (UK) Ltd, Croydon, CR0 4YY

Weidenfeld & Nicolson
The Orion Publishing Group Ltd
Orion House
5 Upper Saint Martin's Lane
London, WC2H 9EA
www.orionbooks.co.uk

The Orion Publishing Group's policy is to use papers that
are natural, renewable and recyclable products and
made from wood grown in sustainable forests. The logging
and manufacturing processes are expected to conform to the
environmental regulations of the country of origin.

To my family in China

CONTENTS

Acknowledgements ix

Introduction 1

WHISPER ONE
China has an ancient and fixed culture 19

WHISPER TWO
The Chinese are irredeemably racist 52

WHISPER THREE
The Chinese don't want freedom 76

WHISPER FOUR
China has the world's finest education system 105

WHISPER FIVE
The Chinese live to work 130

WHISPER SIX
The Chinese have re-invented capitalism 166

WHISPER SEVEN
China will rule the world 193

Conclusion 223

Notes 250

Index 269

ACKNOWLEDGEMENTS

Like most books this one has been a long labour and a formidable number of people have provided gracious assistance along the journey. They are too numerous to list, but I would like to single out Sonny Leong, a tireless champion of the Chinese community's engagement in political life in Britain, for inspiring me to write this book. My thanks also to the *Independent*, particularly my former editor Chris Blackhurst and proprietor Evgeny Lebedev, for generously allowing me a sabbatical from the day job in which to complete the work. I owe a major debt to my agent at HHB agency, Elly James, for her tremendous energy in the early stages of the project, and also to Celia Hayley, for continuing in the same enthusiastic vein.

Extra special thanks are due to Bea Hemming, my editor at Weidenfeld & Nicolson, for her stirring encouragement from the very inception of this project, her instinctive understanding of what the book was trying to say and for her wise technical suggestions on how to present the material. My gratitude also goes to my good friend Sean O'Grady for reading the manuscript and providing useful suggestions and corrections. Any mistakes in these pages, however, are mine alone.

Profound thanks to my wife Hattie for her patience while I shut myself up for interminable periods in the study and, of course, for her loving support through the moments of doubt. And, finally, I would like to convey my gratitude to my family in China who made this book possible through their hospitality and humbling generosity with their time. This book is dedicated to them and their future.

INTRODUCTION

The tiny hamlet of Jung Wo Lei in Guangdong province is, in many respects, a typical slice of rural China. The working-age villagers have all departed to find jobs in the burgeoning cities nearer the coast, leaving the very old to look after the very young. Grandmothers sit on small plastic chairs, gossiping and dandling babies on their knees. Every other house is boarded up or tumbling down. The road leading to the village is a yellow dirt track that winds between vegetable plots. Senescent farmers scratch a living from the land with the same rough tools used by their ancestors in imperial times. A weary man lugs a bamboo pole over his shoulder, with two giant baskets overflowing with freshly harvested sweet potatoes suspended from each end.

At first glance the village looks a timeless plot, a speck of earth where things have never really changed. But in China it often pays to delve a little more deeply. If you were ever to explore Jung Wo Lei you might discover a surprise that confounds your expectations.

Picture a Chinese house. Perhaps it's a traditional one with curved sloping roofs, green tiles and overhanging eaves – the pagoda style familiar from countless Oriental paintings. Or perhaps it is a modern, ugly, breezeblock mansion. Yet here, on the edge of Jung Wo Lei, next to a grove of turquoise bamboo, stands an elegant classical European-style villa with impressive arched windows and a flat, balustraded, roof. Were it not for the bars on the windows, the structure would not look terribly out of place in the Italian countryside. This architectural curiosity is the house that my great-great-grandfather built.

A century and a half ago, when the dam of the rotten old Qing Dynasty crumbled, this region of Guangdong was the source of a mighty flood of Chinese emigration. It was the birthing ground of many of the Chinese labourers who built the American railroads, and fed the boilers of the steamers of the British merchant navy.

Through the door of Guangdong Chinese people flowed to South East Asia, to the Americas, to Europe. For a hundred years the language that was heard spoken in Chinatowns from Manila to Limehouse to San Francisco was not mellifluous Mandarin, but the yakety yak[1] of the local Cantonese dialect. My grandmother's grandfather, Zau Gasam, was among those peasants who set out to seek his fortune in the turbulent denouement of the Qing.

Family history is unclear as to whether Gasam, whose photo shows a kindly looking man with twinkling eyes, went to America or Canada, or what sort of businesses he did when he got there. But by the time he returned to China, not long after the 1911 republican revolution that ended the reign of the emperors, the former penniless emigrant was a wealthy man. Gasam had achieved every Chinese migrant's dream of coming home 'robed in embroidered silk'. Gasam used his capital to set up a shoe factory in the nearby city of Kaiping, helping to feed the growing appetite for Western clothes. By rural standards, the family was prosperous. Gasam wanted a house that advertised his status and cosmopolitanism, so he got hold of designs for balusters and classical reliefs, and in the 1920s commissioned a local builder to throw up this European-style residence in the Guangdong countryside.

In China, however, prosperity is often transient. 'Wealth does not last three generations' goes the old saw, and so it was with my family. Gasam's son, Chernggong, my great-grandfather, was a wastrel who became hooked on opium. Soon after the factory passed into his hands after Gasam's death the business went bust. In 1939 Chernggong died of an overdose. The drug that the British Empire had violently pushed on China in the previous century's Opium Wars had helped to ruin the family. The Japanese occupation of Guangdong and the chaos of the civil war between the nationalist government of Chiang Kai Shek and Mao Zedong's Communist insurgents completed the immiseration.

My grandmother, Chernggong's daughter, and my grandfather (an amateur musician from the neighbouring village) saw the writing on the wall. Just like Gasam two generations before, they wanted out of Jung Wo Lei. Eager to follow the example of a relative who was making money running a laundry in England before them, they set their sights on emigration. With their two young sons, the second of whom was my father, the family packed up their belongings and left China, never to return.

The Chu family knew little about the *Ying Gwok* – England – except that it meant 'brave country' and held out the promise of an existence less beset by poverty and insecurity. They settled in Sheffield in 1960 where my grandfather opened his own laundry. Like so many migrant families, they worked fiercely hard, scrubbing shirts, starching collars and ironing sheets in order to fill the table with food and to create a better life.

Amid the hills of Yorkshire my father met, fell in love with and eventually married my white British mother. In time, the couple moved across the Pennines to Manchester, where, in 1979, I was born. With my older sister and younger brother, we were a half Chinese and half British family: an amalgam of the Orient and the Occident. It was Church of England primary school during the week, Chinese school at weekends; rice on Saturday, roast beef on Sundays.

In 1984 the Orient called my father back. He was posted to Hong Kong by his employer, the engineering conglomerate GEC. In those days the territory, off the southern coast of China, was still under the control of the British crown. But not for much longer. That same year Margaret Thatcher had signed an agreement with the Chinese leader Deng Xiaoping to transfer control of Hong Kong back to Beijing in 1997. So, as the clock of the British Empire ticked down, we lived there in languorous expat comfort for two years, enjoying a life that revolved around country clubs, international schools and holidays in the various luxury resorts of the South China Sea. It was during that balmy time that I first travelled into mainland China to meet the rest of my father's family – the ones who had stayed behind.

They had all left Jung Wo Lei and moved to the province's capital, Guangzhou (once known as Canton). The train journey from Hong Kong to Guangzhou only took a few hours, but in that short journey we seemed to travel back decades in time. The exuberant neon glamour of 1980s Hong Kong melted into a drab, concrete austerity. Roads that had been full of Toyotas and Porsches were now replete with thousands of bicycles. My grandmother's brother, my great-uncle, had a job, working for the Guangzhou government as a cartographer. His wife was employed in a shaving-brush factory. They were comfortable by the standards of most Chinese at that time. And yet their entire family of six people, including my frail ninety-year-old great-grandmother, lived in just three bare rooms of a dank and crumbling housing block. There was no television, no oven, no washing machine. The toilet was shared with a dozen other families. Charcoal bricks fuelled a small stove from which my great-aunt miraculously managed to produce a spread of Cantonese culinary specialities.

I was puzzled at the fact that there seemed to be no beds in the cramped apartment. Where on earth did everyone sleep when we returned to our hotel? Many years later my cousin told me that, at night, the family would pull out a collection of wooden boards from an alcove. With these they would literally make their own beds. I was just five years old but I remember thinking during the visit how few possessions my relatives had compared with us. We were looking at the life that my father probably would have had if he had remained in China.

Since then, of course, there has been a convergence. I've seen how the lives of my relatives in China have been transformed over the years as the country has progressively liberalized its economy. In 1990 the old residential block was demolished to make way for a gleaming new office tower and my great-uncle's family used their savings to buy a new apartment on the other side of town. Their new residence is four times larger and even has a pleasant balcony where my great-uncle grows orchids. The stove runs on gas and the beds do not have to be assembled at night. The apartment has its own bathroom.

The family is not only wealthier; they also have economic self-determination. My cousins have set up their own businesses, one in public relations and one in construction. Other freedoms have materialized, not least the right to travel abroad. My cousin's daughter now lives in New York, where she is an assistant to a Chinese contemporary artist. None of these things would have been possible thirty years ago when I first visited. Life is very far from perfect, but my family in Guangzhou is immeasurably better off than they were in 1984. So if that's what China's economic resurgence means for them, what does it mean for the rest of us?

'CHINESENESS'

After I graduated from university in 2000, I went to work at the *Independent* newspaper in London where, after a few years of learning the ropes, I was allowed to write leading articles for the opinion pages. These are the unsigned columns expressing the view of the paper on the salient issues of the day. Leader writing is an intellectually rewarding and stimulating job that forces you to read widely. Because you might need to rattle out some words on any subject at the drop of a hat it's essential to keep fully abreast of current affairs. And in the first decade of the new Millennium that inevitably included developments in China, the world's fastest-growing economy.

China's boom, the most spectacular in history, has prompted countless news stories, opinion articles, books and documentaries, in recent years. The Global Language Monitor, a media analysis firm, found that 'the rise of China' was the most closely followed topic in newspapers, blogs and social media through the noughties.[2] China's economic boom has inspired even more coverage than the September 11 terror attacks and the invasion of Iraq.

Many of these stories purport to explain what the country is, who the Chinese people are and why it all matters. Among this welter of commentary I noticed some themes kept appearing: an ancient culture, a unified race, a strong work ethic, a population who care more about economic growth than personal freedom, a people obsessed with education. And then there was the most eye-catching observation of them all, and perhaps the unifying, underlying theme: that the Chinese people are destined one day to 'rule the world'.

This sense of being overtaken by China is now constantly promoted in the media. In 2012 the BBC aired a documentary about an entrepreneur from Merseyside attempting to move his cushion factory in China back to the UK. The dramatic tension came from the question of whether the English manual workers would prove the equal of those in China in terms of reliability and cost. 'This is the story of one small town in the North of England,' asserted the narrator, 'and its attempt to take on the economic might of one of the fastest-growing nations in the world.'

The BBC's most feared inquisitor, Jeremy Paxman, took a trip to China in 2012 where he marvelled at the native work ethic. 'The whole economy floats on a sea of migrant workers willing to go any- where for a day's pay,' he observed. 'You can hear them hammering on the construction sites and see them clambering across the half- built highway towers from dawn until long after dusk.' Tellingly, Paxman's thoughts also turned to home. 'It is more than enough to see off soft, Western welfare states which have sold their future for the sake of cheaper televisions and trainers,' he thundered.[3]

The message is reinforced through our political discourse. We're told that we are engaged in a 'global race' with developing coun- tries, China pre-eminent among them. It's a race that we seem to be losing, with commercial bosses hailing China as a more business- friendly environment than our own over-regulated economies. Those sky-high Chinese GDP growth rates that we constantly hear about – notwithstanding the odd wobble – seem to support that picture. The forecasters now confidently predict that China will overtake America as the world's largest economy before the decade is out.

This competition does not only relate to economics. It involves culture and attitudes too. In 2011 Chinese-American academic Amy Chua published a memoir titled *Battle Hymn of the Tiger Mother* in which she chronicled her obsessive approach to parenting, describ- ing it as typically Chinese. This spawned an earnest debate about whether it was cruel or kind to be a Tiger Mother, and, by extension I suppose, Chinese. What no one really doubted was the effective- ness of this kind of parenting in producing high-achieving children. 'The brutal truth [is] that we're being out-educated', argues the American Secretary of Education Arne Duncan.[4]

This is having an impact. I've noticed a growing angst about China, perhaps we should call it Changst, injecting itself into ordin- ary conversations. I recently spoke with a neighbour in London – a rather posh, middle-aged, interior designer – about what a dreadful impact the downturn was having on the young. It was a sympathetic conversation. Then, out of nowhere, she said: 'And meanwhile the Chinese look on, smiling!' She seemed to imagine that the economic mess was some kind of plot devised in Beijing, or perhaps that the Chinese were revelling in our misfortune.

Such reactions appeared to spring from a primal place. A friend of mine, a rational and intelligent person, once quietly told me that he would never visit China. Why ever not, I asked. 'Because I had a nightmare that I went there and the people just swallowed me up.' Not everyone is afflicted by such paranoia, but a fear of the country does loom increasingly large. During conversations about the future – almost any conversation – it is now common for someone to lower their voice as they introduce an awesome and mysterious new influence on the world: 'China'.

And there is some very dark stuff too. In 2010 a two-year-old Chinese girl called Wang Yue was crushed in the city of Foshan, not far from where my family live in Guangzhou, in a backstreet hit-and-run accident. But it was what happened next that was truly horrifying. Closed-circuit television footage showed that no fewer than eighteen people passed the toddler, who was bleeding at the side of the road, without offering help. In the end it was an elderly street sweeper who played the Good Samaritan and came to the child's assistance. By then it was too late. The little girl died of her injuries in hospital. The sad tale became global news. Newspapers and broadcasters from Australia to America picked it up. One journalist from the mass market *Daily Mail* in Britain wondered whether the behaviour of the Chinese passers-by was a 'cultural trait', recalling that Victorian missionaries in the nineteenth century had noted how the Chinese 'lacked moral awareness'.[5]

At first I brushed this off as stereotyping nonsense. Yet what was striking about the horrible story of Wang Yue's death was that many Chinese commentators condemned Chinese culture in similar terms to that *Daily Mail* journalist, arguing that the fate of the poor child was a symptom of a broader social sickness, a reflection of a society that has lost its moral values. Perhaps the stereotype of the 'amoral' Chinese wasn't such a stereotype after all.

Could other aspects of the conventional portrait of the Chinese have substance too? I've been surprised by some of the things my Chinese family and friends have said to me in passing over the years. I remember my father, a mild-mannered man not given to nationalist tub-thumping, telling me that the Chinese people would be an unstoppable force once they got their act together. Recalling that reminds me of those pundits who today herald 'the Chinese century'. There's an ambivalence about personal freedom too. An acquaintance in Guangzhou, an impeccably socially progressive career girl, told me that democracy was probably not appropriate for the Chinese people. 'So many are not educated,' she said. 'You need the government to control them.' Chinese attitudes to race can make you squirm too. I was once told, perfectly pleasantly, by a Chinese friend that I was merely a 'half-blood' because of my British mother. Other elements of the conventional portrait find support among Chinese people too. The most high-profile Chinese Briton today, the television presenter Gok Wan, was impressed by the 'remarkable work ethic' of the Chinese during a recent trip back to his motherland.[6]

In 2004 Tim Clissold, a British businessman who worked for many years in China, produced an enthralling book about his experiences titled *Mr China*. In those pages he wrote of something called 'Chineseness'. Apparently this is 'innate, something that you are born with'. He added: 'It can't be changed by something as ephemeral as a passport or a mere lifetime spent abroad.'[7] That set me thinking. What exactly is this Chineseness? Do I have it? Does my family have it? Is it everything we think it is? This book is, in part, my attempt to reach an answer.

'GREAT IMMORALITY'

According to some historical accounts Chineseness is a rather unpleasant thing. One of the most persistent allegations made against the Chinese by outsiders has been that they are irrepressibly deceitful. The nineteenth-century German philosopher Hegel described the people's 'great immorality'. He wrote that 'friend deceives friend, and no one resents the attempt at deception on the part of another, if the deceit has not succeeded in its object, or comes to the knowledge of the person sought to be defrauded'.[8]

The idea that you can't trust the Chinese was cemented over the centuries. A Spanish historian based in the Philippines, Luis Tejero, described in 1857 how 'they possess the art of disguising their feelings and desire for revenge, hiding all appearances of humility so well that one believes them to be insensitive to all types of outrage'.[9]

The Chinese residing abroad were portrayed in a similarly

unflattering light. In 1870 an American poet, Bret Harte, published 'Plain Language from Truthful James', the tale of a Chinese card shark called Ah Sin who bested two white gamblers at their own crooked game. Harte intended the verses to be a satire on the swelling anti-Chinese sentiment of his native land, but the poem was popular precisely because it articulated the prevalent prejudice of the time: 'For ways that are dark and for tricks that are vain, the heathen Chinee is peculiar.' By the twentieth century Chinatowns in the West were commonly seen as sinks of immorality, nests of vice full of opium dens and the lowest form of criminals.

The Chinese were not just deceitful, but vicious too. The English pulp novelist Sax Rohmer put sadistic infanticide at the heart of his Edwardian fictional super-villain Fu Manchu and, indeed, of all Chinese people. The thin-moustachioed Fu was an 'inhuman being who knew no mercy … whose very genius was inspired by the cool, calculated cruelty of his race, of that race which to this day disposes of hundreds, nay! thousands, of its unwanted girl-children by the simple measure of throwing them down a well specially designated to the purpose.'[10]

It wasn't, apparently, just killing babies that reflected the innate cruelty of the Chinese. The British philosopher Bertrand Russell travelled to China in 1920 and noted their amusement at the plight of tortured animals, relating how 'if a dog is run over by an automobile and seriously hurt, nine out of ten passers-by will stop to laugh at the poor brute's howls'. According to Russell: 'The spectacle of suffering does not of itself rouse any sympathetic pain in the average Chinaman; in fact, he seems to find it mildly agreeable.'[11]

Despite the amusement they seem to take in the pain of creatures, some outsiders doubt whether the Chinese truly find anything funny at all. In the late 1980s the American writer Paul Theroux spent a year travelling by train around China and, by his own estimation, became something of an expert on the Chinese people. He claimed he was able to differentiate between the various Chinese laughs. 'There were about twenty,' Theroux concluded. 'None of them had the slightest suggestion of humour. Some were nervous, some were respectful, many were warnings. The loud honking one was a sort of Chinese anxiety attack. Another brisk titter meant something had gone badly wrong.'[12]

Others are less sure. The most common adjective we use of the Chinese is 'inscrutable'. As a weary viceroy in a Rudyard Kipling poem said: 'You will never plumb the oriental mind, and if you did, it isn't worth the toil.' Nevertheless one writer at the turn of the twentieth century gave it a go. American author Jack London tried to get inside that mind in a short story called 'The Chinago'. A Chinese coolie on Tahiti is given a twenty-year prison sentence by the French colonial authorities for a crime that he did not commit. Ah Cho, however, did not seem disturbed by such a gross miscarriage of justice. 'Twenty years were merely twenty years,' thinks Ah Cho to himself. 'By that much was his garden removed from him – that was all. He was young, and the patience of Asia was in his bones.'[13] Here was exemplified another striking characteristic of the Chinese in the eyes of outsiders. As Bertrand Russell put it: 'They think not in decades, but in centuries.'[14]

Even when the Chinese impressed Western travellers, their qualities were often denigrated. The nineteenth-century French missionary, Abbé Huc, noticed the 'incomparable tranquillity' with which the Chinese met death. This wasn't to be confused with a spiritual peace, said Huc, but rather was a manifestation of their heathen, inhuman, existence: 'The apprehensions connected with a future life, and the bitterness of separation, cannot exist for those who have never loved any one much, and who have passed their lives without thinking of God or their souls. They die indeed calmly; but irrational animals have the same advantage, and at bottom this death is really the most lamentable that can be imagined.'[15] The Chinese spiritual vacuum theme has proved a persistent one over the centuries. Writing in the 1970s, George Kennan, the American Cold War strategist, noted that the Chinese 'seemed to me to be lacking in two attributes of the Western-Christian mentality: the capacity for pity and the sense of sin'.[16]

Some of the abuse was more prosaic. The enlightenment political philosopher Montesquieu believed the heat twisted Chinese brains. 'There are climates where the impulses of nature have such force that morality has almost none.' The Chinese man who could resist the temptation to rape, he asserted, was a virtuous freak.[17]

Adam Smith, the revered eighteenth-century father of free market economics, claimed that Chinese in Canton had lower standards than Europeans when it came to what they put in their mouths: 'They are eager to fish up the nastiest garbage thrown overboard from any European ship. Any carrion, the carcase of a dead dog or cat, for example, though half putrid and stinking, is as welcome to them as the most wholesome food to the people of other countries.'[18]

'John Chinaman', a popular song with miners during the nineteenth-century California gold rush, took on the theme of revulsion at their eating habits and linked it to some other good reasons to despise the Chinese:

I thought of rats and puppies, John,
you'd eaten your last fill;
But on such slimy pot pies
I'm told you dinner still.
Yes, John, I've been deceived by you,
and all your thieving clan,
for our gold is all you're after, John,
to get it as you can.

'Rough on rats – clears out rats, mice, bedbugs, flies, and roaches. 15 cents per box' read an advert for pesticide that circulated in the US city of Boston in the 1880s. Alongside it was an image of a pig-tailed Chinese man, with a golden hat and bright red jerkin, lifting a juicy rodent to his hungry maw.

'OPPRESSED BY A MULTITUDE'

There are just so damn many of them too. Outsiders have always been fascinated with the sheer size of the Chinese population – an obsession that dates from the very first encounters. Galeote Pereira was a Portuguese soldier of fortune, imprisoned in the sixteenth century by the Ming court for smuggling. In one of the earliest European accounts of life in the Middle Kingdom, Pereira wrote how he felt 'loathsomely oppressed by the multitude of people' in the country. 'Out of a tree,' he observed, 'you shall see many times a number of children, where a man would not have thought to have found any one at all.'[19]

The Protestant missionaries of the nineteenth century were just as fixated by China's scale. A Christian periodical, aptly named *China's Millions*, expressed anguish at how much of God's work was to be done in the country. 'During the year represented by this volume [1883] more than eight millions of souls have passed from time to eternity in the Chinese Empire,' lamented the editorial. 'To how few of these millions has there been any adequate presentation of the Gospel of the grace of God!'[20]

In the twentieth century Westerners switched from selling the Chinese millions religion to peddling mammon. In 1937 Carl Crow, an American journalist in Shanghai, wrote a book called *400 Million Customers*, the title deftly chosen to give executives back in the United States wet dreams about the potential to make vast profits from the untapped China market. They are still at it, only the millions have multiplied. *Billions: Selling to the New Chinese Consumer* was the title of a 2005 book by American advertising executive Tom Doctoroff.

Even now we can't seem to make up our minds as to whether the Chinese population is an opportunity or a threat. In the Communist era a Hungarian journalist wrote *Mao Tse-tung: Emperor of the Blue Ants* with the 'swarming' insects in question being the blue-overall-wearing Chinese workers.[21] In 2010 British environmental journalist Jonathan Watts published *When a Billion Chinese Jump* in which he related a myth he remembered being told in his childhood that if all the Chinese were to jump in the air simultaneously they would knock the earth off its axis and destroy humanity. Watts used to fret about 'the possibility of being killed by people I had never seen, who didn't know I existed, and who didn't even need a gun'. Today that childhood nightmare is coming true in the form of China's industrialization, which is accelerating global warming and cooking the planet. 'Now China has jumped,' argues Watts, 'we must all rebalance our lives.'[22]

Great numbers and great peril often seem to be bedfellows. 'It makes a big difference if a fifth of humanity decides to hack you, rather than hire you,' warned the historian Niall Ferguson in his television documentary on China, referring to the supposed proliferation of Chinese cyber criminals.[23] Joel Kotkin, a writer for *Forbes*, describes the overseas Chinese as an ominous-sounding 'Sinosphere' (a club of which I may or may not be a member, depending on whether my 'half-blood' disqualifies me). Other writers casually talk of 'Greater China', an entity that they assume to include Taiwan, Hong Kong and Singapore, as well as the numerous Chinese communities across South East Asia.

What all these images have in common is that they present the Chinese as a giant, homogeneous, mass of humanity – a people we might imagine converting to Christianity in unison, buying Western-made cars in unison, turning Communist in unison, jumping in the air in unison. 'There is a sense,' explained the American missionary Arthur Henderson Smith in 1894, 'in which every Chinese may be said to be an epitome of the whole race.'[24]

We rarely hear such talk about Westerners. There are more than 300 million Americans in the world today and more than 700 million Europeans, but you will search in vain for a reference to 'American millions' or 'European millions'. It probably helps that we can tell Westerners apart. Dip into pre Second World War literature on China and the stereotyping leaps from the page. Again and again the Chinese are described as having 'yellow skin' and 'slant eyes' as if the physiognomy of the population was uniform. But this isn't just about Western racism. What's interesting is how the Chinese are considered to be homogeneous in a way that Indians, or Brazilians, or Russians, for instance, are not. We tend to acknowledge the immense diversity of those nations. We know that there are black Brazilians and white Brazilians and all shades in between. We know that there are Hindus, Muslims, and Sikhs in India. We know that there is a profound difference between a Muscovite and a reindeer herder in Siberia. China, on the other hand, has always been viewed as somehow monolithic.

'THE NOBLEST PART OF THE UNIVERSE'

Of course, there's much more to the encounter between the outside world and China than abuse and what sociologists call 'othering'. It's not all crude stereotyping. There's a powerful attraction, too, an apparent yearning to understand. We must not ignore the fact that Chineseness has, at times, been seen as a quite wonderful thing.

In the thirteenth century, Marco Polo, the first European to travel extensively in China and record his experiences, was full of praise for the emperor who 'surpasses every sovereign that has heretofore been or that now is in the world'.[25] Medieval Europeans lapped up Polo's memoirs, which were translated into numerous languages after the travelogue's first appearance in 1300.

The fascination intensified in the following centuries. 'The noblest part of the universe [and] the seat of that most glorious empire in all natural respects that the sun ever shines upon' was the rapturous description of China by the seventeenth-century Spanish missionary Friar Domingo Navarrete.[26] The German scientist Gottfried Leibniz felt it was difficult to do justice to 'how beautifully all the laws of the Chinese, in contrast to those of other people, are directed to the achievement of public tranquillity and the establishment of social order, so that men shall be disrupted in his relations as little as possible'. To Voltaire, the French dynamo of the Age of Enlightenment, the Chinese empire was quite simply 'the best the world has ever seen'.

Many eighteenth-century thinkers saw China as a land ruled by benevolent philosopher kings, where officials were selected on the basis of academic merit, rather than aristocratic titles; a kingdom where brain, rather than muscle ruled. The Physiocrats, a French school of economists who believed that a nation's prosperity was determined by the quality of its land, also held China in the highest esteem.

Moreover these Sinophiles were not cranks on the edges of the intellectual plain. For a time, monarchs in the West aspired to the China model. In 1756, when Physiocrat ideas were in the ascendancy, the French monarch, Louis XV, was persuaded to emulate the spring ploughing ritual of the Chinese emperor at Versailles. The Austrian emperor also took up the ceremonial Oriental ploughshare a decade or so later. There was a Chinoiserie boom in haute European society. The Royal Pavilion in Brighton, the Prince Regent's eighteenth-century pleasure palace on the south coast of England, resembles an Indian Mughal fantasy from the exterior, with its collection of onion domes. Within the palace complex, however, room after room is filled with emulations of Chinese wallpaper. Goldpainted Oriental dragons glower from sumptuous corners. It was quite a tribute, despite the designers committing a Chinese architectural faux pas by mixing up the dragons with carved serpents.

More recently, even amid waves of bigotry, the Chinese have always had foreign champions. Carl Crow in 1939 described China as 'one vast reservoir of love of beauty, laughter and an optimism which nothing can daunt'. George Kennan might have believed the Chinese to be lacking in any capacity for pity, but they were still 'the most intelligent, man for man, of any of the world's peoples'. Eric Idle of Monty Python simply sang 'I Like Chinese' in 1980.

Western business executives today often enthuse about the country in the manner of the philosophes of old. The American adman, Tom Doctoroff, calls the Chinese 'an amazing, even inspiring people ... analytically and tactically brilliant'. Politicians are by no means uniformly hostile. For every Sinophobic 'dragon slayer' in America's House of Congress there can also be found an enthusiastic 'panda hugger'. Not everyone has a negative agenda. Many of us approach China with nothing except goodwill and a simple desire to understand.

PEOPLE, PEOPLE EVERYWHERE

We should recognize too that the Chinese themselves have long helped to promote some of the conceptions that populate our minds. Amid the many brutal clashes between outsiders and the Chinese in the nineteenth century, Oriental intellectuals began to form not only a view of the character of the invading powers, but also to construct their own self-image. To articulate how they were different from the strange, aggressive foreigners, Chinese scholars were forced to consider what it was that made them Chinese, to describe the essence of their Chineseness. They began to talk about their uniquely continuous five-thousand-year-old culture and their 'yellow' race (yellow being a colour spanning shades from broken white to light brown and with positive connotations in Chinese culture). The picture that they painted influenced the way they were described by the increasing number of Western missionaries, diplomats and soldiers who arrived on Eastern shores.

That tradition of domestic stereotypes reinforcing and interplaying with perceptions held by outsiders continues today. Justin Yifu Lin, a senior official at the World Bank, defected from Taiwan to the People's Republic of China in 1979 by swimming across the strait separating the two territories. All Lin's relatives, except his wife and immediate family, are still in Taiwan. Despite the closer ties between the two territories, Lin has been unable to travel to the island of his birth to visit them. Asked in a recent television interview in Canada how he felt about that enforced separation, Lin replied that a full reunification between Taiwan and China was inevitable and, moreover, that 'China has five thousand years of history so I don't care about waiting a few more months or years.'[27] Is it any wonder that we still talk about the 'patience of Asia'?

The Chinese will wax lyrical about the longevity of their culture. Some speak of the country's collectivist mentality, which is contrasted with that of the individualistic West. Lee Kuan Yew, the founder of modern Singapore, and an ethnic Chinese, has spent many decades promoting the idea that there are special 'Asian values', which he describes as a reverence for family, social order and education.

The Chinese sometimes appear to be as obsessed with the size of their own population as any outsider. 'Ren shan, ren hai' – 'people in mountains, people in the sea' – is the phrase used to lament overcrowding. I once walked down an alleyway in Guangzhou that was almost impassable because fruit and vegetable sellers had colonized so much of the pavement. 'There are so many people here in China,' my cousin remarked to me, apologetically, as we squeezed past the hawkers. Not in this street, or this city, note, but 'in China'.

Chinese often use rather dehumanizing rhetoric about other Chinese people too. Young, poorly paid, graduates surviving in major cities are described in newspapers as 'the ant tribe' or sometimes 'the rat tribe'. Those who emerge from the countryside to find menial work in the megacities are often dismissed contemptuously as faceless 'nong min gong', or agricultural labourers, by wealthy city folk.

China's authoritarian rulers, the Chinese Communist Party, promote many of these ideas too. No foreign power has been more cavalier with Chinese lives than the Party. 'So what if we lose three hundred million people? Our women will make it up in a generation,' said Mao Zedong when he was warned by the Soviet Union that China's aggression towards Taiwan could invite a nuclear strike by the US.[28] 'In China, even one million people can be considered a small sum,' Deng Xiaoping, Mao's successor, was reported as saying during the Tiananmen Square mass democracy protests of 1989, which almost toppled the regime. And it was Deng who established the one-child policy in 1979 – that prevented most parents having more than a single infant – out of a conviction that the Chinese population was too large.

The cadres of Beijing tell us that China is an exception, a place where universal ideas such as human rights simply do not apply. The Chinese people don't, they insist, desire messy Western-style freedom and democracy. And that sense of history and shared culture seems to be unshakeable. Even the Communist Party, whose founders were supposedly inspired by Marx and Lenin, now say that China is a land of Confucian 'harmony'. If the Chinese themselves paint their own nature in such bold colours, why shouldn't outsiders take that portrait at face value?

Can it be true though? Does their culture give the Chinese different values? Do the Chinese care more about social order than freedom? Are they really in love with hard work? Are the Chinese racist? Is China going to rule the world? Being half-Chinese I felt a compulsion to find answers to these questions. After all, what sort of Chinese person doesn't know what Chineseness is?

What I discovered is that the reality is often deeply at odds with the conventional wisdom. I found that China, far from being cut off from the rest of the world throughout its history, has long been shaped by foreign religions. Chinese parents, rather than being beneficiaries of the world's finest education system, are often desperate to send their children abroad to learn because they regard foreign teaching methods as superior. Younger generations, far from being workaholics, are condemned for laziness and lack of drive, just like younger generations everywhere. What began to emerge was a picture of a nation not of fathomless inscrutability but surprisingly familiar to us – rather like my great-great-grandfather's house in Jung Wo Lei. Perhaps most telling of all were the deep historical roots I discovered of the ways – both positive and negative – that we today think about China and its people.

CHINESE WHISPERS

It used to be a party game. A message would be relayed in hushed tones through a long line of people and emerge at the other end amusingly garbled. Most of us have found alternative amusements nowadays, but the name Chinese Whispers survives as a figure of speech; an idiom used to signify how facts or a story tend to get twisted over time and distance.

Why 'Chinese' though? There seem to be no concrete answers. One theory has it that messages relayed between the lonely watchtowers of the Great Wall of China suffered this kind of distortion. Another is that China was once a byword for misunderstanding and confusion in the West, something to do with that old inscrutability. It doesn't seem to be a very old usage, with the first references only appearing in the middle of the twentieth century. Whatever the provenance of Chinese Whispers, there's something appropriate about the name.

These pages will examine the stories that we whisper to each other about China. They will show how ideas about the Chinese have historically been warped when passing through the long chains of people that have mediated between China and the outside world – and how they were often twisted once again when they arrived. Much the same thing happens today. In our interpretation of China and its people, powerful currents in the waters of our thoughts seem to keep yanking us in the same directions. Often, just as in a game of Chinese Whispers, we end up hearing what we want to hear. Now, with China poised to become the world's largest economy and an ever more profound influence on all of our lives, it is time to reconsider what we think we know.

CHINA HAS AN ANCIENT AND FIXED CULTURE

In July 1851 Charles Dickens visited an exhibition of Chinese crafts and curiosities at a small gallery in London's Hyde Park Place. Among the works on display were painted lanterns, clay teapots and delicate ornamental balls of carved ivory. There was, however, some intimidating local competition for tourists that summer. Down the road, in the green lung of Hyde Park itself, stood the Great Exhibition. Under the canopy of a magnificent 'Crystal Palace' were arrayed all the fruits of Victorian industrial and scientific genius from steam locomotives and centrifugal pumps, to agricultural engines and electrical telegraphs.

Dickens did not feel it made for a flattering contrast. In a review of the two shows in his own journal, *Household Words*, the novelist, who had published *David Copperfield* to critical acclaim the year before, was overflowing with contempt for the works of the Orient. 'Consider the greatness of the English results, and the extraordinary littleness of the Chinese,' he wrote. 'Go from the silk-weaving and cotton-spinning of us outer barbarians, to the laboriously-carved ivory balls of the flowery Empire, ball within ball and circle within circle, which have made no advance and been of no earthly use for thousands of years.' There were, felt the celebrated author, profound conclusions to be drawn about the nature of China's culture from this juxtaposition. China had violated the 'law of human progression':

> Well may the three Chinese divinities of the Past, the Present, and the Future be represented with the same heavy face. Well may the dull, immovable, respectable triad sit so amicably, side by side, in a glory of yellow jaundice, with a strong family likeness among them! As the Past was, so the Present is, and so the Future shall be, saith the Emperor. And all the Mandarins prostrate themselves, and cry Amen.[1]

Quite an outburst, but one that would have sat snugly with the prejudices of many of Dickens' readers. His themes – ancient China,
static China – constituted the conventional wisdom of the age.
Indeed, it was the view of China held by generations of outsiders
before him. And in some respects it remains our perspective today.

THE PERMANENT PHENOMENON

Open any travel guide, history book or newspaper that takes China
for its subject and you'll read the same assertion: this is the 'oldest
continuous civilization', the most 'ancient culture' on the face of
the earth. China is, we tend to assume, antiquity itself. While other
great empires have been torn apart over the centuries by revolution
and the entropic forces of history, China, uniquely, has endured.

'Since the days of Confucius,' wrote the philosopher and mathe-
matician, Bertrand Russell in 1922, 'the Egyptian, Babylonian,
Persian, Macedonian and Roman empires have perished; but China
has persisted.'[2] It is as if the citizens of Rome, or the subjects of
the pharaohs, were walking among us, still locked into the same
grooves of life as their ancient ancestors. Writing more recently,
Henry Kissinger goes even further in his estimation of Chinese antiquity. Richard Nixon's old adviser puts China on a par with the
trade winds or the rising of the sun, describing the country as 'a
permanent natural phenomenon', a civilization-state that 'seems to
have no beginning'.[3]

As remarkable as the longevity of the Chinese civilization is its
permanence. 'They have continued the same with regard to the
attire, morals, laws, customs, and manners, without deviating in
the least from the wise institutions of their ancient legislators,' said
the Jesuit historian Jean-Baptiste Du Halde in 1738.[4] The American
novelist Jack London in 1904 described the Chinese as 'dozing …
through the ages'.[5] The Chinese are, in the words of the Protestant
missionary Chester Holcombe, 'the very incarnation of conservatism'.[6] The view has endured. 'China has *been* Chinese, almost from
the beginnings of its recorded history,' claimed the anthropologist
and popular science writer Jared Diamond as recently as 1998.[7]

China never changes because it is the most fixed and resilient culture on the planet. The country might have succumbed to foreign

invasions by various barbarian tribes over the centuries but those invaders were themselves always conquered, in a kind of reverse takeover, by the overpowering institutions and magnificent culture of their prize. This idea goes back at least to Voltaire in the eighteenth century. In his play *The Orphan of China*, the French Enlightenment philosopher engineers a culmination in which Genghis Khan, the Mongol conqueror, witnesses an act of native Chinese virtue and proceeds to bow before the moral superiority of the people that he had won through force of arms:

> You have subdued me, and I blush to sit
> On Cathay's throne, whilst there are souls like yours
> So much above me; vainly have I tried
> By Glorious deeds to build myself a name
> Among the nations; you have humbled me,
> And I would equal you.[8]

A hundred years later a Catholic missionary to China, Abbé Evariste Régis Huc, described how a different set of the country's conquerors, the Manchus from north of the Great Wall, had made little impact on peoples of their new territories. 'The Manchu race has … imposed its yoke upon China but has had scarcely any influence on the Chinese mind,' he wrote. Huc even sounded a note of pity for China's new masters, whom he described as 'isolated and lost in the immensity of the empire'.[9] The American philosopher and poet Ralph Waldo Emerson described how the 'elemental conservatism' of the Chinese had ensured that 'the wars and revolutions that occur in her annals have proved but momentary swells or surges on the Pacific Ocean of her history, leaving no trace'.[10]

The idea that Chinese conquerors over the centuries all ended up 'Sinicized' remains widely accepted to this day. Twentieth-century historians suggested that external invasion by the likes of the Mongols and the Manchus merely made Chinese culture more cohesive, by forcing its people to find refuge in social institutions. John King Fairbank, the last century's doyen of American scholars of China, argued that these waves of conquest had prompted the Chinese to develop a 'culturalism', which he described as a binding communal identity as strong as the patriotism that unites other peoples.[11]

This deep sense of cultural unity has been posited as a reason why China has been so resistant to foreign religions. 'It is almost impossible for Christianity ever to be established in China,' predicted Montesquieu. The Gospels, he said, would only win Chinese souls if there were a total revolution in their customs, and given the fixed nature of Chinese mores that was inconceivable. The failure of Catholic missions, from the sixteenth-century Jesuits onwards, to prise hundreds of millions of heathen Chinese souls from the clutches of native Taoism and Confucianism seemed to bear this out.

Protestants were just as unsuccessful. The London Missionary Society sent out their first man to China in 1807. Asked whether he expected to have any spiritual impact on the country, Robert Morrison replied with indomitable confidence: 'No, but I expect God will.' Some three decades later the Protestant church had no more than a handful of converts.[12] The message is clear: China doesn't change. China changes you.

China's long unbroken history has also apparently imbued its people with a remarkable 'historical mindedness',[13] a profound understanding of their place in the continuum of their own national story. 'Only in China can one interview an official charged with civil service reforms who, in describing these reforms, recalls how officials of the Han Dynasty dealt with the problem of nepotism,' noted the journalist Jasper Becker.[14] This has engraved self-confidence, arrogance even, on to the Chinese mind. The Chinese believe themselves to be 'more intelligent, more cultured, and more capable than any other people' observed the American sinologist Herrlee Creel.[15]

This colours the Chinese attitude to the rest of the world. 'China regards all other states as various levels of tributaries based on an approximation for Chinese cultural and political forms,' according to Henry Kissinger. The more 'Chinese' you are, the more civilized you are in the eyes of Beijing. China's very name for itself – 'The Middle Kingdom' – seems to reflect an assumption of cultural superiority, the ingrained belief that the world revolves around China.

This is not merely the impression of outsiders; the Chinese themselves subscribe to it too. 'Barbarian tribes with their rulers are inferior to Chinese states without them,' said the Chinese sage Confucius in the fifth century before Christ.[16] Some Chinese intellectuals claim that no other country is so wrapped up in its own history. 'Chinese history is the very flesh and blood of China ... [it] is the place where we see most clearly that the human being is *homo historiens* through and though,' argues Huang Cheun-Chieh of National Taiwan University.[17] Chinese officials seem to be forever paying homage to China's long cultural and historical continuum, while ambassadors from the Middle Kingdom in foreign capitals miss no opportunity to lecture their hosts on the special historical status of their nation.

Chinese and the rest of us thus appear to be united in regarding China as something different. We see an ancient people unified by a Bronze Age writing system, enduring values that go back to the teachings of Confucius, and the ancient native spiritual guide of Taoism. China seems a uniquely self-confident, culturally self-assured, often profoundly arrogant nation.

In fact, when one looks a little closer this sprawling empire's cultural unity turns out to have been grossly exaggerated. China, far from being a 'permanent natural phenomenon', does not even date back five thousand years. Assertions of the country's uninterrupted political history make little sense, and the theory of China's age-old imperviousness to external religious influence is as fragile as one of Dickens' disappointing ivory balls.

ESSENTIALLY THE SAME?

'Chinese, regardless of whether they live in China, Taiwan, or Hong Kong, are essentially the same' writes the Shanghai-based advertising executive Tom Doctoroff.[18] That seems a stretch when millions of Chinese cannot even speak to each other in a common tongue. China's education ministry reported in 2007 that only around half of the country's population could communicate effectively in standard Mandarin. The figure in cities was 66 per cent, while in rural areas it fell to just 45 per cent.[19] Hundreds of millions of Chinese rely on local dialects and languages for everyday communication.

In my father's ancestral village of Jung Wo Lei the locals speak Toishanese. A Cantonese-speaking friend came on a trip to the village last year. As we sat at a table of a roadside restaurant, which creaked under the weight of local dishes such as lotus-root chunks

and cloud-ear mushroom soup, he remarked that he couldn't understand a word that the Toishanese next to us were saying. This
despite the fact that he lives just two hours away by car. Drive east
through Guangdong for a few more hours and you come to the city
of Chaozhou where yet another language is spoken, which no one
else in the region can understand.

And this is within just one of China's twenty-two provinces.
According to some estimates there are as many as three hundred
different languages, or dialects, across China. This remarkable linguistic diversity is one of the reasons it is misleading to think about
this country as a Western-style state. China has roughly the same
landmass as the United States, around 9,800,000 square kilometres,
but an American would expect to be understood in every corner of
the country. In China a traveller can move from one province to the
next and feel as if he or she has passed into another land entirely,
rather like travelling through Europe. Yet how many of us would
describe all Europeans as 'essentially the same'?

FIVE THOUSAND YEARS

He was the man of the moment and the world was waiting to hear
him speak. Xi Jinping stepped onto the stage within the cavern-
ous Great Hall of the People in Beijing on 15 November 2012 after
being unveiled as the new leader of China's Communist Party. The
fifty-nine-year-old was expected to outline his direction for the
country, but first Xi, like all new Chinese leaders, was required to
pay homage to the nation whose reins he now found in his hand.
'During the civilization and development process of more than five
thousand years, the Chinese nation has made an indelible contribution to the civilization and advancement of mankind,' was how
he began.

Of all the bland things Xi said that day, that was probably the
blandest. The idea that Chinese history extends back five millennia has been repeated so often that it is now taken for granted. It
shouldn't be. The claim is predicated on the existence of a so-called
'Yellow Emperor', who is said to have ruled three thousand years
before the birth of Christ. As well as bringing the Chinese nation
into existence, this God-like founding father is supposed to have

taught his people how to grow crops, domesticate animals and even to clothe themselves.

There is no archaeological or written evidence that such a figure ever existed. So to argue that Chinese history 'begins' at this point is akin to claiming that King Arthur was the first British sovereign, or that the mythical Trojan hero Aeneas was the founder of modern Italy. It is the stuff of legend, not history. If David Cameron started talking about the Knights of the Round Table, or an Italian prime minister were to make earnest reference to King Priam, they would open themselves to ridicule. But in China a myth is embedded in mainstream political rhetoric, and few Western writers have shown any inclination to challenge it.

In fact the claim is relatively recent. The China scholar Kerry Brown has noted that before one of Xi Jinping's predecessors, Jiang Zemin, made an official visit to Egypt in the late 1990s, the Beijing authorities tended to talk of three or four thousand years of Chinese history. It appears that in Egypt someone brought to Jiang's attention that there, on the Nile Delta, was a civilization that could claim even more venerable origins than the Middle Kingdom. So Chinese leaders unilaterally awarded the country an extra thousand years of history in an act of international one-upmanship.[20]

Not that those lesser claims were any sturdier. The foundation of the Xia Dynasty was put at 2100 BC by China's earliest chroniclers, but there is very little archaeological evidence of the existence of such a state. The earliest written records date from the era of the Shang Dynasty in 1600 BC. 'Oracle bones' – the shoulder blades of oxen with a primitive Chinese script engraved upon them – appear to have been used by rulers for divining the future. As the Shang only covered a relatively small region of modern-day northern China, it is not clear why they should be regarded as the founders of the modern nation, rather than just an early people who lived within the geographical borders of the present state.

So what about two thousand years of continuous history? This has more force, given that 221 BC saw the Qin unification of the warring fiefdoms and principalities that comprised a significant area stretching from modern-day inner Mongolia to Hunan province in the south. Qin Shi Huangdi, the man who accomplished this feat, styled himself the 'first emperor', and his surname became the root of the European name 'China'. Unlike his predecessors, Qin had manifest ambitions to build a mighty nation and bind it tightly together. He standardized weights and measures, dictated the width of the axles on chariots, established a common currency and oversaw the imposition of a single script that forms the basis of today's writing system. More miles of road were built in China under the Qin than in Europe under the Romans. The Qin emperor was certainly a blessing to the future Chinese tourism industry. He commenced the construction of a 'long wall' to keep northern raiders out, the predecessor of today's Great Wall. It was in Qin's necropolis in Xi'an that thousands of terracotta warriors were discovered in 1974. He was less of a blessing, however, to his contemporary subjects. Legend records that he ordered dissident scholars and unfortunate concubines to be buried alive, and used slave labour on his grand construction projects.

For all its horrors and achievements the Qin Dynasty itself only lasted fourteen years before it was swept away by a peasant uprising, which installed the Han Dynasty. The Han, in turn, broke up after four hundred-odd years. Then came the Jin, the Tang, the Song, the Yuan, the Ming and the Qing, all separated by periods in which no single dynasty ruled the geographic region we now call China. This catalogue of dynasties, punctuated by disintegration, raises questions about what we mean by terms such as 'continuous' when we talk of Chinese civilization. If we were to substitute the adjective 'fractured', the description would be closer to the truth.

Some historians, alive to this conceptual wrinkle, maintain that while dynasties came and went the Chinese system of political administration remained constant. This however does not stand up to scrutiny. The celebrated Confucian exam system, the supposedly meritocratic means of selecting officials, was only fully developed in the seventh century, more than a thousand years after the death of Confucius. When the Ming toppled the Yuan Dynasty they also shook up Chinese governance institutions, establishing a hereditary military caste of soldiers to prevent a resurgence of the Mongols they had vanquished.[21] The Qing too were innovative in matters of governance, imposing their own system of tribal loyalty, termed the 'Eight Banners', over the existing state institutions.[22]

If it is legitimate to talk of China's 'continuous' political history stretching back for two millennia, then so, equally, might we speak of a continuous European history over that same period. In theory there is a continuous two-thousand-year-old European civilization, from Imperial Rome, through the Holy Roman Empire, to today's European Union. If it is culture, rather than politics, that constitutes the glue of continuity, then Europe might be said to have the shared philosophical heritage from Ancient Greece, reinforced by Christianity, then the Renaissance and finally the Enlightenment. Of course this would mean turning a blind eye to the Dark Ages, the Hundred Years War, the Thirty Years War, and the two shattering conflicts of the twentieth century. Such omissions would be ridiculous. Yet by accentuating China's historic 'continuity' we do something very similar. The innumerable catastrophic collapses of the Chinese polity, from the warring states period when Confucius was alive, to the era of feuding warlords in the early twentieth century, become mere footnotes in our teleological vision.

THE LAUGHING BUDDHA

What about cultural imperviousness, the argument that China has never been much altered by foreign ways of thinking? Well, that's challenged by my great-uncle's sideboard in his home in Guangzhou. On that sideboard sits a porcelain figure of a shaven-headed man with a benevolent smile and a gigantic exposed belly. Small children are climbing delightedly on his corpulent frame. My family tell me that this charm – known as '*do jai fat*', or 'many children bring luck' – attracts prosperity and fertility to a household.

The tubby man is a character from a tenth-century Chinese folk tale. There was a monk from modern-day Zhejiang province who performed small wonders during his life and, as the legend goes, revealed himself on his deathbed to be an incarnation of the Buddha. This laughing Buddha today can be found in homes across China. The original Buddha, of course, wasn't born in China.

The Chinese first had contact with the alien creed called Buddhism in the first century AD. It had made its way northwest out of India to modern-day Pakistan and Afghanistan. The Chinese encountered it through trade with Central Asians on the Silk Road. Siddhartha Gautama Buddha was an Indian nobleman turned ascetic who lived in the sixth century before Christ. He had taught that there was a way to find perfect inner peace and enlightenment. This promise of mental release from a turbulent and cruel world proved attractive to a Chinese people who were, at that time, boiling in a cauldron of civil strife during one of the empire's periods of breakdown.

The Chinese used terms from the local Taoist religion, which bore some resemblance to the new philosophy, to translate Buddhist spiritual concepts from the original Sanskrit. Some have suggested that Buddhism was thus assimilated into traditional Chinese culture, rather than fundamentally altering the host nation. But this is to ignore the clear challenge that Buddhist teachings posed to the dominant Confucian tradition. In the universe of Confucian values the family was of supreme importance. The only time a man realized himself to the full was in mourning his parents.[23] To fail to produce children was considered a betrayal of one's forebears. Buddhism, by contrast, recommended a complete severing of all family ties – and monks were supposed to be celibate.

That was not the only clash. Confucius argued that contemplation, in the absence of extensive study, was useless. 'I once spent all day thinking without taking food and all night thinking without going to bed, but I found that I gained nothing from it,' as he put it. 'It would have been better for me to have spent the time in learning.'[24] Instead Buddhism recommended pure meditation as the road to enlightenment. It seems safe to assume that Confucius and the Buddha would not have seen eye to eye.

Nevertheless this alien spiritual morality is embraced by 'Confucian' Chinese society. One of the central characters in the *Water Margin*, one of the sturdy pillars of Chinese literature from the fourteenth century, is a Buddhist monk called Lu Zhishen. Lu, whose title 'the flowery monk' came from the floral tattoos that covered his torso, was considered to be the embodiment of the value of loyalty. The Buddhist influence extended to architecture. The quintessentially Chinese pagoda is a multi-storied version of the Indian stupa burial mound.[25] Buddhism is flowering in China today: temples are flush with donations and China's expanding middle classes have taken up the religion as a means of demonstrating their cultural sophistication. Official estimates put Buddhist followers at around one hundred million; unofficial counts suggest the figure is three times that. No one disputes that it is the largest single religion in the country. The teachings of a foreigner from the Indian subcontinent helped to revolutionize Chinese spirituality. As the twentieth-century historian and liberal reformer Hu Shih put it: 'India conquered and dominated China culturally for twenty centuries without ever having to send a single soldier across her border.'

Buddhism isn't the only foreign religion that has successfully pierced the supposedly impenetrable bubble of Chinese culture. The foundations of the Huai Sheng mosque in Guangzhou were laid in AD 627, five years before the death of Muhammad. It is a fascinating melange of Chinese and Arabic architectural styles, with a stone minaret that, until just thirty years ago when the sky-scrapers arrived, was still the tallest structure in the city. Islam, like Buddhism, entered China through trade, arriving from the Middle East via the sea commerce routes during the Tang Dynasty, when Muslim traders married local women. The religion spread further through China during the thirteenth century under the patronage of the Mongol Yuan Dynasty.[26]

One Muslim rose remarkably high under the early Ming too. The fifteenth-century explorer-general Zheng He, a figure now cele-brated in China as a national hero, was the son of a Muslim lord in Yunnan, in the far southwest of China. After his father was defeated by the Ming imperial forces the eleven-year-old Zheng suffered the brutal, but not uncommon, fate of the offspring of disloyal vassals: he was castrated and sent to be a slave in the imperial court. Yet Zheng's misfortune turned into an opportunity when he became an adviser to a Ming prince who later became the Yongle emperor. The young Muslim proved his prowess in battle and was put in charge of a grand imperial naval expedition. Zheng's giant fleet of 300 ships and 28,000 crew – one of the world's earliest blue water navies – sailed as far as the Horn of Africa in a spectacular demonstration of China's technological prowess. Today there are some twenty million Muslims in China, spread across almost every province. Except for those in Xinjiang, who have a distinctly Central Asian culture, many of the followers of the Prophet Muhammad in China are impossible to distinguish from the dominant Han ethnic group in their lan-guage and dress. Even their wedding and funeral rites are the same.

However their faith in a religion founded in the Arabian Peninsula still endures.

Other world religions have left their mark on China – for both good and ill. There were Christians in China long before the Jesuits arrived in the fifteenth century. Those European missionaries assumed that they were the first to preach the gospel of Christ in the Far East, but a stone tablet unearthed in Xi'an documents the presence of Nestorians – Persian Christians – in China from the seventh century.[27] The Mongols patronized Christianity too. The mother of the great Mongol emperor of China, Kublai Khan, immortalized in verse by the pen of Samuel Taylor Coleridge as the commissioner of the 'stately pleasure dome', was a Nestorian. Winston Churchill in his *History of the English-Speaking Peoples* depicts the Mongols as 'heathen hordes from the heart of Asia', but they were religiously tolerant heathens. And Marco Polo, who was appointed as an administrator in the city of Yangzhou by Kublai, suggested that the Grand Khan himself might have converted to the cross if the Vatican had sent a sufficient number of missionaries over.[28]

Christianity has also shaped China's modern history. The Taiping Rebellion against the Qing Dynasty in the middle of the nineteenth century was led by a Christian convert called Hong Xiuquan. Hong's thirteen-year revolt convulsed China and left some twenty million dead. To put such a figure in context, the American Civil War, which raged at roughly the same time, is estimated to have resulted in a death toll of 750,000. Such was the monumental scale of the Taiping slaughter that some historians have suggested that the conflict ought to be regarded as China's equivalent of the First World War. And the man who lit the fuse had been inspired by pamphlets produced by Protestant missionaries preaching in Guangzhou.

Hong was not, it is true, sponsored by the Church; he was a millenarian fanatic, rather than a recognizable Christian. But China's rulers nevertheless came to identify the spread of foreign faiths in those years as an existential challenge to Confucian civilization. 'This is not just a crisis for our Qing Dynasty, but the most extraordinary crisis of all time for the Confucian teachings,' warned the leader of the anti-Taiping forces, Zeng Guofan.[29] Even though Hong was ultimately crushed, Zeng was right to fear the revolutionary potential of Christianity because the man who led the movement that ultimately deposed the crumbling empire in 1911 and became China's first president, Sun Yat Sen, was a Protestant. Sun had converted while studying medicine in Hong Kong during the 1880s. In China today there are around forty million followers of Christ. Underground churches – Christian congregations that refuse to register with the authorities for monitoring – are also flourishing. My aunt in Guangzhou became a Catholic in 2010. She told me she was inspired by the message of human compassion in the Gospels. Foreign religions have long shaped spiritual belief in China and continue to do so.

Evolution has been essential to the survival of spirituality in China. The Falun Gong, which advocates a mixture of Taoist and Buddhist philosophy together with an emphasis on meditative exercises, has been savagely repressed by the state. But between the sect's foundation in 1992 and the turn of the Millennium, when the Falun Gong was forced underground, it was believed to have attracted one hundred million adherents in China – more than the entire membership of the Communist Party.

One might look at the laughing Buddha on my uncle's sideboard and see the fat monk as China and the scrabbling children as the world's religions, competing, with varying degrees of success, to get his attention.

BUTTONS AND PIGTAILS

The idea that the Chinese civilized their conquerors through their superior culture is no sturdier than the proposition that the great walls of Chinese life have never been breached by foreign religion. The Mongol emperors of the thirteenth century ruled fairly tolerantly, making no attempt to overturn the traditional bureaucracy of the majority Han people (although they did ban the imperial examinations). Voltaire's caricature was right up to a point. But the heirs of Genghis Khan were not assimilated, or 'civilized' as Voltaire imagined. Nor was their dominion merely shrugged off by the Chinese. For one thing the Mongols helped overhaul China's wardrobe. Before the Mongol Yuan Dynasty the Chinese kept their robes tied with belts. The Mongols introduced the distinctive toggle-and-loop buttons – accessories that are now, ironically given their origins, seen as quintessentially Chinese.[30]

The warriors from Manchuria who established the Qing Dynasty in the seventeenth century also successfully preserved their own distinctive culture. Indeed, they were jealously protective of it. Marriage between Manchus and Han Chinese was forbidden and the Qing emperors kept their own language alive as a means of secret military communication.[31] Visitors to the Ming emperors' Forbidden City, if they examine the blue and gold signs above the many courtyard gateways, will see a strange script next to the more familiar Chinese characters: Manchu. The Qing had inscribed their own culture into the symbolic heart of their new empire.

The classic image of 'old China' is a man with a shaved forehead and a long braided pigtail. This was not, however, an ancient Confucian fashion statement, but something enforced, upon pain of death, on the majority Han people by their Manchu overlords. It is a curious kind of cultural assimilator who is compelled to shave off half of his hair. The Manchus also demanded that all Han get rid of their old robes and wear the cheongsam. A slim-fitting version of this full-length dress, with its split down the leg, is most commonly associated with the femme fatales of 1920s Shanghai, but this classic item of 'Chinese' clothing was once an item of Manchu sartorial oppression.

The early Qing emperors were, however, essentially pragmatic. Like the Mongols, they ruled China as a multicultural empire, recognizing that this was the only way they could hope to hold together this diverse and naturally fractious political entity made up of Christians, Muslims, Buddhists and a host of different groups and tribes. It is said that the Qing governed as Confucians in China, Mongolians on the northern steppe and, unlike today's Communists, actively sponsored Tibetan Buddhism, with its worship of the Dalai Lama.[32] Early Qing rulers even made an effort to become multilingual. The emperor Qianlong explained how his statecraft worked: 'I use their own languages and do not rely on an interpreter ... to conquer them with kindness.'

This pragmatism extended to foreign relations. The so-called Chinese 'tributary system', under which neighbouring Asian states were required to deliver regular gifts to the emperor, is often cited as a manifestation of China's cultural superiority complex. Yet these states received lavish gifts in return for this tribute. Some China scholars now regard the tribute system as a cover for an expansion of foreign trade, or possibly a face-saving way for emperors to buy protection from aggressive northern raiders. In the words of the historian Joanna Waley-Cohen, 'for tributary states the entire process primarily represented a peaceful way to acquire essential Chinese goods without having to steal them in border raids'.[33]

We often hear that China arrogantly refused to acquire technological expertise from the West when it had the chance and paid a heavy price. This interpretation draws a straight line between the moment a British trade mission, led by Lord Macartney, was dismissed empty-handed by the Qianlong emperor in 1794, and the appearance of British gunboats off Canton in 1839 to blast open the gates of China to international commerce. 'We possess all things. I set no value on objects strange or ingenious, and have no use for your country's manufactures,' Qianlong wrote to Lord Macartney's patron, King George III, in a missive that has gone down in history as the final word in deluded hubris.

However the Qing emperors were not so closed-minded as this rebuff would suggest. The Qing, like the Ming before them, had patronized Jesuit missionaries and commissioned them to transfer Western technologies such as cannon manufacture and cartography. Indeed, a number of the Chinese cannons captured by European powers in the invasions of the nineteenth century and transported back to museums for display had been designed for the Qing by the Flemish missionary Ferdinand Verbiest two hundred years previously. These examples of 'Chinese' technology were in fact a testament to China's willingness to absorb expertise from the West. Jesuits were also appointed to senior positions in the state astronomy bureaucracy. The Qianlong repudiation of Macartney's overtures might have been a calculated move against a rival power rather than an example of supreme complacency.

In another of history's great ironies, a wing of the Qing emperor's Old Summer Palace, which was burned down by British and French soldiers in the second Opium War in 1860, was a neo-classical structure, designed by two Jesuits. The voluted chunks of masonry that can be seen heaped up on the site of the ruined palace to this day in northwest Beijing are an eloquent testament to the fact that China's emperors were not, in fact, as insular as their European detractors (including some of the very soldiers who looted the palace) insisted. Indeed, they might be seen as the mirror image of their Western monarchical counterparts who began to commission grand works of Chinoiserie in the late eighteenth century.

Nor were all the Chinese so hubristically convinced of the superiority of Chinese culture and technology as the caricature might suggest. As early as the First Opium War in 1839–42 there were instances of Qing officials attempting to replicate Western military technology. As the belligerent British advanced up China's eastern seaboard they discovered paddleboats fitted with brass guns in Wusong, and in Xiamen they came across a replica of a British man-of-war. Even during these first bruising contacts the Chinese were copying foreign technology.

The Guangxu emperor of the later nineteenth century also failed to fit the Victorian stereotype of the reactionary and closed-minded Chinese autocrat. Not only did he appoint radical intellectuals to enact deep political reforms, he also wanted to shed some of the old rhetoric about China's cultural superiority over its Asian neighbours. When Guangxu's ministers brought him the diplomatic instructions of the new ambassador to Korea, the emperor ordered the removal of a phrase suggesting that he should be described as existing in a plane well above the Korean sovereign. His explanation was simple: 'Korea is independent and no longer a vassal to us. What's the use of affecting such hollow forms of arrogant pride?'[34]

The empress dowager Cixi, with the help of Manchu nobles, repressed the reformers and deposed Guangxu. Yet even this old reactionary agreed to scrap the imperial exam in 1905. Cixi also celebrated her sixtieth birthday in 1897 watching ballroom dancing in the neo-classical Astor House Hotel in Shanghai. Perhaps, as she gazed on the twirling Western-dressed dancers that night, she puffed on one of her preferred 'Peacock' brand of cigarettes, imported especially from Japan.

THE NEW CULTURE

We tend to think of China as a place determined not to change. 'After every successive revolution this extraordinary people has applied itself to re-constitute the past, and recall the antique traditions, in order not to depart from the rites established by their ancestors,' said the missionary Régis Evariste Huc. In reality, a closer look at its twentieth-century history reveals a nation engaged in a long struggle to throw off the chains of its traditional culture. The founding father of the republic, Sun Yat Sen, made a point of wearing Western clothing and implored his countrymen to do the same. To Sun, who is the one nationalist leader still esteemed by the Communist Party, China did not float separately to the rest of humanity and world history but was very much a part of it. In 1912, upon the foundation of the republic, Sun declared that the Chinese were 'continuing the historic struggle of the French and American peoples for republican institutions'.

This struggle went on long after the downfall of the Qing Dynasty. The May Fourth Movement came together on that day in 1919 when students learned that, despite China's support for the allied forces in the First World War, chunks of Chinese territory annexed by Germany were to be arbitrarily transferred by Europeans to Japan. The indignant nationalism of the students was fused with a campaign for cultural reform. The students and urban intellectuals who led the movement were unsparing in their criticism of traditional ways of thinking, which they believed had led China to humiliation after humiliation. Traditional Chinese culture was reviled by Chen Duxiu, the editor of the radical magazine *New Youth*, as 'hypocritical, conservative, passive, constrained, classicist, imitative, ugly, evil, belligerent, disorderly, lazy'. A 'New Culture' movement in these years strove to replace the classical written language with a democratizing vernacular style, accessible to all. 'Down with the ornate obsequious literature of the aristocrats – up with the plain expressive literature of the people!' urged Chen.

This was a time of intellectual challenge to old civilization across the board. Historians of what became known as the 'Doubting Antiquity School' started to look sceptically on the works of some of their ancient predecessors such as Si Ma Qian of the Han Dynasty, who is one of the few sources for much of what we know about the Xia and Shang Dynasties. These scholars insisted that lists of ancient kings could no longer be taken on trust. Everything was to be challenged.

It was in these radical years that one of China's most celebrated writers, Lu Xun, wrote *The Real Story of Ah-Q*. Published in 1921, it is the tale of a delusional Chinese scoundrel who convinces himself of his moral superiority, even in the throes of humiliation and oppression. After one beating, Ah-Q imagines himself to have been a father slapped around by his sons, and thus egregiously wronged under the Confucian moral code. If his assailants where in the wrong, he reasons, that must put him in the moral right, something from which he draws some strange comfort. Ah-Q is also, however, an awful bully to those he considers weaker than himself. The tale ends with the pathetic anti-hero executed by revolutionary forces after being framed for a robbery in which he had no part. Lu Xun conceived the story as a satirical critique of what he saw as the craven Chinese national character. It was remarkably successful: the term 'Ah-Q mentality' is still used in China to describe people who are stuck in the past and unable to face reality.

Lu Xun was explicit in his objectives. Studying at a medical school in Japan in 1906, he was stunned by the impassive reaction of his fellow Chinese students when they were shown a slide of one of their countrymen, identified as a spy, being beheaded by a Japanese soldier. That incident put Lu off a career in medicine. He told himself that however rude a nation was in physical health, if its people were intellectually feeble, they would never become anything other than cannon fodder or gawping spectators. His calling, he realized, was to change the Chinese national spirit through literature. As he wrote: 'I reinvented myself as a crusader for cultural reform.'

But it was the Communists who really took the knife to traditional China. While some senior cadres such as Liu Shaoqi tried to find a justification for the Communist revolution in quotations from the Confucian sage, Mencius, a historical and ideological rupture, rather than continuity, was the dominant goal of those who seized power in 1949. Mao Zedong's chilling poem distils the destructive essence of his regime:

A revolution is not a dinner party,
or writing an essay, or painting a picture,
or doing embroidery.
I cannot be refined, so leisurely and gentle,

so temperate, kind and courteous, restrained,
and magnanimous. A revolution is an insurrection,
an act of violence by which one class,
overthrows another.

The first line is well known, but the rest is just as important. Temperance, kindness, courtesy and magnanimity were all instantly recognizable Confucian virtues. Mao was very clear about where he stood: he 'hated Confucius from the age of eight'. For Mao 'the struggle between the old and new cultures is to the death'.[35]

He practised what he preached. The Maoist campaign against the 'four olds' – the ideas, culture, customs and habits of the exploiting classes – during the Cultural Revolution of the 1960s and 70s was an explicit attack on Confucianism. Under the Qing a son who struck his father could face decapitation under the law. In the Cultural Revolution, children were encouraged to denounce their own parents as class enemies. Confucius taught reverence for teachers and learning; Mao told Chinese youth that 'to rebel is justified'. In the years of chaos between 1966 and 1976 educators were beaten and tormented, sometimes to death, by their own students.

Some would like to write off those years as a nightmare imposed on an unwilling Chinese people by a small clique of ideologues. Sadly, that's not so easy. Much as it is regretted now, the Cultural Revolution captured the imagination of a mass audience in China. It fed on old divisions and ancient tensions in Chinese society. According to Mobo Gau, a Chinese historian who lived through those days, the Cultural Revolution 'involved a huge number of ordinary people who lived their lives based on the choices available to them and from the beliefs and values that had been accumulated for years.'[36]

The social madness faded after the death of Mao, and the Communist Party's assaults on China's traditional culture were toned down, but the intellectual challenges to what was considered a backward and suffocating culture have continued. In 1984 the Taiwanese writer and novelist Bo Yang wrote *The Ugly Chinaman* in the same angry spirit in which Lu Xun had composed *Ah-Q* sixty years earlier. 'This culture from the time of Confucius onwards, hasn't produced a single thinker!' he complained. 'Everyone who can read is occupied in annotating the theories of Confucius or those of his followers; they don't have their own independent opinions because our culture doesn't allow them to, and so they can only try to survive somehow in this pool of stagnant water.' Bo described Chinese culture as a vat of rotten soy-bean paste. 'Whenever the vat emits a stink, it makes Chinese look ugly,' he asserted.[37]

The Beijing authorities banned imports of Bo's book, but a similar intellectual spirit was moving on the mainland too. In June 1988 a six-part documentary called *River Elegy* was shown on Chinese television. The thesis of the series was that China had been oppressed by its traditional culture, as represented by the muddy Yellow River. The iconoclasm was unrelenting. Nothing was spared from attack, not even the Great Wall, which the documentary described as standing only for 'isolation, conservatism, and ineffective defences'. Just as radical was *River Elegy*'s solution. The documentary urged the country to create a new culture and open up to the blue oceans of the outside world: 'The Yellow River has given us all it could. It cannot give birth again to the civilization created by our ancestors. We must create a brand-new civilization, one which cannot flow from the Yellow River. The dregs of the old civilization, like the silt in the Yellow River, have built up in our nation's blood vessels. It needs a scrubbing by a great flood.'

The documentary precipitated a national debate and fed the mood of political radicalism among students, which exploded in the mass pro-democracy demonstrations of 1989.

TARNISHED GOLDEN LILIES

Cultural practices in China have always evolved as the country's society and economy have shifted. For hundreds of years, female foot binding was prevalent throughout much of the country. Some say it began when a Song emperor enthused about the sexual allure of a young concubine with tiny feet. Others suggest it became fashionable after a princess was born with a club foot. Whatever the origin, the practice became widely socially desirable, and not only among wealthy elites, but the lower gentry too, who wanted to marry their daughters into the higher classes. Mothers would break their daughters' tiny bones, fearing that without bound feet, they would never marry up the social scale and be consigned to a life of drudgery and near starvation.[38] By the mid nineteenth century it is estimated that fifty per cent of Chinese women had their feet deformed from a young age.

In 1905, however, the practice was outlawed. Today it is completely gone, its disappearance unlamented. No Chinese, no matter how traditionalist, wants to resurrect the repellent practice of crushing a woman's foot into a three-inch 'golden lily'. The disappearance of foot binding is a very good example of how culture *does* change in China.

The only foot abuse that takes place today is when young Chinese women, like their western counterparts, squeeze their toes into tight-fitting high heels. It is one of many fashion revolutions. The colour white is highly inauspicious in Chinese folklore, being commonly associated with death, yet today you can see young Chinese brides posing for photos on the iron Waibaidu Bridge in Shanghai clothed in gleaming white Western-style wedding dresses. Thinness was traditionally associated with poverty in China, but now there are adverts for slimming products pasted on metro billboards across the country. Young Chinese have very similar fashion tastes to their Western counterparts.

This younger generation will determine China's future cultural development. By 2015 there will be five hundred million Chinese under the age of thirty. What characterizes this youthful cohort, perhaps more than anything else, is a powerful attraction to Western culture. The basketball player Yao Ming is loved and revered, long after retirement, because he became a star of the National Basketball Association in America, playing for the Houston Rockets. Yu Keping, a professor at Beijing University, describes how 'the American dream is the highest ideal for the young generation that grew up since the [1979] reforms. Everything in the USA, including American people, institutions, economy, culture and country is so perfect that the American moon has become more round than the one in China!'[39]

The culturally protectionist Chinese government allows just twenty foreign-made films to be shown in China every year. Despite this, in 2010, imported releases constituted 55 per cent of cinema ticket sales. Once, as we sat in Guangzhou's best noodle house, near the churning Shangxiajiu shopping district, I fell to discussing films with a Chinese friend. While he liked the work of contemporary Chinese directors such as Zhang Yimou, what really enthused him was Tom Cruise's *Mission Impossible* franchise. It was a passion only rivalled in his affections by English Premier League football.

Modern Chinese culture is fed by the West. Yu Hua's 1992 novel *To Live*, a harrowing sweep through the traumas of the twentieth century related by a stoic peasant, is one of the most influential Chinese works of fiction of the past two decades. Yu was inspired to write the work when he heard 'Old Black Joe', a song about a dying slave by a white nineteenth-century American composer.[40]

At a more prosaic level, Chinese television draws on Western influences too. The televised singing talent competitions pioneered in the UK saturate the channels. There is a Chinese version of the *Antiques Roadshow*, with participants bringing jade Buddhas and Celadon vases to be valued rather than grandfather clocks and Wedgwood Toby Jugs. The Chinese have the same type of cheap soap operas as in the West, although period costume dramas are also very popular. They have imports too – Chinese parents can watch a dubbed version of *Supernanny* to see how much trouble Westerners have controlling their toddlers. A Chinese version of the show is in production.

What of everyday life? Our guidebooks, desperate to spare us a traumatic culture shock, are full of little notes about Chinese manners. They tell us that spitting in the street is acceptable, blowing one's nose with a hankie is considered disgusting and that pushing in queues is tolerated. This picture isn't wrong. The males in my Guangzhou family enjoy a good belch at the end of a meal to show their satisfaction. There is still much hacking and expectorating on Chinese streets in winter. But even here there are changes afoot. My aunt shudders whenever she sees someone putting their feet up on a table in a hotel lobby. Hong Kong natives have been scandalized by mainland women holding babies over gutters to allow their children to defecate. Chinese manners, following the pattern of all other industrializing nations, are evolving.

There are new social complexities too. China's linguistic diversity is creating fresh social tensions as people mix more. The local Shanghainese language, known as Wu, was suppressed under the

Communists, but is now being tentatively re-introduced in the city's public transport announcements, alongside Mandarin.[41] The older generation are pleased, but the massive population of migrant workers in the city, who already suffer discrimination, fear it could be a prelude to further exclusion. Mandarin-speaking mainlanders, at least those who don't have much money, experience a similar hostility in Cantonese-speaking Hong Kong. Some residents of the territory funded an ugly newspaper advertising campaign in 2012 depicting mainlanders as locusts, who had come to exploit Hong Kong's social services. Such tensions are easily missed if we assume that the Chinese are all 'essentially the same' in their ways of life.

SWEET POTATOES AND STARBUCKS

Charles Lamb, the nineteenth-century English essayist, came up with an amusing story about the origins of roast pork. The house of a Chinese swineherd was once accidentally burned down. Returning to the scene of devastation, the farmer touched the flanks of one of his burned pigs, looking for signs of life. Thrusting his scorched digits into his mouth to soothe the pain, the man became the first person on earth to discover the succulent delights of crackling. From that moment on the swineherd dined regularly on roast pig. The trouble was that every time he wanted to prepare the delicious meal he had to burn his house down.

This little fantasy reinforces the idea of China as a discrete culture, evolving in its own eccentric way. When we think of Chinese food we don't think of cultural fusion. Peking duck, sweet and sour pork, egg fried rice, spare ribs and spring rolls seem to belong to a hermetically sealed culinary world. In truth, the history of Chinese food culture demonstrates a different story; it shows a considerable degree of influence from outside the country's borders.

The Chinese did not drink hot water mixed with tea leaves as an everyday beverage until the Tang Dynasty, more than a thousand years after Confucius. Sorghum was introduced in Mongol times. Later, under the Ming, a great revolution in the Chinese diet came from the introduction of crops discovered in the Americas. Staples such as corn and potatoes, which produced higher yields than rice and wheat and grew in previously marginal land, contributed to a massive jump in the Chinese population, which rose from around 150 million in 1700 to 450 million in 1850. One of the favourite traditional dishes of my family in Guangzhou is a grey stew made with sweet potatoes and arrowroot. And these new crops didn't just mean more bulk, they deeply influenced the style of Chinese cooking. Anyone who visits Sichuan will know how dominant the chilli pepper is in that Western region's cuisine. These ferocious red vegetables only arrived in the Ming era. The culture continues to evolve. Peking duck is, it is true, a quintessentially Chinese dish, but around a quarter of the crispy-skinned birds carved in China's restaurants are now a special low-fat breed, imported all the way from Lincolnshire in Britain.[42]

Western food outlets are multiplying across China. Despite China's celebrated tea culture, Starbucks coffee is a particular favourite. My Guangzhou cousins were delighted when the first branch opened in the city centre ten years ago. Once, before a long road trip, my aunt insisted on stopping the car on one of Guangzhou's dangerous highways, in the middle of the morning rush hour, so she could rush into the local branch and get her latte fix.

The proliferation of McDonalds, Pizza Hut and the like across China, as well as the growing popularity of potato crisps and fizzy drinks, are creating the same kind of health problems among the urban wealthy in China as can be found in the West. Some 120 million Chinese are obese. Around 10 per cent of urban Chinese are diabetic, including the former premier Wen Jiabao. China has gone from famine to gluttony in a single generation. Other culinary changes are more encouraging. The Chinese fetish for consuming endangered species does not seem to have passed to the younger generation, at least if my cousins' disgusted reaction to the idea of eating bear's paw or shark's fin is anything to go by.

CONFUCIAN CONFUSION

'It is still impossible to understand modern China without understanding Confucius,' according to the BBC journalist Andrew Marr.[43] That's certainly what Beijing would like the outside world to believe. The government has established hundreds of 'Confucius Institutes' in foreign cities, to promote Chinese culture internationally,

modelled on Germany's Goethe Institutes. The sage was ostenta-
tiously celebrated in the spectacular opening ceremony for the 2008
Beijing Olympics.

Yet Confucian values have an ambiguous status in modern China.
Some argue they are making a comeback as the country tries to fill
the moral vacuum created by the state's de facto jettisoning of Communist ideology after the death of Mao in 1976.[44] In 2007 a book
called *Reflections on the Analects of Confucius* by a Beijing University
literature professor, Yu Dan, became a bestseller in China, shifting
more copies than any tome since Mao's Little Red Book, and was
followed by a TV series. The appeal was Yu's application of Confucian wisdom to modern situations, making the ancient teachings
seem accessible and relevant.

Nevertheless other intellectuals continue to attack Confucianism
in the same manner as the iconoclasts of the May Fourth Movement
we met earlier in this chapter. Jiang Rong in his bestselling 2004
novel *Wolf Totem* contrasted the traditional values of China most
unfavourably with those of the nomads of the Mongolian steppe,
and he has explicitly linked Confucianism with China's history of
repression. 'Confucianism wants people to become sheep,' according to Jiang. 'Its central tenet is obedience, following the emperor
... In essence, the political system during the Cultural Revolution
was the same as that of the last several thousand years: Both were
autocratic, totalitarian and dictatorial.'[45]

There are Confucian revivalists who argue that China should
re-embrace the traditional values from which it has become alien-
ated, but their opponents counter that without democracy and the
rule of law, a Confucian revival can only serve the interests of the
repressive authority. The fact is, one cannot understand modern
China simply by learning about Confucius. One also has to grasp
this long-running intellectual battle over the country's Confucian
heritage.

So what is the role of Confucianism in everyday lives? When I
asked one young Chinese friend from Beijing whether she and her
friends would ever quote from *The Analects* she shot me a look as
if I was crazy. Another friend from Shanghai told me that Confucian values, for him, meant children sitting on a separate table from
adults at dinner. Rather like Christianity in the West, Confucian

values in China cover a wide spectrum, ranging from daily literal devotion to the equivalent of an annual trip to church on Christmas Eve to sing carols.

Filial piety, the value that says children should respect and honour their parents, does still exist, but it is important to recognize that it is evolving in response to changed circumstances. Many of my friends in China say they are determined to look after their parents when they become old and frail. However, that does not necessarily mean taking their parents into their own home, as would once have been automatic. It might, for instance, mean paying for a carer or a nursing home. Indeed, retirement homes are increasingly common in China. One recent survey showed that only 45 per cent of urban dwellers expect to live with their children when they reach retirement and only a fifth expect any financial support from their offspring.[46]

THE EUROPEANS ARE VERY QUIET

It should not be hard to grasp these truths about China. The impact of Buddhism, a testament to the adaptive capabilities of that culture, is evident in the impressive temples found in many Chinese cities. One need only dip into any history of modern China to learn of the struggles of would-be modernizers to tear up China's traditional culture. The incorporation of new world vegetables into its cuisine should be obvious whenever one bites a chilli in a Sichuanese restaurant. So why is this apparently such a difficult lesson to learn? Why do we assume China's culture is immutable?

A clue might lie in our own history. Wars of religion have been fought for hundreds of years in Europe, with adherents to different branches of Christianity savagely persecuted. From the Crusades era to the 1529 Ottoman siege of Vienna, Islam has been regarded as an external military threat. The livid scars of sectarianism are still visible across the continent today. And America was, of course, settled by Protestant nonconformists who abandoned Europe in search of freedom of conscience. Religious strife defines our history.

China, by contrast, has a much more flexible and tolerant religious tradition. There was certainly repression of Buddhism at times. A ninth-century imperial edict instructed Christians to 'cease polluting the customs of China'. Missionaries were banned from provinces by Qing emperors. All religions were comprehensively repressed under the Communists. Nonetheless religious tolerance has been more common throughout China's history than repression. Within ten years of Louis XIV's 1685 Revocation of the Edict of Nantes, which made French Protestants targets once again for pogroms, the Chinese emperor Kangxi issued an edict of toleration for Catholics. 'The Europeans are very quiet,' the emperor's 1692 judgement read. 'They do not excite any disturbances in the provinces, they do no harm to anyone, they commit no crimes, and their doctrine has nothing in common with that of the false sects in the empire, nor has it any tendency to excite sedition.'

Many Chinese studied Taoism and Buddhism side by side. Despite their very different messages, there were Buddhist temples erected to Confucius. Ma Dexin, a nineteenth-century Muslim scholar, even tried to find accommodation between Islam and Confucianism. The late Qing reformist martyr, Tan Sitong, said: 'The founders of the three religions [Christianity, Confucianism and Buddhism] are all one. When I worship one, I worship them all.'

That liberal and non-dogmatic approach to matters of faith is still tangible today. On my uncle's sideboard in Guangzhou the laughing Buddha statue sits happily next to three cheery Taoist deities called Fuk, Luk, and Sau.[47] They represent happiness, wealth and health respectively. Another popular Buddhist deity in China is the white-robed goddess of mercy, Guanyin, who bears a resemblance to the Virgin Mary.

That kind of spiritual syncretism is alien to the Western tradition. In his influential 1993 essay predicting a 'Clash of Civilizations', the American political scientist Samuel Huntingdon based his case, in part, on the logical incompatibility of religious values. 'A person can be half-French and half-Arab and simultaneously even a citizen of two countries' he argued. '[But] it is more difficult to be half-Catholic and half-Muslim.'[48] That probably seems self-evident in the European/American mental universe. In China, as we have seen, it is anything but.

We find it difficult to accept that China can have absorbed these divergent faiths without experiencing its own shattering wars of religion. Because it makes China easier to understand, we also

accentuate a single strand of China's spiritual heritage, generally
Confucianism or Taoism, and ignore or downplay the others. But
could there be something else, something more unpalatable, going
on too?

THE ETERNAL STANDSTILL

It all goes back to an old insult. Writing about China in the middle
of the nineteenth century, John Stuart Mill painted a picture of a
people incapable of change. 'They have become stationary – have remained so for thousands of years,' he argued. 'They have succeeded
... in making a people all alike, all governing their thoughts and
conduct by the same maxims and rules.'[49] The historian Leopold
Von Ranke echoed this, calling the Chinese 'The peoples of an eternal standstill'. 'An embalmed mummy, wrapped in silk and painted
with hieroglyphics' was the description of China offered by the
German poet Johann Gottfied von Herder.

This was always over the top. As Joanna Waley-Cohen has pointed
out, there was plenty of evidence in the late eighteenth century,
at the time of the Macartney mission's failure, that China's rulers
were not, in fact, closed to Western technology. Europeans seized
on the Qianlong rebuff as evidence of an entire mental attitude of
'ingrained xenophobia and a concomitant resistance to progress'. As
she puts it: 'in the Age of Progress, such an attitude led automatically to the assumption that the Chinese were inferior beings.'[50]

Prejudice justified violence. Chinese cultural 'arrogance' became
one of the rhetorical tropes used by public advocates of those punitive expeditions launched to open up China to the opium trade. In
1841 *The Times* urged Britain's military to terrorize the Chinese out
of their faults. 'Something approaching to absolute terror must be
inflicted before arrogancy so great and self-confidence so deeply-
rooted can be expected to give way,' the newspaper thundered.[51]

Cultural stasis became a justification for imperialism. Popular
writers like Charles Dickens, as we saw earlier, helped spread the
message on the home front. Christians in China tended to be less
bloodthirsty, but many nevertheless concurred with the underlying
message. During the Second Opium War of the late 1850s the Protestant missionary lobby in Britain insisted, with sincere regrets, that

the Chinese had it coming. 'We weep over the miseries let loose [on the Chinese] but we cannot shut our eyes to the fact that nothing but the strong arms of foreign power can soon open the field for the entrance of the Gospel,' said a journal. 'If pride goeth before destruction and a haughty spirit before a fall, then it was inevitable that chastisement from some power would sooner or later result.'[52] American missionaries were preaching from the same gospel of force more than forty years later. 'China can never be reformed from within,' insisted Arthur Henderson Smith in 1894. What Smith called 'Christian civilization' would need to be imposed on the country by Europeans.[53]

Some things have changed. We now talk about China's ancient culture in a tone of admiration rather than echoing the contempt of many Victorians. We have slipped back into an older tradition, exhibited by the French philosophes, of venerating the country. When we refer to China's cultural self-confidence, we feel that the country has a perfect right to that pride, given the country's economic resurgence. But our analysis, particularly the Victorian idea that the Chinese consider themselves made of finer stuff than the rest of humanity, is surely no less suspect in light of the vigorous internal challenges to China's own traditional culture over the past century. There remains something dubious about the view that Chinese culture is rigid and unchanging.

Various European-style architectural enclaves have been built in China in recent years. There is a 'Thames Town' in Shanghai, modelled on an English village, and a village in Guangdong based on the Austrian mountain retreat of Hallstatt. Homes in these projects are, admittedly, rather kitsch, not to mention unaffordable to most Chinese. But Western media outlets have also ridiculed these construction projects as 'inauthentic', or as a *Washington Post* headline put it: 'Developers build ersatz European, American Communities'. This inadvertently reveals an unconscious prejudice. Presumably to be 'authentic' these communities would need to have Westerners living in them, to be built by Westerners. Chinese people in such communities must be acting out a role, rebelling against their true cultural nature. The idea that a Chinese person might simply want to live in a Georgian terrace or an Alpine chalet seems scarcely possible, even though the father of the republic, Sun Yat Sen, set up home in a European-style house in Shanghai's French Concession during the 1920s. My great-great-grandfather did not consider himself any less Chinese for living in his classical-style villa in Guangdong.

This urge we feel to put an entire people into the iron cage of a rigid culture and an ancient history throws up many bitter ironies. It's not too hard to see why the Communist Party itself has relentlessly propagated the idea of China's cultural homogeneity. If a regime can convince the world that China has a monoculture, rather than a fractious collection of diverse territories, it bolsters its own international legitimacy. That's why it has swallowed some of its old anti-Confucianism to promote a message of 'harmony'. For a regime interested in, above all, preserving its monopoly on power, that perception matters more than any Marxist ideological purity. The regime has a clear interest in promoting a narrative of cultural relativism, hence its mouthpieces are fond of arguing, in a transparently self-serving fashion, that democracy and human rights are alien conceptions that cannot be grafted onto China's culture.

But do those of us who repeat the mantra that China has a monolithic and static culture realize we are inadvertently serving the purposes of the Communist regime? By glossing over the manifestly distinctive cultures of the Dalai Lama followers of Tibet and the Muslims of the far western province of Xinjiang we implicitly accept the right of the regime in Beijing to sacrifice the separatist ambitions of those regions on the altar of China's national unity. And by trumpeting China's cultural specialness we underwrite the claptrap that says democracy can never be accepted in China.

Everyone now scorns the memory of the 'useful idiots' – Lenin's label for those European intellectuals who naïvely sang the praises of the Bolshevik regime in Russia before the Second World War. Yet are those of us who overemphasize China's cultural homogeneity today any less useful to a distant repressive regime?

NEW CHINA

It would be fatuous to argue that there is no such thing as a recognizable Chinese culture in everyday life in large swathes of the country. Feng Shui philosophy, superstitions about numbers, ancestor worship are all vividly present, even as China's urban centres become increasingly Westernized. Many buildings in China have no marked fourth floor, since the number four sounds similar to the word for death. My aunt in Guangzhou is ruthlessly practical when it comes to running her public relations business, but she still hired a Feng Shui consultant for advice on laying out her new office. When I leave my relatives in China they light a joss stick at an all-purpose family shrine and pray for my safe arrival home.

It is also true that the Chinese written language constitutes a powerful cultural and national adhesive. Many people from across the broad empire might not be able to understand each other's dialects, but they can generally read the same newspapers and follow the same television subtitles. The effort at literary homogenization goes back to that first Qin emperor; and Mao forced the teaching of Putonghua, the 'common speech' of Mandarin, in schools. If there is a single story that supports the claims to China's cultural continuity, it is this literary unity.

There is genuine cultural pride too in China's history and achievements. Sun Yat Sen and Mao were always careful to pay homage to the strengths of Chinese tradition, even as they sought to overturn it. Mao might have scorned the 'feudal' emperors but he wanted to recapture the pomp of their glory years. Sun argued that China's ancient philosophy was actually similar to the principles of Western democracy.[54] His former protégé, Chiang Kai Shek, who headed the nationalist government after Sun's death, founded a New Life Movement in the 1920s to resurrect traditional Chinese values. Attacks by radical intellectuals on backward aspects of China's culture have always been countered by other intellectuals who have pointed out that culture's valuable philosophical contribution.

There are limits to historical revisionism. It is clear that China's conservative political culture strangled progress at various times, just as Chinese reformists themselves have argued. After the pioneering fifteenth-century voyages of Zeng He, the Ming Dynasty turned inward, deciding not to sponsor further long-distance naval expeditions, even formally outlawing trade with immediate neighbours in Japan. In the nineteenth century, Qing rulers, for whatever internal reasons, closed themselves off from cultural exchange with the European world. It is telling that there was no foreign ministry in Beijing until 1861, and the ban on migration was only lifted in

1893. Those late imperial rulers were complacent and arrogant too. This mindset was brutally exposed by a military defeat by the Japanese in 1895, a people who China's ruling class, up to that point, had foolishly looked upon as inferior in every respect.

Advocates of reform in the late imperial era faced huge resistance too, born of a quasi-religious attachment to tradition from large sections of the elite. Reformers had to sweeten their calls for modernization by stressing 'Chinese learning for the substance, Western learning for the application'. Other non-Western empires in the nineteenth century, such as the Ottomans on Europe's eastern borders, managed to achieve modernization with much less of a struggle. Japan, with its Meiji Restoration, also showed that it was possible for Eastern societies to reform.

Despite all this, we should not be misled by those who have fashioned sweeping conclusions about the insular 'Chinese mind' from this elite history of political conservatism. At the turn of the twentieth century, at a time when the Dowager Empress Cixi was backing the anti-foreigner Boxer pogroms, tens of thousands of poor Chinese were emigrating to the Americas and the Caribbean in search of work, people like my great-great-grandfather Zau Gasam. The ability of the empire to keep them shut in had evaporated and they seized the opportunity. Ordinary people in China were open to the outside world, even if their rulers in Beijing were not.

We should note too that that bastion of Chinese culture, the written language, has also adapted considerably in the modern era. Children today are taught the language with 'pinyin', Chinese sounds expressed by the Western alphabet. Chinese people also use pinyin when texting on their mobile phones and typing on their computers. The script itself was simplified in the 1950s, cutting down the number of strokes in each character. Though there are some who regret the cultural loss entailed by that simplification, very few Chinese who use the script for everyday communication wish to turn the clock back.

The Japanese have helped shape the language too, more than many of today's sabre-rattling Chinese nationalists would care to admit. A host of phrases were taken from classical Chinese by Japanese scholars after the Meiji Restoration and applied to modern Western concepts such as 'society', 'economics' and 'environment'.

These words were then re-exported to China in the late nineteenth century as scholars travelled to Japan to study the new scientific disciplines. Modern spoken Chinese languages are also liberally sprinkled with English words.

In the end we see that Chinese culture did not spring up fully formed from the banks of the Yellow River, as legend suggests. Instead, it has been continually shaped by outside forces over many centuries. Historically it has evolved through adaptation, sometimes revolution. Modern nationalism is as powerful a force in modern China as ancient Confucianism. Sun Yat Sen's 'Three Principles of the People' lectures (which were, incidentally, inspired by Abraham Lincoln's Gettysburg Address) are now just as much a part of Chinese political culture as the *Analects*. Chinese culture is also heterogeneous to a far greater extent than assumed. Different parts of this vast and varied land have sharply divergent traditions and outlooks. It makes more sense to speak of China's series of interlocking cultures, rather than a single dominant value system, or way of life.

Meanwhile, China's attitude to its history is a contradictory phenomenon. Sometimes China repudiates the past; at other times it embraces it. Sometimes the government has a great reverence for its heritage, imposing the death penalty on those who smuggle antiques and artistic treasures out of the country, yet at other times it acts like a cultural vandal, as shown when the Beijing authorities tore down the historic Hutong alleyways in the capital ahead of the 2008 Beijing Olympics.[55] This contradiction can be found in popular attitudes too. Speak to Chinese people today and, it is true, they will often talk about what an ancient nation they are, seeming to support the idea of their great 'historical mindedness', but at other times they will emphasize how 'new' their country is and how far they have to go to catch up with the West.

Most important of all, China has a contested culture, not a universally accepted one. There has long been a struggle over what to retain, what to cast off, and because of that struggle the culture is still changing. Like the Yellow River – that age-old symbol of China – it flows and winds. We should resist lazy assumptions about where it will travel next.

THE CHINESE ARE IRREDEEMABLY RACIST

Hou Dejian was an unlikely-looking pop star. With his oversized spectacles and a bouffant mop of black hair, the twenty-two-year-old singer songwriter looked more like a nerdy student than a celebrity. But genius can be delivered in unlikely forms. Despite his some-what unpromising appearance, Hou scored a gigantic hit in China in 1978 with a patriotic composition called 'Heirs of the Dragon'. The song was a mystical paean to China's racial unity:

> In the ancient east there is a dragon, her name is China
> In the ancient east there is a people, they are all heirs of the
> dragon
> I grew up under the claw of the dragon,
> after I grew up I became an heir of the dragon
> Black eyes, black hair, yellow skin, forever and ever an heir of
> the dragon.

What made Hou's success even more surprising was that he lived on the contested island of Taiwan. At that time official relations between Taipei and Beijing were still in the deep freeze. The nationalist forces of Chiang Kai Shek had fled to the island in 1949 after the Communists prevailed in the civil war. Mao had been plotting to take back the renegade province, which enjoyed the military protection of the United States, for decades. Unlike today, travel between the two jurisdictions – the one authoritarian capitalist, the other authoritarian Communist – was strictly forbidden. That meant Hou, whose parents had fled to Taiwan along with Chiang, had never even been able to visit the motherland whose glories he extolled.

But the sentiment he expressed in that song, that the Chinese no matter where they live are all 'heirs of the dragon', resonated deeply on both sides of the Taiwan Strait. Soon it was everywhere. Hou made a music video where he appeared in a traditional Chinese gown of gleaming gold, beside lithe dancers, urging the 'mighty dragon' of China to 'open your eyes, forever and ever open your eyes'. Hou seemed to give new expression to what the Chinese had long known in their bones: that they were an indivisible and glorious race of people.

We tend to take it for granted that the Chinese, if perhaps not quite heirs of the dragon, are a formidably unified tranche of humanity. The racial homogeneity of the Chinese was assumed in the West during the nineteenth century. The American sociologist Gerrit Lansing, in an 1882 essay on the Chinese, wrote that 'the development of a society from a single race, under one government, with constantly similar surroundings and but little subject to the influence of foreign races or nations, has produced a homogeneous society.'[1] Bertrand Russell, at the commencement of the twentieth century, described 'the unrivalled national cohesiveness' of the Chinese.[2] More recently, historian Eric Hobsbawm called China an 'extremely rare example' of a nation that is 'ethnically almost or entirely homogeneous'.[3] To Sinologist Lucian Pye it was 'self-evident that the Chinese people share the same blood, the same physical characteristics, the same ancestry'.[4] We seem to agree with Sun Yat Sen, the earnest leader of the republican movement that brought down thousands of years of imperial rule in 1911, who proclaimed that the Chinese were 'a single pure race' with 'common blood, common language, common religion and common customs'.[5]

With racial unity comes racial pride and the conventional wisdom is that, alas, the Chinese people's ethnic and biological cohesiveness has bred a streak of ugly chauvinism in the national character, particularly towards those peoples of the world with darker skin.

RACISM WITH CHINESE CHARACTERISTICS

In the Communist view of history Africa and China had much in common. Both had been carved up by rapacious capitalist powers throughout the nineteenth century. Both were now throwing off the colonial yoke. This was a relationship that Mao Zedong sought to nurture after taking power in 1949. During the 1960s and 70s

many young Africans from friendly regimes were invited to study at
Chinese universities. On the surface it was a gesture of anti-imperial
solidarity, although Mao mainly saw it as way to assert China's pri-
macy among Communist states around the world and to irritate his
rivals in Russia.

In the event, solidarity among ordinary Chinese and their African
comrades turned out to be in short supply. Resentment between the
visiting dark-skinned foreigners and the local students grew over
the decades, exacerbated by the fact that the foreign scholars enjoyed more generous grants than domestic youngsters. Finally, over
the winter of 1988, the situation exploded. After an altercation at a
Christmas party in the city of Nanjing hundreds of angry Chinese
students went on the warpath, besieging visiting Africans in their
dormitories. The anti-African riots soon spread to major university cities across China, including Beijing, Shanghai and Wuhan.
Many terrified African students were forced to seek refuge from
the violence and intimidation at their own national embassies and
consulates. The slogans chanted by mobs that winter of student discontent – 'Down with the black devils', 'Black devils go home' – left
no doubt that this was an outbreak of racial bigotry.

The Chinese authorities regained control. A few Africans were
turned into scapegoats for starting the trouble and swiftly deported,
but the racial tensions continued to bubble away beneath the surface of Chinese society. They oozed out again when Condoleezza
Rice, the African American US foreign minister, made an official
visit to China in 2005. The Chinese Internet overflowed with racist
venom. 'How come the United States selects a female chimpanzee
as Secretary of State?' asked one anonymous online commentator.
Others labelled Rice a 'black female dog'.

Another typhoon of racial abuse broke in 2009 when a Shanghai
student called Lou Jing, whose father was an African American, appeared on *Go Oriental Angel*, one of China's many televised singing
talent shows. The treatment of the pretty twenty-year-old by the
producers was cringe-worthy. 'Her chocolate-coloured skin lights
up her sunny character,' exclaimed the host. The reaction on the
Chinese Internet to Lou Jing was still more offensive. 'All those who
come from mixing yellow and black blood are truly ugly,' complained one person. 'If I were that girl, I would be so low key. How

could I possibly come out and expose my face seeking attention and sympathy?' asked another.

Hostility to foreigners extends well beyond the anonymous netizenry of China. Yang Rui, the middle-aged host of *Dialogue*, an English language discussion programme on Chinese state television, normally comes across as a sober and urbane figure. But in 2012 the presenter unleashed a rant to his 800,000 followers on the Chinese social networking site, Weibo, that stunned many Westerners living in China. 'Americans and Europeans,' Yang claimed, 'come to China to traffic people, misleading the public and encouraging them to emigrate.' After railing against 'foreign spies', he suggested: 'we should make everyone who demonizes China shut up and get out.' This was the equivalent of a senior mainstream media figure – Jeremy Paxman in the UK or Larry King in the US – morphing into a xenophobic demagogue. The fact that Yang often invited Western guests on his show made the incident all the more alarming.

Perhaps the most disturbing modern tale of Chinese racism involved the British author Martin Jacques. His Malaysian wife, Harinder Veriah, who was of Indian heritage, was admitted to Ruttonjee Hospital in Hong Kong on the first day of the new Millennium after suffering an epileptic fit. She died the following morning from respiratory failure. Jacques recalls his wife complaining of racist prejudice and neglect from doctors and nurses in the hours after she was admitted. Despite a coroner finding no evidence of negligence, Jacques sued the hospital and in 2010, after a protracted legal struggle, a settlement was reached. This traumatic episode has helped to lead Jacques to the conclusion that Hong Kong, and indeed the Chinese nation as a whole, is in the grip of what he terms 'racial hubris'.

He is by no means the only Westerner to have identified an ingrained xenophobic mentality among the Chinese. In 2012 Mark Kitto, a former publisher, wrote of his decision to leave China after sixteen years. One of his reasons he gave was that 'all non-Chinese are, to the Chinese, aliens in a mildly derogatory sense'.[6] Kitto also spoke of his anxieties, suggesting that if the regime in Beijing ever collapsed one of the consequences would be violence directed at foreigners.

This evokes memories of the Boxer Rebellion at the turn of the twentieth century, when angry nativist mobs of rural Chinese massacred Christians and besieged terrified Europeans in the international settlement of old Beijing. Rather than suppressing the Boxers, the Qing rulers sided with the rebels. This prompted a military intervention from a multinational coalition to protect Europeans residing in the capital. Some have wondered whether a 'clamp down on foreigners' campaign launched in 2012 by the Beijing municipal authorities aimed at deporting those non-Chinese who have overstayed their work visas could be a harbinger of resurgent Boxerism.

Other suspicions have been kindled. The Beijing regime's one-child policy introduced in early 1979 looks to some like a policy to improve the 'quality' of the Chinese race. The propaganda that has accompanied the policy has stressed the importance of fewer but 'better' children. And in 1994 the regime passed a eugenics law, requiring all pregnant women to undergo embryo screening and to abort foetuses with genetic disorders. Richard Lynn, a professor of psychology at the University of Ulster, claims that, as a result of these policies, a super-intelligent Chinese race will emerge over the next two decades.[7] Lynn is a fringe figure in science and as an enthusiastic advocate of eugenic policies himself he plainly has an agenda. All the same, the idea that China is going to show its true racially intolerant colours to the world does seem to be growing in popularity. One serious academic has estimated that the number of Chinese who harbour sympathies for racial chauvinism 'could number in the millions, if not tens of millions'.[8]

In his 2008 bestseller, *When China Rules the World*, Martin Jacques concluded that: 'The rise of China as a global superpower is likely to lead ... to a profound cultural and racial reordering of the world in the Chinese image. As China draws countries and continents into its web ... they will not simply be economic suppliants of a hugely powerful China but will occupy a position of cultural and ethnic inferiority.'[9] Never mind 'Socialism with Chinese characteristics', this sounds alarmingly like National Socialism with Chinese characteristics. Can this dark prophecy be true?

RACIAL PURITY?

The first thing to say is that Sun Yat Sen was wrong. China is very far from being the 'single pure race' with 'common blood'. Rather, it is a land of vast variety. The state itself recognizes no less than fifty-six different minority 'nations' who live mainly in China's borderlands. These range from the Mongols from the grassy steppes in the north, the Manchus of the Korean border in the northeast, Tibetans in the Himalayan west, and numerous groups such as the Miao and the Zhuang in the tropical south on the border with Burma and Vietnam. Their ethnicities, from the Islamic Uighurs in Xinjiang, to the animist Li people of Hainan Island, are profoundly different. And they are numerous too. There are, for instance, twice as many ethnic Mongols in China as there are residing in Mongolia itself. As has been remarked many times of China, it is not really a nation, but rather a multi-ethnic empire masquerading as a nation.

Some respond that these minorities constitute just 105 million out of a population of 1,300 million and that 93 per cent of Chinese citizens identify themselves as a single group, the Han. Yet this is another mistake, for it misses the cultural and indeed genetic diversity among the Han themselves. We have seen in the previous chapter how there is as much variety in language among the various populations of Han China as there is among the peoples of continental Europe. The idea that the Han are in a biological sense a single group does not stand up either. Research on populations throughout China has found that the Han Chinese who live in the north tend to have different genetic features from those who live in the south, suggesting that the two populations had separate geographic origins.[10]

There are some fascinating pockets of diversity too. The Han inhabitants of Liqian, on the edge of the Gobi desert in China's arid northwest, are renowned for their striking green eyes and light hair. Legend has it that a band of Roman soldiers fled to China after the army of Crassus was scattered by the Parthians at Carrhae in 53 BC. In the 1950s Homer Hasenphlug Dubs, an Oxford professor of Chinese Studies, came up with a theory that this lost legion ended up in Liqian.[11] Dubs suggested that some unusual military formations described in ancient Chinese texts could have been Roman attack techniques. Sadly for the professor's disciples, no Roman coins or Latin inscriptions have been unearthed to support his theory. But the fair-haired Chinese of Liqian do, nevertheless, suggest that the genetics of Han China are fuzzier than many would like to believe.

Though they might share some physical traits, the idea that the Han Chinese constitute a 'race' is as fantastical as the notion that they are all descendants of an ancient dragon. Like the 'Anglo-Saxons' or the 'Hispanics', the Han are a purely imagined biological community.

A LOOSE SHEET OF SAND

Of course, what people believe can often matter more than the truth, and the Chinese sense of themselves as a discrete branch of humanity has deep roots. Frank Dikotter, a historian at the University of Hong Kong, has shown in exhaustive detail that hostile attitudes to outsiders, particularly nomadic tribes from the north, were rife in elite intellectual circles long before Europeans kicked in the door of imperial China in the middle of the nineteenth century.[12] Northern tribes were routinely dehumanized in texts, likened to savage or domesticated beasts. Chinese scholars even used brush strokes that signified animals when they invented characters to denote these peoples. The concept of 'Sinicization' – outsiders enveloped by the Chinese cultural universe – was equated with the concept of humanization. So when officials of the besieged Qing regime said that European invaders belonged in the same lowly category as dogs and horses they were drawing on a long-established tradition of bigotry.

Things were just as ugly after the empire fell and China moved into its republican era. Newspapers and popular novels in the early decades of the twentieth century were full of racist language and imagery, and school textbooks were strewn with passages such as this:

> Mankind is divided into five races. The yellow and white races are relatively strong and intelligent. Because the other races are feeble and stupid, they are being exterminated by the white race. Only the yellow race competes with the white race. This is so-called evolution ... Among the contemporary races that could be called superior, there are only the yellow and the white races. China is the yellow race.

Despite this long history of xenophobia the Chinese people's perception of themselves as a 'race', in the biological sense, is a relatively recent phenomenon. Late nineteenth-century European scholars such as Thomas Huxley and Herbert Spencer used a bastardized reading of Darwin's natural selection to come up with the theory of human racial difference and natural competition between nations. These ideas were transmitted to China in the translations of Spencer and Huxley by the Chinese scholar Yan Fu (who had studied at the Naval Academy in Greenwich). It was Yan Fu's translations that popularized notions of the Chinese race and its supposed struggle for survival, a struggle that seemed all the more tangible to native intellectuals in the light of China's various military defeats at the hands of European powers throughout the century.

It would be too simplistic to argue that an innocent Chinese mind was infected by European racism, but racial thought was, nevertheless, another example of the Chinese appropriation of a Western intellectual innovation. Hard as it might be today to imagine, at one time theories of racial and national unity were at the bleeding edge of progressive and scientific thought. Spencer and Huxley were not reviled in Victorian society as racists, but respected as serious scientific thinkers. And so it was in China.

That progressive association of race was the reason the notion featured so prominently in Sun Yat Sen's vaunted 'Three Principles of the People' manifesto for a vigorous republican China. Sun regarded building a Chinese racial consciousness as a central part of his nation's modernization. As he travelled the world seeking to raise money for his rebellion, his mind was always on China. Though he claimed he was attempting to tap into some primal feeling of Chinese solidarity based on common blood and the yellow soil of the north China plain, Sun was in fact trying to build a modern Chinese state in the manner of a Bismarck in Germany or a Mazzini in Italy. As Sun put it, he wanted to make concrete out of a Chinese population that he characterized as an easily divided 'sheet of loose sand'.

Persistent Japanese aggression against China in the years before and following the establishment of the republic added further urgency to these nation-building efforts. Tokyo attempted to justify the invasion of Manchuria in the 1930s on the spurious grounds that they were merely helping the minority peoples of Tibet, Mongolia and, particularly, Manchuria achieve self-determination and to throw off the ancient burden of Chinese domination. That threat from Japan made it all the more important in the minds of nationalist leaders to build a sentiment among the Chinese that they were a single and unified race. It was not merely China's prosperity that seemed to depend on building a sense of racial unity, but her very continuance as a nation. As the historian Wang Gungwu has put it, bringing the Chinese together seemed 'the only way to save the country from being declared unfit to survive'.[13]

In some ways the nationalists were remarkably successful. Chinese people today sometimes describe themselves as 'sons and daughters of the Yellow Emperor'. This is often said with such conviction that we tend to assume this is a folk belief in a common racial origin that stretches back deep into China's long history. In reality the cult of the Yellow Emperor was largely created in the early twentieth century. It was the centrepiece of a propaganda exercise by the republican government of Sun and his successors. There were sixteen official addresses between the 1911 revolution and the fall of the republic in 1949 declaring the Yellow Emperor to be the progenitor of the Chinese state. Officials were ordered to gather at the reputed site of the deity's tomb in Shaanxi province to pay their respects. The mythical figure was even assigned a birthday, 4 April, and it was declared a national holiday.[14]

Yet in other ways the nationalists' attempts to build a sense of racial unity yielded only confusion. Sun Yat Sen's writings, which had been awarded the status of scripture by the republican government, had been built around the common blood of the Han. There was no room in this Chinese racial nation for the Manchu minority, from whom the emperors of China's Qing Dynasty had been drawn and whom the nationalists blamed for leading the country into a state of semi-colonial servitude. The other ethnic minorities were also excluded. But this presented a complication: if these groups were not part of the Chinese racial nation there was no strong argument for them to remain part of the Chinese motherland. This seemed to invite colonial powers, not least Japan, to start breaking them off, dismembering the Chinese territory.

The nationalist regime never coalesced around a satisfactory answer to this conceptual problem. Some scholars tried to show that all the peoples of China, including the minorities, had always been united by common blood. Others began to argue that a host of different populations in the region had been 'melded' over the centuries into what had become a racially unified population. Both couldn't be true, of course. Moreover, both ideas clashed with Sun Yat Sen's sacred racial definitions.

This mess of contradictions was hardly surprising, given that the agenda of Chinese racial categorization was being driven by politics, rather than science. The objective of these scholars was not to portray reality, but to show that the sprawling and diverse empire that the nationalists had inherited after the 1911 revolution was based on something more substantial than a series of arbitrary military conquests by the Qing rulers who preceded them.

Some independent-minded scholars rejected the idea that the Chinese were a homogeneous race of people and argued that the government should seek honest ways to build a sense of national unity and resistance to the depredations of foreign powers. The revisionist historian, Gu Jiegang, for instance, deplored the republican government's 'lie' that all Chinese are descended from the same ancestor. He asked a question: 'Once the people become intelligent, can this trick still deceive them?' It is a question that, as we shall see, continues to hang over China to this day.

HAN ACTORS IN THE BIRD'S NEST STADIUM

The Communists who toppled the nationalist government in 1949 began with a different, and in some respects refreshing, outlook on race. Guided by orthodox Marxist theory, they dismissed the idea of race as bourgeois claptrap. People were workers or capitalists. The former were exploited by the latter, and that was the extent of human differences in the world. Mao Zedong's early rhetoric was resolutely internationalist. The Chairman made Norman Bethune, a Canadian doctor who had died fighting with the Communist forces against Japanese occupation in 1939, into a great symbol of solidarity. 'What kind of spirit is this that makes a foreigner selflessly adopt the cause of the Chinese people's liberation as his own?' he asked in a speech that year. 'It is the spirit of internationalism, the spirit of communism, from which every Chinese Communist must learn.' Mao went on to call for the unification of the Chinese 'proletariat' with those of all other nations, from Japan and Britain to Germany and the United States. This international coming together, he argued, was the only way to overthrow the global oppression of imperialism. The Communists also criticized the nationalist anthropologists who had been busily cooking up theories of racial distinction.[15] Mao promised independence to China's ethnic minorities upon assuming power in 1949 and a few years later warned against 'Han chauvinism'. The sun seemed to be setting on a long day of racial dogmatism.

But the day was soon extended. Once settled in power, the Communists broke their promises of independence for minorities. In 1950, Tibet was occupied and China's other ethnic minority regions were soon enveloped in an iron grip. Even after 1976, when China opened up, the door of self-determination remained firmly closed to minority peoples. The authorities in Beijing have sent tens of thousands of Han Chinese to live and work in Tibet and Xinjiang, calculating that this demographic shift will strengthen their hold over these strategically important regions. This influx, combined with preferential official treatment for the incomers, helped spark race riots between Uighurs and Han in the Xinjiang capital of Urumqi in 2009. It is true that some affirmative action policies for minorities, remnants of the Communists early policy of multiculturalism, continue. The official rhetoric of harmony in diversity also lingers on, as when some minority children were paraded at the opening ceremony of Beijing's 2008 Olympics. But the phoniness of these exercises was perfectly illustrated when it turned out that the colourfully dressed minority children who trooped through the Bird's Nest stadium that night were, in fact, Han actors.[16]

The Communists were racial nationalists in other ways. Since 1955 they have refused to allow any Chinese to hold dual citizenship. If a Chinese person today wants to take out a passport from another state they must emigrate for good. Paradoxically, this refusal on the part of the regime to accept that a person can owe allegiance to two nations has also given rise to the suspicion that the authorities in Beijing, deep down, regard all overseas Chinese as merely confused sheep that have strayed from the flock. This attitude was inherited from the imperial era, when the authorities insisted that the Chinese abroad remained subjects no matter how much distance they put between themselves and the motherland. This is a feeling that persists. Even today some members of the diaspora nurse the fear that if they return to visit their birthplace as legitimate tourists they might not be allowed to leave again.

Mao's successors have also adopted the racial propaganda of their nationalist predecessors. They have, for instance, smiled on the tenuous theory that the Chinese people did not emerge from Africa along with the rest of the human species. In the 1920s early hominid remains dating back approximately 750,000 years were dug up in caves near Beijing called Zhoukoudian. This 'Peking Man' was said to be an ancestor of the Chinese people and seized upon by some scholars as evidence of the discrete nature of the race. In 2011 the Communist authorities designated Zhoukoudian as a 'site of patriotic education'. State media in recent years have also shown a consistent preference for highlighting research that seems to support the theory that the Chinese people had exclusive evolutionary origins.[17]

The modern Chinese narrative on blood and soil is, as we have seen, confusing and contradictory. The Chinese people seem to be simultaneously sons of the dragon, sons of the Yellow Emperor, and also descendants of Peking Man. And while not everyone in China is of the Chinese race, all the territory of modern China is, apparently, inherently 'Chinese'. It is hard to take this seriously, yet anything that might help sieve this strange soup of ideas still makes today's regime jumpy.

The Tarim mummies are a good example. Beijing claims that the Han Chinese had a presence in the sprawling Western province of Xinjiang dating back 2,200 years. But in the twentieth century archaeologists discovered a cemetery in the Tarim Basin of Xinjiang containing bodies that were 4,000 years old. Furthermore, it was observed that their features looked rather more European than Oriental. Genetic tests on the bodies have suggested that the mysterious tribe indeed had Western origins.[18] This, in turn, implied that Europeans were travelling the Silk Road for hundreds of years longer than historians had previously thought, raising the possibility that Europeans arrived in Xinjiang before the Han. The present Uighur inhabitants of Xinjiang only arrived in the ninth century AD, but the Tarim mummies nevertheless threatened to provide a fillip to their modern separatist movement. In 2011 a Chinese touring show of the United States called 'Secrets of the Silk Road', exhibiting the Tarim mummies, was abruptly curtailed. The show's organizers cited the fragile condition of the bodies, but the strong suspicion was that someone in Beijing had decided that this remarkable archaeological discovery, which shed light on the early history of a disputed region of Chinese territory, should receive no further publicity.[19]

CARIBBEAN REGGAE TO MALAYSIAN PORK

Some Westerners seem almost umbilically connected to China. Lucian Pye was born in 1921 in Shanxi province to two Protestant preachers. He grew up to become one of the world's foremost China scholars with a professorship at the Massachusetts Institute of Technology. Pye, for one, was convinced about the centrality of the concept of race in Chinese culture and thinking. This, he believed, defined not only the Chinese in China but the great Chinese diaspora too, which at around fifty million is the largest in the world.

'The Chinese,' Pye noted, 'see such an absolute difference between themselves and others that even when living in lonely isolation in distant countries they find it appropriate to refer to those in whose homeland they are living as "foreigners".'[20] This perception of the aloof Chinese abroad has a long history. The Chinese coolies in the US during the nineteenth century were accused of sticking together, rather than mixing with other labourers. And it remains so today. We hear complaints that Chinese labour teams sent to Africa by their government to work on infrastructure construction projects such as dams, roads and power stations do not patronize local shops, but instead shut themselves off in their fortress-like compounds until their work is done and they can return to China.

There is, however, another side to Chinese diaspora which conflicts with this image of an inherently insular and chauvinistic people. My Chinese-born father married my white British mother in Sheffield in the 1970s. Far from being rejected, it was a union that received the enthusiastic blessing of my father's immigrant parents, and my parents were the beginning of a trend. The 2001 UK census shows that 20 per cent of Chinese Britons are in mixed-race relationships.[21] Moreover the 2011 census is expected to show an increase in mixed-race marriages involving Chinese Britons. Virtually every young Chinese person I know in the UK is in a relationship, or married, to a non-Chinese. Contrary to the stereotype of the immigrant parents who are hostile to their children 'marrying out', the older generation in my experience could not be happier about the choices their offspring have made.

Chinese assimilation is not just a British phenomenon. Asian Americans, of whom Chinese Americans are a significant group, are the racial group most likely to have partners from outside their ethnic group. From the 2010 cohort of newly-weds, 28 per cent of Asians married someone of a different ethnicity.[22] This compared with 9 per cent of whites, 17 per cent of blacks and 26 per cent of Hispanics. Women were especially likely to marry outside their ethnic group, with about 36 per cent of Asian female newly-weds marrying non-Asians.

In other parts of the world, the Chinese have shown themselves still more likely to assimilate. Coolie labourers from China, mostly from the Hakka minority, travelled to the Caribbean in the nineteenth century to work in sugar plantations. These itinerant workers put down roots rapidly, marrying local women and seizing opportunities to go into business for themselves. By some estimates 20 per cent of Jamaicans have Chinese ancestry. The Chinese language has pretty much died out, but the old surnames remain. A Chinese Jamaican called Randy Chin was a key figure in the commercialization of the island's reggae music, recording among many others, a young Bob Marley at his Kingston studio. The Chinese had a lasting impact across the Caribbean. Sir Solomon Hochoy, the first post-independence Governor General of Trinidad and Tobago in 1962, was of Chinese descent.

The biggest Chinese diaspora is in South East Asia. There are between eighteen and twenty million ethnic Chinese spread over Indonesia, Thailand, Malaysia, Singapore, the Philippines, Burma, Vietnam, Laos and Cambodia. Some are said to have arrived in the region more than a thousand years ago, during the Tang Dynasty, but the majority came from southern China amidst the upheavals and civil wars of the nineteenth century. It is this group that is frequently depicted as 'sojourners', a people just passing through with no intention of assimilating into the culture or life of the host country. They have also been called the 'Jews of the East' for their dominant role in commerce and their perceived loyalty to the international ethnic group, rather than the nation state.[23]

Tong Chee Kiong, of Singapore University, who has conducted extensive research on the Chinese diaspora in the region, has demonstrated that the reality is far more complex than this caricature of a perennially aloof people allows. He notes that in Thailand the Chinese have managed to integrate with the local community while also retaining their distinctive group identity. 'Most Chinese in Thailand today can speak Thai, go to Thai schools, join Thai associations, celebrate Thai festivals and would consider themselves Thai citizens,' he points out. 'At the same time, Chinese schools and associations persist, Chinese religious rituals are still practised on a daily basis, and most Chinese would consider themselves Chinese.'[24]

There has also been extensive marriage across South East Asia between these supposedly aloof sojourners and local populations. José Rizal, the great nationalist martyr of the Philippines who was executed by the Spanish colonial authorities in 1896, was of Chinese descent. The great-grandfather of the first female president of the former colony, Corazon Aquino, was a Chinese immigrant. And the man whose title evoked countless guffaws across the English-speaking world – Cardinal Sin, the late Archbishop of Manila – was the son of a junk dealer from Xiamen. The great-grandfather of the present Thai prime minister, Yingluck Shinawatra, was also Chinese.

In Malaysia and Indonesia the descendants of Chinese migrants who married local women are known as 'peranakans', or 'children of the soil', in an acknowledgment of their local roots. Malaysian peranakans use the native language, but with a few words from Chinese dialect sprinkled around. And while they use Malaysian cooking styles, they cook with pork, which is forbidden by the religious strictures of the country's Islamic majority. The extent of the cultural assimilation and the reason it has been greater in some nations than others remains a subject of academic debate, but the notion that the Chinese of South East Asia have hermetically sealed themselves off from the native populations of the lands in which their ancestors settled, motivated by some sort of racial contempt for the locals, is hard to sustain.

The story seems to be the same in new frontiers of emigration.

We often think of Africa as an imperial project for the Chinese, with huge amounts of investment and manpower flowing to the continent from the East each year but precious little mixing. Yet here too the common image of the Chinese refusing to assimilate is misleading. An increasing number of Chinese small traders in Africa are marrying local women, just as their predecessors did in South East Asia, Europe and America. In a far cry from the stereotype of a people who cannot leave behind the ways of the old country, the Chinese have proved themselves rather good at mingling in the new lands in which they make their homes.

'CHOCOLATE CITY'

There is no disputing that casual racism and reflexive xenophobia are depressingly common features of modern Chinese life. Around Tong Xin Road in Guangzhou, where my great-uncle lives, the air is often thick with smoky aromas as white-capped Hui muslims barbecue skewers of lamb on street corner stalls. Despite the presence of Muslims in this great trading city since the seventh century, many locals still look upon them with suspicion. One evening in Guangzhou as our family chatted on the pavement after visiting a local restaurant one of my cousins started fussing about, urging us to return home and take care of our belongings. At first I wondered what the hurry was, but then I realized what was bothering him: the street was full of Muslims.

Amble through the maze of surrounding streets in the Xiaobei district of the city and you can find Middle Eastern shopkeepers selling cheap clothes and mobile phones. But Guangzhou's biggest immigrant population is African; there are 20,000 in the city according to official statistics, hailing from Nigeria, Cameroon and Mali and a host of other nations. And these Africans are in China not to sell, but to buy. They purchase cheap clothes, usually seconds from the province's many factories, and transport them to their home countries, where they are able to sell them on at a decent profit. These modern-day merchants do not pay for bulk shipping like the Western multinationals that use China as their workshop. Instead their goods go in the hold of commercial airplanes.

Africans can be seen queuing up at Guangzhou international

airport most weeks. Massive bales of clothes wrapped into tight green plastic are perched precariously on their trolleys. This is their 'luggage' and they are waiting to check it in. It all seems a tremendous hassle, but importing cheap clothes from China is a lucrative trade and the numbers of new traders arriving from Africa rises each year. Xiaobei has now become known as 'Chocolate City' by the city's taxi drivers.

As with the Muslims, there is Chinese suspicion of this community too. Locals say the area is rife with drug dealing, theft, illegal immigration and disease. In the minds of many locals, Africans and criminality seem to go together. In the summer of 2009 Chocolate City almost melted down when a Nigerian called Emmanuel Okoro fell from a second-storey window while attempting to evade immigration police. His compatriots took the unconscious Okoro to the local police station and staged an impromptu protest against official harassment.[25] The traffic on one of Guangzhou's eight-lane mega highways was blocked for three hours, prompting a predictable debate in the Chinese media about the 'African problem'.

There are parallels with Chungking Mansions, a shabby block of cheap hostels and shops that most visitors to Hong Kong's Kowloon district will probably have passed. Those who venture inside this twenty-first-century Tower of Babel will find Indian restaurants serving up curries on formica tables, Africans flogging mobile phones from cramped booths, sari shops stuffed to the rafters with colourful fabric and Nepalese knock-off DVD emporiums. Like Xiaobei, Chungking has a poor reputation among the local Chinese, who see it as a nexus for drugs and crime. Chungking Mansions also gets special attention from the local police.

Political correctness when it comes to race is an alien concept in China. The old term 'foreign devil', which first came into fashion in the nineteenth century, still slips thoughtlessly from the lips of even the most ostensibly enlightened and polite of Chinese. Patronizing attitudes to China's ethnic minorities and the Japanese, or the 'little Japanese' as they are frequently referred to in another slur dating back to the imperial era, are common. There can be quite stunning insensitivity: 'Black People toothpaste', which shows an image of a top-hatted minstrel figure with gleaming teeth on the packaging, is still on sale in Chinese supermarkets. Many African students complain of a depressing sense of alienation. Others report being refused jobs on account of their skin colour.

None of this racism should be downplayed, but it is important to acknowledge some context too. From the 1950s to the later 1970s China was a closed society. Chairman Mao turned the country into a giant jail, much like North Korea today. The few foreigners who penetrated its high walls were not permitted to stay for an extended period, let alone marry. While the population of expats in China is growing, it remains relatively small, at around one million. The old tendency for Chinese people to stare at white people and other foreigners with curiosity is dying out; in large cities it perished some time ago, but it is still not completely gone. In 2012 in a holiday resort in the hills above Shenzhen a series of smiling Chinese tourists wanted to have their picture taken standing next to my white British wife – for no other reason than she was an unusual foreigner. Others took more discreet snaps from afar.

It is also worth remembering, as context, that Britain was a land of rampant racism as recently as the 1950s, with dark-skinned immigrants from the Caribbean and Pakistan facing routine discrimination over the allocation of housing and jobs. This was the era of signs on boarding houses that read: 'no dogs, no blacks'. And in America state 'anti-miscegenation' laws (which forbade marriage between different races) of many states were not ruled unconstitutional by the Supreme Court until 1967. It took time for attitudes and laws to begin change in the West.

Can the same happen in China? There are already some tentative signs that it is. Barry Sautman, an academic based in Hong Kong, has been studying race relations in China for two decades. He conducted a series of interviews with African students in China after the riots of 1988, chronicling the racism and hostility they experienced from the host population, and he has continued to interview African visitors in the years since.[26] Sautman argues that there has been a considerable improvement in relations. In the late 1980s and 1990s the African population often feared to go to certain places within the cities where they were living because of the threat of physical violence from locals. But things have got much better. 'No African student that I have interviewed in recent years has reported that there is any place in the country they cannot go and feel safe,' he told me.

This picture is supported by Loretta Evans, an African American who has been in China for eight years. She summed up her experience in 2012 speaking to CNN: 'Yes, I've sometimes had people stare or touch my skin, as if to see whether it's going to rub off. But I think this comes from curiosity not negativity.' She even suggested that attitudes to black people in China are, in some ways, preferable to those in America: 'Here I don't feel the racial tension I feel back home. I've done things, such as setting up my own geophysics company, which as a black woman I might not have been able to do in the States. Yes, I'm treated differently from Chinese people. But here I'm different first, black second.'[27]

The testimony of Lou Jing, the Shanghai girl with an African father who was racially abused online after appearing on a TV talent show, also merits attention. She says she was stunned not so much by the bigotry of the online commentators but because she had never experienced racist hatred like that before in China. 'I have never felt different because of my skin until now,' she told an interviewer. 'I get the odd person pointing in the street and saying I have dark skin, but not in a nasty way.'[28] It is worth noting too that black contestants have sometimes done well on Chinese TV talent contests. A Liberian singer came second in CCTV's *Star Walk* in 2006, and a man from Sierra Leone came fourth in 2007. Both were popular among viewers and were even invited back to appear as judges.

Sautman and a team from Guangzhou University researched the attitudes of locals towards African immigrants in 2009. What they found was that those Chinese who had worked alongside black people, as brokers and shopkeepers, tended to have a more favourable attitude to the community than those Chinese who merely noticed their presence around the city. The more time people spent with them, the more their prejudices about the criminality of black people eroded.

This makes Sautman relatively optimistic about the future of race relations in China. 'There's no evidence that as the years have gone by the Chinese have become more xenophobic. And there's no evidence that Chinese are particularly xenophobic compared to other people,' he says.[29] That view is echoed by Yan Sun, a professor of political science at the City University of New York, who also feels that further contact will help reform attitudes. 'As market and globalizing forces cause the Chinese to interact more with foreigners from abroad, conflict will be inevitable, but so is progress,' she says.[30]

There are increasing flickers of that progress too. Since the election of President Obama in 2008, views seem to have become more favourable to black people, at least if the Chinese Internet is any indication. When Michelle Obama spoke at the 2012 Democratic convention in support of her husband, many Chinese netizens were full of admiration, noting that it would be unthinkable for one of their leaders' wives to speak in public in this way. 'China, when can we have a great first lady like her?' asked one. It was a far cry from the abuse heaped on another African American woman, Condoleezza Rice, seven years earlier.

Love is also tearing down barriers. Mixed ethnicity marriages are rising in China, especially in the big cities. The numbers of Chinese tying the knot with foreigners has more than doubled from 22,000 in 1985 to 49,000 in 2010.[31] There is a high-profile example. Barack Obama's half-brother is married to a woman from Hunan province. Mark Okoth Obama Ndesandjo, a business consultant and fluent Mandarin speaker who lives in the southern city of Shenzhen, seems pleased with his reception in China. Shortly before the half-brothers were reunited in 2009 he told *Time* magazine: 'I'm so happy my brother is coming to China because I've experienced the warmth and the graciousness of the Chinese people.'[32]

My own family told me excitedly of an elderly man in our ancestral village in Guangdong whose granddaughter has married an African doctor who works at Guangzhou hospital. These sorts of stories are increasingly common and my sense is that they are rapidly losing their capacity to scandalize Chinese people.

THE YELLOW RACE

It would be naïve to argue that greater contact with outsiders will, of itself, reform Chinese racism. Hong Kong was a multiracial entrepôt under British rule. Its seven million people have long had exposure to citizens of creeds and colours from all over the world. Europeans, Indians, Pakistanis, Filipinos, Indonesians, Thais, South Africans and Nepalese make up 5 per cent of the population. They are an

integral part of the territory's life and culture. The much loved Star
Ferry Company, which transports passengers between Kowloon and
Hong Kong Island on its jolly green-and-white vessels, was founded
by an Indian merchant in 1888. And yet after the handover of the
region to Beijing's control in 1997, the Hong Kong authorities dis-
couraged Indians from taking up Chinese citizenship. The many
South Asians who work as maids for wealthy residents in the city
continue to complain of racial harassment. The public school system
discriminates against ethnic minority children with poor Chinese
language skills. The Cantonese phrase '*gwei lo*', 'ghost man', used to
describe white people, is so ubiquitous that most people aren't even
aware of its insulting etymology.

Nevertheless, the former colony can be regarded as an example
of how change is indeed possible in China. The publicity around
the case of Harinder Veriah, who died in Ruttonjee Hospital after
she complained of racially motivated neglect, created such a public
uproar that the authorities finally passed an anti-racial discrimination law in 2008. The law is far from perfect, not least because it
excludes government agencies, including the police, from its provi-
sions, but campaigners regard it as a start. It is now no longer legal,
for instance, for Hong Kong landlords to refuse to let a property to a
resident purely on account of the colour of his or her skin. And this
is how progress will come in the rest of China, through civic campaigns and public education. That is, after all, how our own societies
have been prosecuting the war on endemic racism.

The good news is that racist attitudes in mainland China no
longer go unchallenged. After the Lou Jing affair, the *China Daily*
columnist Raymond Zhou told his readers: 'It is high time we introduced some sensitivity training on races and ethnicities if we are
going to latch on to the orbit of globalization. People should realize
that if you have a right to discriminate against another race you have
automatically given others the right to discriminate against you.'

It is sometimes noted that the anti-African student riots of the
winter of 1988 were followed by the student pro-democracy protests of 1989. Many of the same students who were chanting for
the removal of the 'black devils' were six months later chanting for
free speech and human rights. Some have even implied that this
constitutes some sort of racist original sin for China's democracy

movement. Yet this ignores that reform activists have also played a role in challenging Chinese racism. In 2005, when Condoleezza Rice was abused on the Chinese Internet, a hero of Tiananmen Square, Liu Xiaobo, wrote an impassioned article deploring the bigotry that had been displayed by his compatriots.

Also encouraging is the growing tendency of other online commentators to criticize the racists. Many netizens actually came to the defence of Lou Jing. 'Don't discriminate against outsiders, everyone is equal', 'Everyone, there's no need to talk about her like this', 'She is local born and raised Shanghainese' were a few of the supportive comments. What this demonstrates is that Chinese society is having an internal debate about racial prejudice. The bigots do not, contrary to what we sometimes assume, have it all their own way.

Modern pop music and culture casts an ambiguous light on modern Chinese racial attitudes. Xie Tingfeng has the handsome visage of a classic idol of Cantopop, as the Hong Kong music industry is known. For much of the last decade he was most famous for dating actresses and crashing expensive cars, but in the build-up to the Beijing Olympics in 2008 he reinvented himself as a nationalist champion with a bombastic song called 'The Yellow Race'. In the music video terracotta warriors disinter themselves from a desert, form into the ranks of a mighty army and, led by Xie, advance towards the camera. The song included the phrases 'the yellow race descended to earth, puff out your chest' and 'only us Chinese will exert ourselves selflessly'. The spectacle seemed designed to push all the buttons of our paranoia about Chinese racial triumphalism.

However, there is another point about Chinese attitudes to race that is often missed. The attitude is not always one of belligerence as exemplified by Xie. A sense of introspection is sometimes at play. In 2001 the Hong Kong hip hop group Lazy Mutha Fucka (LMF) released '1127', a song about the martial artist Bruce Lee. Lee was the first Chinese actor to become a Hollywood star. In the song (which is named after Lee's 27 November birthday) LMF lauded him for making the Chinese feel proud through his success in a Western film industry where the Chinese were traditionally portrayed as villains, and also for articulating a positive philosophy of experimentalism and self-belief. I have vivid memories of a friend belting out a karaoke version in a hotel in the southern city of Dongguan.

He didn't need the subtitles. Every word was emblazoned on his memory.

'WHETHER YOU ARE WILLING OR NOT'

The late Chinese Premier, Zhou Enlai, Chairman Mao's right-hand man, once boasted that racism is 'uniquely absent' from China. That was always complacent and self-deceiving rubbish. Xenophobic currents flowed through imperial China, and after the fall of the empire the nationalist propaganda, guided by Sun Yat Sen's conviction that the Chinese were engaged in a global racial struggle, helped to entrench such sentiments. Today the Communist authorities, more subtly but no less insidiously, pander to these same prejudices.

Yet fears that the Chinese are, beneath the surface, a nation of ferocious Boxers waiting to slaughter foreigners at the first opportunity are paranoid delusions. However unpleasant and heavy-handed official raids on suspected visa over-stayers have been in recent years, such enforcement drives are common in the supposedly racially enlightened nations of the West. Moreover, there are no grounds for believing that grassroots Chinese xenophobia is incapable of being reformed. 'Scientific' racism took hold in China at the same time as it gripped Europe and America. And just as in the West, attitudes can be reformed through popular pressure and public awareness campaigns. It is impossible to see anything in Chinese culture that makes racism there uniquely ineradicable.

What is true is that China has a great deal of catching up to do, thanks largely to its decades of seclusion from the global flow of people and ideas. But then in some ways China has a smaller mountain to climb than our own societies did when it comes to eradicating racial prejudice and stamping out its attendant evils. China never generated the systemized political racism of twentieth-century Europe or America. It has no crime in its history to compare with the transatlantic slave trade, the destruction of the way of life of American Indians, the segregation of the southern states of America, or the Holocaust. The fact that the regime in China has excluded minority peoples from the one-child policy belies the notion that Beijing today is implementing a grand programme of racial 'improvement'.

An appreciation of context is necessary too. The Chinese Internet can often seem like a racist sewer, but so, equally, can a great chunk of cyberspace elsewhere. Attitudes in our own societies are not as enlightened as we like to think. A poll in 2009 found that 51 per cent of White Americans believed racism was still widespread in the US. Some 59 per cent of Hispanics and 78 per cent of blacks believed the same to be true.[33] This doesn't of course excuse Chinese racism, but it reminds us that there's nothing unique about it.

Economic forces, too, are working on the side of reform in China. The Beijing government is keen to encourage more direct investment from abroad and to persuade more foreigners with technical expertise and specialist knowledge to arrive. Its reformist wing regards both as important drivers of the modernization of the Chinese economy. A land of backward and unreconstructed views on race does not offer much of a welcome mat. The line used to prepare the Chinese for the influx of foreigners during the 2008 Olympics – 'Is it not a joy to have friends come from afar?' – was an ancient saying, taken from the first verse of Confucius's *Analects*, but the sentiment also underlines a very modern economic imperative.

In a strange way Hou Dejian demonstrated how progress is possible. After the success of 'Heirs of the Dragon', the singer emigrated to China in the early 1980s to the fury of the Taiwanese authorities. But Hou soon set about irritating his new hosts too. Instead of relaxing into an easy life as a bard of racial pride, Hou became involved in the student protest movement. He was one of the unofficial leaders of the Tiananmen Square demonstration in 1989. There, in that crucible of democratic activism, Hou came into contact with many representatives of China's ethnic minorities. That was when he realized that not all heirs of the dragon are necessarily endowed with 'black hair, black eyes, yellow skin'. 'Heirs of the Dragon' was still immensely popular and became one of the anthems of the students of the Tiananmen protests, with the song drifting on the summer breeze across the vast expanse of the Beijing square. And so Hou decided to revise his famous lyrics: 'Black eyes, black hair, yellow skin, forever and ever an heir of the dragon' was transformed into 'whether you are willing or not, forever and ever an heir of the dragon'.[34] A song that began life as a simplistic racial fantasy took on a more nuanced meaning. China can learn from that example.

THE CHINESE DON'T WANT FREEDOM

In the early months of 2011 hundreds of thousands of ordinary people across the Arab world, quite unexpectedly, rose up and toppled the authoritarian regimes that had held power over them for decades. In doing so they also toppled a dogma: the conviction that the people of those nations did not want self-government. The Arab Spring showed that the democratic optimists had been right: while ordinary people could be suppressed for an age they could not be beaten down for ever and one day they would take to the streets to claim their freedoms. In that heady atmosphere of vindication some dared to suggest that the next authoritarian domino to fall might be the greatest of them all: China.

Some Chinese democracy activists certainly hoped so. 'Today we are all Egyptians' typed the artist and activist Ai Weiwei on his Twitter microblog as the crowds in Cairo's Tahrir Square celebrated the final capitulation of the dictatorship of Hosni Mubarak. 'It only took 18 days for the collapse of a military regime which was in power for 30 years and looked harmonious and stable. This thing [the Communist Party] that has been for 60 years may take several months.' It was a joke, but his words also seemed to be a digital rallying cry for a Chinese Spring. The call was answered. Internet activists declared 19 February a day of 'Jasmine Revolution'. Peaceful demonstrations would be held in major cities across China. The hope was to emulate the street protests that kicked off the mass movements in the Middle East, to bring down the Communist Party with people power.

And then? Well, nothing much. Around two hundred people turned up in Wangfujing, Beijing's shopping district. According to reporters on the scene it was difficult to distinguish the protestors from shoppers hunting for bargains in the shadow of the gigantic billboards. Perhaps one hundred arrived in Shanghai's People's

Square. In many cities, the police and foreign journalists outnumbered the protestors. The activists chanted their slogans. The police made a few arrests. Ai Weiwei was taken into custody for attempted political subversion. And then life clattered on. Democracy's spring never arrived in China; the Jasmine did not bloom.

Here, it was suggested, was evidence that China was different from other nations. 'China won't be having a revolution any time soon' was the verdict of Melissa Chan of Al Jazeera's English language TV station.[1] 'Why the Chinese are not inspired by Egypt' ran a headline in the *Financial Times*.[2] While the mighty world spirit of revolution roused oppressed people from their slumbers across the Middle East, China remained unaffected. Why? Could it be that most Chinese don't care about democracy? Was the movement that found its voice in Tiananmen Square in 1989, only to be savagely beaten down, just a curious aberration? Do the Chinese not want freedom?

A SERVILE SPIRIT

Our assumption that the Chinese like being told what to do is centuries old. The nineteenth-century German philosopher Georg Hegel knew all about the world spirit, or *'weltgeist'*. His vision of history as an unfolding phenomenon propelled by a grand dialectic of spiritual forces and ideas was taken by Karl Marx, turned on its head, and fashioned into the more influential theory of dialectical materialism.[3]

Hegel never visited China, but that didn't prevent him maintaining strikingly firm opinions about the Chinese character. 'It appears nothing terrible to them,' he wrote in his lectures on the *Philosophy of History* in the 1820s, 'to sell themselves as slaves, and to eat the bitter bread of slavery.'[4] Hegel was picking up a theme advanced by Montesquieu in the seventeenth century, who suggested that 'there reigns in Asia a servile spirit, which they have never been able to shake off, and it is impossible to find in all the histories of that country [China] a single passage which discovers a freedom of spirit; we shall never see anything there but the excess of slavery.'[5]

Where did Montesquieu get this idea? Like Hegel he had never visited China and nor did he read Chinese. It's possible that he was recycling the ancient Greek philosopher Aristotle, who said that 'the natives of Asia are intelligent and inventive, but they are wanting in spirit, and therefore they are always in a state of subjection and slavery'.[6]

But Hegel was probably also influenced, like everyone else in Europe in that era, by the dispatches of Matteo Ricci, the seventeenth-century Jesuit missionary to China. Ricci, who served at the Ming court, painted a picture of a people devoid of complaints about their rulers. 'They are quite content with what they have,' he observed. 'In this respect they are different from the peoples of Europe who are frequently discontent with their own governments.'[7]

Nineteenth-century Protestant missionaries concurred, depicting the Chinese as forever willing to bow down to authority. In their reports, the kowtow, where a person would knock their head on the ground, became the quintessential 'Chinese' act. Karl Marx might have subverted the Hegelian idealistic tradition but his own concept of the 'Asiatic mode of production', which depicted China as still stuck in a pre-feudal regime of forced labour, also left no room for a Chinese pursuit of liberty.

However the notion arose, for centuries thinkers in the West believed in the politically passive nature of the Chinese. For some, like Hegel and Montesquieu this servility was backward and loathsome. Others, though, quite admired the Chinese way. In his influential work *The Despotism of China*, eighteenth-century French economist François Quesnay urged European monarchs to learn something from the institutions and philosophies of what he called 'the most flourishing kingdom known'.[8]

The thesis that the Chinese don't care for liberty in the way that we do endured after the imperial era. 'The Chinese always have had masters and they always will' are the words that William Somerset Maugham puts in the mouth of a hypocritical Socialist called Henderson in his 1922 collection of short stories inspired by a visit to China.[9] Henderson sounds rather similar to the American Sinologist Lucian Pye, who argued, more recently, that 'the Chinese demand rule by men, not just law'. According to Pye, the Chinese expect that 'all power should emanate from above ... a fact that is acknowledged by the entire population'.

'Let the ruler be a ruler, the subject a subject, a father a father, and a son a son,' said Confucius according to the *Analects*.[10] For Pye, this teaching from the great Chinese sage has always found expression in Chinese political arrangements. 'The unrelenting emphasis on filial piety prevents the Chinese in early life from expressing aggression against the natural targets of authority,' he argued. The Chinese obediently follow leaders because political rulers are 'an amplification of the Confucian model of the father as the ultimate authority in the family'.[11] 'Confucian democracy', according to the political theorist Samuel Huntingdon, whose 'Clash of Civilizations' theory many people still find compelling, is 'clearly a contradiction in terms'.[12]

Lloyd Eastman, another American Sinologist, agreed, adding that whenever China has experimented with democratic structures the results have been disastrous. 'Because of the nature of Chinese society and of its political traditions, it is perhaps one of China's tragedies during the twentieth century that, in the quest for a viable political system, attempts had been made to erect democratic institutions,' he wrote in the 1970s. His conclusion? 'In a profound sense Anglo-American democracy was not suited to China.' Eastman's advice was for the Chinese to stick to what suited them, namely autocracy. Such a system of government in China was 'better able to produce the greatest happiness of the greatest number'.[13]

These ideas about the antipathy between the Chinese and liberty have penetrated the mainstream. In his 2012 television series on China the historian Niall Ferguson concluded: 'the way the Chinese think is as different from the way we think as the way they write'. As he put it: 'All the basic assumptions I've grown up with – particularly individual freedom – just don't apply here.'[14]

In the West, governments acquire legitimacy by winning elections. Not so in China, apparently. Daniel Bell, a professor of political theory at Tsinghua University, tells us that the Communist Party achieves popular acquiescence though 'non-democratic methods'. Because the Party has overseen rising living standards over the past three decades it has 'performance legitimacy'. And because the Party is a 'political meritocracy', allowing those with talent to rise up its ranks into leadership positions, the Chinese accept its right to govern the country. 'The Chinese care more about having high-quality politicians than about having procedural arrangements to choose their leaders,' Bell explains.[15] And do the Chinese even need Western-style liberty? It's sometimes argued that the Chinese, unimpeded by the bureaucracy and regulation prevalent in advanced countries, actually enjoy a larger personal economic freedom than we do, even if they can't vote.

Some say that Chinese political forms have always been roughly the same and will ever remain so. In 1957 the historian and refugee from Nazi Germany, Karl Wittfogel, identified ancient China as a 'hydraulic empire'. This meant the state in imperial times was shaped by the dominant economic importance of water. The dry climate of northern China made massive irrigation works – canals, dams, levies – necessary to boost agricultural production to a level capable of sustaining the population. These irrigation works were so monumental that they could only be undertaken by rulers who enslaved peasants, forcing the population to work in the service of the polity. This system of compelled labour could only be effectively administered through an efficient public bureaucracy. And this efficient bureaucracy, in turn, made it possible for rulers to strangle at birth any independent civic institutions, such as professional societies and merchant guilds, that might emerge to challenge their personal authority.

Wittfogel, who was a vehement anti-Communist writing at the height of the Cold War, identified a connection between ancient hydraulic empires and the bureaucratic totalitarianism of modern China and Russia. 'Like the tiger the engineer of power must have the physical means with which to crush his victims,' he said. 'And the agro-managerial despot does indeed possess such means. He exercises unchecked control over the army, the police, the intelligence service; and he has at his disposal jailers, torturers, executioners, and all the tools that are necessary to catch, incapacitate, and, destroy a suspect.'[16] So the techniques of the old emperors and the modern Communist autocrats were remarkably similar; both were practitioners of what he termed 'Oriental Despotism'. Thus Mao's Communist Party, for all its modern trappings, seemed to become, in Wittfogel's analysis, merely the latest imperial dynasty to rule China.

Reform looks a remote prospect. It was once assumed that China's economic liberalization would propel political liberalization too; that as the country's middle classes moved further away from enervating poverty, they would inevitably start to demand more political liberty. That idea – known as 'modernization theory' – is now roundly dismissed as wishful thinking. The American political theorist Robert Kagan argues that, in practice, the opposite seems to have happened. 'The richer a country gets the easier it may be for autocrats to hold on to power,' he suggests. 'More money keeps the bourgeoisie content and lets the government round up the few discontented who reveal their feelings on the Internet.'[17] Charles Kupchan, Professor of International Affairs at Georgetown University, similarly sees China's middle class as 'a defender of the status quo, not a force of political change'.[18] On a visit to China in 2012 the BBC presenter Jeremy Paxman noted the lack of fervour for political reform among the young people in Beijing he spoke to. 'Not a single young person talked, even in their cups, of revolution,' he remarked. Paxman's conclusion: 'Right now there are too many people doing too well for such thoughts.'[19]

The days when our public intellectuals would confidently predict the demise of the Communist Party and the arrival of democracy in China have disappeared. One is now more likely to hear predictions of Beijing exporting its own model of authoritarian capitalism to other emerging nations than of China liberalizing from within. In the mountains of analysis produced by economic consultancies, the possibility of a political earthquake in China is barely mentioned. Continued one-party rule is assumed.

Even advocates of reform within China appear to subscribe to this pessimism. Han Han, the country's most popular blogger, seems to believe that the Chinese are, if not slavish, then certainly hopelessly selfish. 'Most Chinese people don't care about the lives of others,' he argues. 'They only holler when they get abused themselves. They will never manage to unify ... China is the least likely nation in the world to have a revolution.' For Han Han democracy is just a fetish of a handful of out-of-touch intellectuals:

> Over the years, I have visited more than one hundred county cities of all types. They are not especially isolated or impoverished. I have spoken to people from all walks of life in those places. Their quest for democracy and freedom is not as urgent as intellectuals imagine ... They don't care about restricting or supervising the authorities; they pick up the vocabulary about democracy and

freedom only when ill luck befell them and they need to petition their causes. If the government pays them enough, they will be satisfied.[20]

Han Han is no mouthpiece of the Communist authorities. He regularly scorns them on his blog, and he has consistently championed greater press freedom. Yet even Han Han dismisses the introduction of free elections and competing political parties in China as 'not realistic'.[21]

This is a common view inside China. One constantly hears that representative democracy would lead to violent chaos. Free elections would open the door to dangerous populism, possibly even a return of Maoism and greater assaults on human rights. The rabble-rousing of the former Chongqing party secretary Bo Xilai, who staged a mini Maoist revival and fostered a personality cult before he was ruthlessly purged by his Beijing rivals in 2012, is held up as a warning of what could happen nationwide if the gates of political reform were to be flung open.

Another ubiquitous fear is that a democratic China would emulate the descent of Russia into gangsterism and social breakdown following the collapse of the Soviet Union. Pan Wei, a professor of political science at Peking University, has forecast that China would 'disintegrate' if the country were to stage free elections. Some see democracy sending China down a xenophobic and externally aggressive road, menacing the country's neighbours and undermining stability throughout Asia.

Of all people it was the comedy Kung Fu actor Jackie Chan who summed up all this foreboding when he told an audience on Hainan Island in 2009 that the Chinese, unlike other peoples, simply could not be trusted with liberty. 'I'm not sure if it is good to have freedom or not,' he confessed. 'I'm gradually beginning to feel that we Chinese need to be controlled.'[22]

SEAMLESS AUTOCRACY?

To stand at the north end of Tiananmen Square in Beijing is to straddle the historical fault line that separates two Chinas. To the north is the opulent and vermillion-walled Forbidden City, the enormous palace complex constructed by the Ming emperors in the fifteenth century. To the south lies the almost equally vast concrete expanse of Tiananmen Square, one of the largest public spaces in the world, commissioned by Mao Zedong. The architecture comes from two profoundly different eras, one imperial, the other Communist, and yet the sensation for the individual as he gazes north, and then south, is rather similar. The scale of both the square and the palace is intimidating. Both, in their own ways, project a cold and ruthless power. Both plant a feeling of insignificance into the soul of the individual. On this spot the Wittfogel proposition, that Chinese political history is one long and seamless story of autocracy, feels plausible.

We continue to favour the notion that the strongmen who have ruled China since 1949 are merely modern manifestations of an ancien regime. Mao is often still described in Western newspapers as 'China's last emperor'. Indeed, perhaps this is hardly surprising since the Chairman himself revelled in the comparison. Mao was open in his admiration for China's first emperor, Qin Shi Huang, who, as we have seen, was famed for his cruelty.[23] But it's not just Mao. The American political theorist Francis Fukuyama saw the purged Bo Xilai as another potential 'bad emperor' who needed to be deposed by more responsible elements in the regime.[24] And journalists continually draw analogies from deep in Chinese history when analysing contemporary politics.[25] In 2010 *The Economist* profiled the rising man of the Party, Xi Jinping, under the bold front-page headline 'The next emperor'.[26] It is as if the Qing Dynasty never really fell in 1911, but rather continued by other means.

Yet there lies a danger in our tendency to analyse twentieth-century China through this lens. Joseph Needham was a biochemist and Sinologist who wrote a magisterial seven-volume history of the scientific achievements of China. He documented that, among other things, the stirrup, printing, the compass, gunpowder and the ploughshare (all once thought to have been Western inventions) had their origins in China. And Needham didn't care for Wittfogel's argument that twentieth-century bureaucratic totalitarianism was among those early Chinese innovations. He pointed out that the mandarins of the old Chinese court were often permitted to oppose the emperor and that China had a level of intellectual freedom that allowed native science to advance spectacularly until the fifteenth century. 'The civilization which Professor Wittfogel is so bitterly attacking was one which could make poets and scholars into officials,' protested Needham.[27] And was ancient China really a totalitarian hydraulic empire? The irrigation works in the Yellow River valley in that era tended to be small scale, rather than monumental. The more one looks, the more holes one discovers in the Wittfogel hypothesis.

But the Wittfogel thesis is misleading in a more profound way, because it minimizes the novelty of the apparatus of terror and control created by the Communists in China (strongly influenced by those developed by the Bolsheviks in Russia). There were certainly despotic horrors in China's history such as the castration of scholars like the court historian Sima Qian for speaking out of turn. Qin Shi Huang's use of slave labour to construct the foundations of his proto-Great Wall seems to have analogies with the Cultural Revolution work camps. The first Ming emperor, Hongwu, killed a hundred thousand people in various purges, including not only disloyal officials but their families too. The imperial bureaucracy was indeed sophisticated and often repressive, yet the old emperors never came close to achieving the overhaul of all aspects of Chinese life as the post-1949 autocrats did.

The social shocks imposed by the Communist command economy in the twentieth century were on a far larger scale than any before in Chinese history. And they were only made possible by modern communications technologies – newspapers and radio – and other new repressive state apparatuses, particularly the rigid Communist party hierarchy. The mania of the Great Leap Forward, when peasants were ordered to melt their cooking pots to make steel in backyard furnaces and to scour the countryside slaughtering sparrows to prevent the birds from stealing seed grain, was unprecedented. The society-shredding terror of the Cultural Revolution, when students were encouraged to beat their teachers, and former landlords were vindictively tortured, must also be understood as something new in Chinese history. Chinese emperors of the past had no equivalent of Mao's personality cult. Violent as they often were, China's old rulers never turned society on its head by encouraging the people, as Mao did, to smash anything associated with the old culture.

When we look for ancient origins for twentieth-century Chinese totalitarianism we risk misunderstanding both the past and the present. Mao may have likened himself to China's old rulers, but why should we read much into the self-descriptions of a homicidal tyrant? Mao was not an emperor. His style of rule owed more to Joseph Stalin than Qin Shi Huang. As for the gang of autocrats who constitute the current Communist Party Politburo, however much they gush about the virtues of 'harmony', they are not Confucians. Their totalitarian one-party rule has more in common with the hard men who control North Korea than it does with the scholar bureaucrats of the Qing or the Ming.

One can make another, quite different, argument from history. Before the twentieth century China lacked the independent centres of civic power that facilitated the growth of democracy in the West. There were no proud merchant societies, no bourgeoisie that could appeal to independent courts for protection from arbitrary official power. There were no scurrilous popular news-sheets that challenged and mocked the institutions of authority, no coffee shops where liberal ideas could be exchanged. However, it is a travesty to present, as Hegel and Montesquieu did, the history of Chinese thought as one long apologia for tyranny. One can find in Confucius and the rest of the canon of classical thought not just respect for authority but a humanist creed urging respect for mankind. In *The Book of Mencius*, one of the classic ancient philosophical texts of China, there are clear delineations of the right of people to rebel against rulers who forfeit the 'mandate of heaven'. The Qing scholar Kang Youwei interpreted Confucius, in his time, as a reformer, not a reactionary. It would be going too far to present Confucius and Mencius as proto-democrats, but what matters is that Chinese people have interpreted these ancient texts in different ways. They did not all accept the canon as some sort of moral blueprint for repressive rule.

In any case, from the late nineteenth century democracy formed a central element in the Chinese political discourse. As a mere merchant, Zheng Guanying had no standing in intellectual or official circles. Nevertheless the self-taught Shanghainese comprador became a champion of political reform in the late Qing era when he published his 1893 tract *Words of Warning to a Prosperous Age*. The title was dripping in irony since China was, at that time, anything but prosperous, having been ransacked by foreign powers and broken by a tumultuous civil war. Yet Zheng's call for domestic political reform was entirely serious and struck a resonant chord. Among those who took up Zheng's ideas for political reform were Kang Youwei and his protégé Liang Qichao. They made for an odd couple: Kang was an utopian dreamer and Liang was a radical journalist. But during the Hundred Days Reform movement of 1898, the pair spearheaded the bold attempt to transform the Dragon Throne into a constitutional monarchy with limits on imperial power. Kang and Liang were given their head by the young Guangxu emperor, who could see the writing on the wall for the imperial regime. With this support Kang and Liang set about remaking the Chinese state in a strikingly liberal image.

The reformers were crushed by the power behind the throne, the Dowager Empress Cixi, who headed a faction of conservative Manchu aristocrats. But the reactionaries only delayed the inevitable. Indeed, by resisting organic reform, they ensured total rupture. The republican forces led by the revolutionary Sun Yat Sen – guided by the same conviction as Zheng, Kang and Liang, that political reform was essential to save China – dealt the coup de grâce to the empire in 1911. The provisional constitution that Sun established to take its place was a model of liberal democracy, with guarantees for an uncensored media, an independent judiciary, free trade unions and space for competing political parties. The franchise was, it is true, restricted to literate and propertied males, but this was no different from the practice in European democracies in that era.

Sun's liberal democracy soon broke apart, giving way to the rule of a military strongman, of whom more later, but these founding liberal principles of the republic were never rejected. Indeed, the fact that the forms of constitutional government were kept on, even when they were empty, represented a tacit acknowledgement of their legitimacy, just as hypocrisy is the tribute that vice pays to virtue. And the pressure for political reform did not abate. The New Culture movement of the 1920s, led by young Chinese students who had studied abroad, made political reform their lodestar, calling for the replacement of 'Confucius and Sons' with 'Mr Science' and 'Mr Democracy'.

Even the Chinese Communists, at least in theory, espoused

government based on popular sovereignty. Mao Zedong was in-spired by the writings of Kang Youwei in his youth. After taking power in 1949, when asked in an interview how the Communists would avoid falling into corrupt decay like all other Chinese gov-ernments of history, Mao insisted, 'we have found a new path; we can break free of the cycle. The path is called democracy. As long as the people have oversight of the government then the government will not slacken in its efforts.'[28]

The constitution of the post-1949 People's Republic makes re-peated reference to democracy. To this day Mao's successors often talk about the centrality of popular sovereignty to their vision. 'There is no modernization without democracy,' stressed the former Chinese president Hu Jintao in 2006. 'The people's wishes for, and needs for, democracy and freedom are irresistible,' echoed his pre-mier, Wen Jiabao, in 2010. This sort of speech, coming from a party that will brook no opposition to its monopoly on political power, sounds, of course, like Orwellian doublethink,[29] yet there is a ghost of sincerity flitting through the rafters of this rhetoric. The Commu-nist Party emerged from the same reformist early twentieth-century milieu as the Hundred Day Reformers and the May Fourth Move-ment, which both placed political reform at the heart of its vision of a modernized China. The founder of the CCP was Chen Duxiu, the leading light of the May Fourth Movement. The point here is not to exonerate the Communists for their betrayal of those promises of democracy, but to rebut the notion that self-government is an alien concept that has never been accepted by the inflexible and servile Chinese mind. On the contrary, democracy was at the very heart of the reform movement that laid the ideological foundation of the modern Chinese state.

DISCONTENT AND MAOSTALGIA

In late 2011 an insignificant fishing village called Wukan, secreted in the lush tropical hills of the southern province of Guangdong, all of a sudden became the most significant scrap of territory in China. The residents of Wukan got wind that Party officials were planning to sell off the village's communal land in a deal with some property developers. The villagers assumed that the officials would, as usual, pocket the profits for themselves rather than distributing them. But this time they weren't going to stand for it. A large crowd set off to protest at the two local centres of power: the office of the Communist Party secretary and the police station. The first was trashed and the second was mobbed.

The authorities wasted no time in striking back. A quiet man with a square face called Xue Jinbo had reluctantly agreed to speak on behalf of the protestors. One evening he was accosted and bundled into the back of an unmarked minibus and taken to the police station. Xue never came out alive. The police said he died of a heart attack, but when Xue's family came to collect the body it was clear to them that he had been beaten to death. The villagers exploded with anger. This time they drove all Party officials and police out of the village entirely and barricaded the roads. The authorities massed outside and stopped all supplies going in. Wukan was under siege. Everyone knew what to expect next. The state would surely move in with overwhelming force and crush all opposition, just like Tiananmen in 1989.

Yet Wukan was not crushed. What it got instead was redress. The Party chief of Guangdong, an ambitious man called Wang Yang, embarrassed by the global media attention Wukan had attracted, promised to investigate the original land deal that had sparked the violence. The villagers were permitted to stage new elections too. There have been village elections in China since the Maoist communes were disbanded in the early 1980s, but these have been phoney exercises in local democracy with candidates vetted in advance by Party officials. Wukan's election was different: it was free and fair. The villagers fashioned new wooden voting booths and 85 per cent of the seven thousand registered voters turned out. For a people culturally indisposed to democracy, the villagers of Wukan seemed remarkably enthusiastic about exercising their voting privileges.

Of all the silly things we assume about modern China perhaps the most foolish is that its people are uniformly content and endlessly grateful to the Communist Party for delivering rising living standards. What was unusual about Wukan was not the revolt, but the fact that the rebels managed to get their message out to the global media before the authorities could pummel them back into their box. Desperate villagers across China revolt against the authorities with increasing regularity. The precise numbers are, for obvious reasons, kept quiet, but there is little doubt that there are tens of thousands of uprisings every year, with the majority, as in Wukan, provoked by local government corruption. The Chinese Academy of Social Sciences estimated that there were more than 90,000 'mass incidents' in 2006, up tenfold over the decade. In 2010 Sun Liping, Professor of Sociology at Tsinghua University, put the annual number of disturbances at 180,000, which would break down as around 500 every single day of the year. Many of these are revolts by people who have been pushed to the point where they will risk their lives and livelihoods to express their anger. And millions more are boiling in quiet desperation at their dispossession by corrupt local Party bosses.

Swelling social anger in China extends much further than villagers. In thirty years China has gone from being a society in which virtually everyone was poor to one of the largest income gaps in the world.[30] There are now more than a million US dollar millionaires in China.[31] At the same time around 170 million people scrabble by on less than two dollars a day.[32] And the middle classes are just as furious about this spiralling inequality as the very poorest because they tend to be more aware that the incomes of China's super rich are, often, the fruits of nepotism and corruption rather than the rewards of hard work.

This was brought home to me at the Guangdong Museum of Art in 2012. One striking piece of contemporary sculpture showed a gold brick levitating above a pile of rubble. I couldn't see what the work was saying at first, but my Chinese friends, who had come along for the visit, instantly understood. It was, they told me, an indictment of modern China; the artist was depicting a gilded minority pulling away and leaving everyone else on the rubbish heap. I've never seen a work of contemporary art have such a visceral impact on an audience before.

This pervading sense of economic injustice is having some strange effects in parts of society. Many visitors have been intrigued, indeed alarmed, by a wave of Mao nostalgia in China in recent years. The Chairman's 'Little Red Book' of supposedly stirring quotations was the bestselling book in all of China in the 1960s and 70s. That was because its purchase was compulsory for virtually the entire population. The publishing royalties made Mao a privately wealthy man in an impoverished and often starving country. But in recent years sales have risen even though the Chinese are no longer forced to participate in a personality cult. There has been an upsurge of visitors to Mao's birthplace in Hunan. There are even some 'red' restaurants, which stage Cultural Revolution-themed cabarets in which evil landlords are subjected to 'struggle sessions' by actors in fancy dress. Most Chinese people I speak to put this enthusiasm for a man who inflicted such pain on Chinese society down to increasing disaffection with the corruption of the present regime and the massive inequality it has created, rather than any genuine desire to plunge back into Communism.

The inequality dimension is crucial. The city of Chongqing, under the rule of Bo Xilai, saw the most significant upsurge in popular Maoism recently, witnessing mass choruses of dredged-up Cultural Revolution-era anthems. Part of the explanation is likely to be that Bo wrapped popular local initiatives designed to help the poorest, such as an increase in the provision of cheap housing, in Maoist rhetoric.

The novelist Yu Hua, who was himself one of the vindictive young Red Guards during the dark days of the Cultural Revolution, sees this popular egalitarian impulse as the root of contemporary Maostalgia. 'Although life in the Mao era was impoverished and restrictive', he says, 'there was no widespread, cruel competition to survive, just empty class struggle, for there were no classes to speak of in those days and so struggle mostly took the form of sloganeering and not much else.'[33]

Does popular anger though, spell revolutionary intent? The people in Wukan rose up against their local Party chiefs, but they did not call for the downfall of the Communist Party itself. Rather, they appealed to the authorities in Beijing for protection against the local strong men. Some argue that pockets of anger will always, in the end, be brought off and that the position of the Communist Party itself, for all the popular discontent, is under no serious threat.[34] Yet it seems to me this overlooks the deep reserves of contempt that ordinary people have for the entire political system. In my experience there are very few Chinese people who, whatever they might judiciously say in public, are so naïve that they believe that the ills of the country are entirely a consequence of the misbehaviour of regional officials. They know that corruption has eaten its way through the entire Communist Party, hollowing out its claims to govern selflessly on behalf of all Chinese. An online poll conducted by the *People's Daily* in 2010 seemed to support that impression. It showed that 91 per cent of respondents were of the opinion that all wealthy people in China have political backgrounds.[35] 'Who has more power, businessmen or politicians?' I once asked my aunt. 'Politicians, by far,' was her unambiguous reply.

The 70 richest delegates in China's National People's Congress have a collective estimated net worth of close to $90 billion. Compare that with the $7.5 billion net worth of the 660 top officials in the US government. And that includes not only the American legislature, but also the executive and judiciary.[36] A visiting alien from another planet might be puzzled to learn that, of the two, the Chinese regime is the Communist one.

The revelations of the massive graft of the family of Bo Xilai have hammered the corruption point home. Until 2012 Bo was an ascendant star of the Party firmament, with a reputation for busting crime, redistributing wealth and delivering stunning growth in the province of Chongqing. He managed all of this while displaying an unusual amount of charisma for a senior Communist apparatchik. But the edifice collapsed when Bo fell out with his police chief, Wang Lijun. Wang, fearing for his life, tried to seek asylum in the American embassy where he reportedly made many allegations of corruption and other criminality against the Bo family. Outraged at this embarrassment, the authorities in Beijing moved swiftly to take Bo down. He has been stripped of his Party position. His wife has been found guilty in the courts of the murder of a British businessman. Bo himself is awaiting trial.

Who knows how many lies have been thrown at the Bo family by the regime to blacken its name? But the details that have emerged certainly look damning. Bo's official salary as Party secretary of Chongqing was just $1,600 a month, but his family appears to have amassed assets of more than $100 million. One minute Bo was touted as a great champion of the people. The most senior Party leaders from Beijing travelled to Chongqing to praise his good work in the city. The next he was disgraced and jailed. The Chinese people are not stupid. They know Bo did not go from being a hero to a villain overnight. If he was corrupt, so was the system that saw him ascend so high. If he was innocent, a corrupt system has engulfed him.

Is China, as Han Han argues, the least likely place in the world to witness a revolution? Flashes of skin from the country's so-called 'naked officials' suggest otherwise. These are bureaucrats who are known to have sent almost all their relatives and money abroad. This is hardly behaviour that bespeaks great confidence in the stability of the regime. Roughly 90 per cent of members of the ruling Politburo have family members living or working overseas according to one Hong Kong magazine. Between 1995 and 2008 up to 18,000 officials left China, taking $130 billion in assets with them, equivalent to 1 per cent of China's 2012 GDP.[37]

The wealthy are also looking for the exit. A survey in 2011 found that 14 per cent of Chinese dollar millionaires had emigrated, or were in the process of doing so. Half were considering leaving. And a third had assets overseas already in the form of property or cash.[38] One UK-based Chinese businessman told me of the paranoia he regularly encounters among wealthy people when he returns home. 'They worry that something might happen like in the Middle East and that all their money will be seized,' he said. 'So they buy property abroad and if something happens at least they have an investment to live on.'

It's not just the super rich who are looking for a way out. I have several young friends working in Europe, America and Canada who are exploring ways to help their parents back in China emigrate. Ask them why their parents would want to leave what we are constantly told is a great land of opportunity and you will get a look of bemusement. I have yet to meet a Chinese person who would argue that life in China, for all its spectacular economic growth, is better than life in democratic Europe or America.

GRASS MUD HORSES

Guo Jingming does not, it must be admitted, cut a revolutionary figure. The delicately featured twenty-seven-year-old, who is China's bestselling author, is more interested in photo shoots than showdowns with the Communist Party. 'I don't understand June the Fourth [the date of the Tiananmen Square crackdown],' he says. 'I don't know too much about it. I don't like history or politics. I just want to have a good career and expand my company.'[39] Guo's literature is politics free, which seems to be how his legions of teenage female fans like it. Read his tales of young heartache, stuffed with references to luxury clothing brands, and the image of modern Chinese youth as supremely apathetic seems real enough.

We tend to assume that this generation, the sibling-less progeny of the state's one-child policy, inherited none of the radical instincts of the students who filled Tiananmen Square in 1989. Spurred into action by the death of the deposed senior liberal Communist leader Hu Yaobang, the younger generation took to the massive Beijing square in their hundreds of thousands to demand political reform. They erected a 'goddess of democracy' statue and called for full political rights. The protests spread across some four hundred other Chinese cities. The students were joined by factory workers as their support swelled. The Communist leadership was split and it looked at one point as if the democracy movement would prevail. But the paramount Deng Xiaoping and other hardliners in the regime prevailed over their more liberal colleagues. On 4 June Deng sent in the army to clear the square and the surrounding avenues by force. Unarmed protestors were machine-gunned or crushed to death by tanks. The final death toll is unknown, but it is very likely that hundreds died. As a result, the democracy movement was driven underground.

Does anyone care now? Growing up in the warm bath of rising prosperity seems to have soaked all political idealism out of the minds of today's younger generation. The activities of high-profile fifty-something dissidents from 1989 such as Liu Xiaobo prompt only a shrug of the shoulders and perhaps a yawn. All the well-chronicled human rights abuses of the modern Chinese state – the forced sterilizations of rural women who have breached the one-child rule, the torture of Falun Gong members, the smashing of traditional Tibetan culture, etc – simply don't matter to them. Nor does the plain fact that they cannot choose their own political leaders.

Melissa Chan of Al Jazeera paints a picture of comfortable

apathy. 'Chinese students would probably riot if you took away their iPhones with the Angry Birds computer game on it, sooner than they would rise up to demand greater human rights,' she says. 'This is because college students are privileged. They are comfortable and middle-class, and have too much to lose to bother rabble rousing.'[40] We think of this generation as not only uninterested, but self-censoring too. They don't talk about politics because they've been conditioned to avoid the topic. As Jiang Fangzhou, a twenty-three-year-old literary prodigy who published her first book when she was just nine years old, puts it: 'They do not stray from the orthodoxy for even one millimeter when they are still ten meters away from crossing the line.'[41]

But look below the surface and the paint of this portrait of bovine, apolitical, youth begins to peel off. In particular, look online. The Internet, through micro-blogging sites such as Weibo, has created an unprecedented outlet for political dissent in China, and the young have been especially keen to seize it. It is true that the state's vaunted 'Great Firewall of China', which blocks access to Western news sites – and Twitter and Facebook to boot – is an obstacle to free expression online. So are official algorithms that seek out and shut down web pages where contentious subjects such as 'Tiananmen' are discussed. Type in the names of senior politicians and Chinese search engines yield no results. The reputed thirty thousand cyber-police employed to monitor discussions and identify any politically subversive or sexually explicit comments make life a bore too. Yet any technologically savvy young Chinese person can jump the automatic firewall with relative ease by using proxy servers. And there are other more subtle ways to evade and mock those massed ranks of censors. A few years ago the Chinese Internet was full of creatures called 'cao ni ma', or 'grass mud horses'. They looked a bit like llamas. But the point was the sound of the word. Change the tones slightly and you get 'Fuck your mother'. 'We talk about political leaders in puns that would not be detected by the censors,' one young Chinese person told me. 'We can basically say anything we want. Sometimes we will just post the picture of the grass mud horse next to a picture of the politician to make the point.'

The Internet has also facilitated a frank discussion about China's traumatic twentieth-century history that would never have been possible in previous decades. In 2012 there were extensive online debates about the great famine of the late 1950s and the Communist Party's culpability for that disaster. The Internet brings repressed history to the surface. Young netizens were able to read first-hand testimonies from people who were reduced to eating mud and tree bark to fill their bellies, or who witnessed their relatives starving to death in front of their eyes.

Microblogs, which allow only 140 characters per post, are also especially well suited to the Chinese language. In English, 140 characters is merely a sentence, but in Chinese it's a decent-sized paragraph. In Europe and America microblogs are often portals to blogs with more content, but in China they usually contain the content themselves. 'It's the first time a public sphere has happened in China,' according to Zhao Jing, who blogs in China under the name Michael Anti. 'It's like a training of their citizenship, preparing [people] for future democracy.'[42]

In some ways cyberspace is now the primary battleground for China's political future. On the one hand there are the liberal bloggers, who use their sites to make passionate arguments for radical political reform that would never be published by the loyal official print media. And then there are the reactionary bloggers who defend the status quo. The latter are supported by the '50 cent party' who fill discussion sites with supportive comments about the government. That name was invented by liberals who accused their opponents of receiving half a yuan from the government for every loyal post they deposit in cyberspace.

These online skirmishes are spreading into the real world too. In the summer of 2012 there was a confrontation in Beijing's Chaoyang Park between liberal and reactionary bloggers after a particularly acrimonious cyber row. Some have suggested that the reason the attempts to instigate a Jasmine Revolution in China came to nothing was that it was led by Chinese activists living abroad, using websites that are still difficult to access inside the country.[43] Might things have turned out differently if the demonstrations had been domestically organized? With the Chinese blogosphere expanding rapidly – in 2010 there were 40 million Weibo accounts, now there are more than 300 million – the potential for organized dissent is growing. Michael Anti argues that the phenomenon is still only in its early stages: 'More and more Chinese intend to embrace freedom of speech and human rights as their birth right and human right, not some imported American privilege,' he says.

Technology and public anger have already been coming together in powerful ways. In 2007 a chemical manufacturing plant was planned for construction in Xiamen in coastal Fujian province. The city government was four-square behind the project and the local press agreed that it was a fabulous idea. But one local professor raised concerns about the potentially harmful impact on public health. Those concerns were picked up and spread by bloggers. The opposition grew and, in the end, a group of eight thousand citizens, mobilized by cell phones and the Internet, marched through the streets of Xiamen in a massive show of popular anger. They made sure they got maximum publicity too by sending messages to bloggers in Guangzhou who created real-time reports for the rest of China to read. In this way, the web enables people to bypass the traditional media. 'The Chinese government controls the press, so the news circulated on the Internet and cell phones. This showed that the Chinese people can send out their own news,' explained one blogger.[44] The Xiamen authorities ultimately decided to reject the plant.

It is an increasingly common story. A petrochemical factory in the northern city of Dalian was shut in 2011 after twelve thousand residents marched to protest about the fumes. A solar-panel plant in Haining City, Zhejiang, was closed the same year after evidence emerged it was poisoning local rivers. The construction of a copper alloy factory in Shifang in Sichuan province was halted after an opposition campaign led by bloggers. And so on.

Some campaigns are smaller scale. There has been a burgeoning of grass-roots opposition campaigns against local construction projects that threaten historic neighbourhoods that young people think should be protected. It is impossible to predict what causes will grab public attention. In 2011 many people in Guangzhou came together to oppose an innocuous plan by the city government to erect lights along the banks of the Pearl River. One activist Ou Jiayang explained: 'I am not saying "no" to this project. But the government spent 200 million yuan on a similar project last year. I want the government to tell me why the city needs more lighting along the river bank.'[45] This is a fascinating shift. For centuries the Chinese had to accept what they were given by officialdom. Now, on just about any matter that touches on their environment, the Chinese people automatically expect their voices to be heard by those with the power.

And they are insisting on accountability too. In July 2011 a high-speed train careened into the back of another in the suburbs of the city of Wenzhou, leaving 40 people dead and 192 injured. The railways ministry blamed the disaster on a freak lightning strike that had incapacitated one of the trains. The national government, which had just invested billions in the high-speed rail network, ordered state media to downplay the story. The TV networks obliged. But the Chinese blogs didn't. They reported the full details, including that one of the derailed carriages was quickly buried at the scene rather than properly examined for clues as to the cause of the accident. The government was ultimately forced to conduct a full investigation into the crash, which identified multiple failures of management in the railways ministry. When the full facts came out, even the normally supine state media, for once, did not hold back from lambasting the government.

ASIAN VALUES?

Lee Kwan Yew, the grand old man of Singaporean politics, has a tendency to leave Western politicians smitten. 'There is no better strategic thinker in the world today,' gushed Henry Kissinger.[46] Tony Blair, the former British prime minister, described Lee as 'the smartest leader I think I ever met'. Such veneration might be considered rather distasteful, considering that Lee's Singapore is not what Amnesty International and other human rights groups consider a free country. The small city state at the tip of the West Malaysia peninsula restricts the press, curbs association and metes out judicial canings for petty criminals. Singapore also has a tendency to send troublesome authors who criticize the state to jail, or to hound them out of the territory.

Perhaps these grand Western admirers of Lee were convinced by his 1992 explanation of why democracy simply does not gel with what he terms 'Asian values'. Democracy had not generally brought good government to new developing countries, he explained: 'What

Asians value may not necessarily be what Americans or Europeans value.' According to Lee, 'Westerners value the freedoms and liberties of the individual.' As an Asian of Chinese cultural background, said Lee, 'my values are for a government which is honest, effective and efficient'.[47]

Let's examine this. The idea that Chinese cultural values are incompatible with democracy is a testable proposition. If Lee were correct about the Chinese people's cultural rejection of democracy we would expect to find the diaspora having little to do with voting or civil rights around the world. The reality is very different. Until the mid-1980s, Taiwan was an authoritarian state, the legacy of the nationalist strongman leader, Chiang Kai Shek. But in 1996 the island introduced elections and a multi-party political system and the twenty-three million Taiwanese, many of whom are from families that fled mainland China in 1949 when the nationalists were defeated in the civil war, have become very attached to it. Taiwanese democracy is far from perfect. There have been major corruption scandals and the former president, Chen Shui Bian, is serving a nineteen-year prison sentence for bribery. Nevertheless Taiwan is very far from being the anarchic disaster that the mainland Chinese media, conscious of the views of the CCP, relentlessly portrays.

Chinese communities in Britain and America are sometimes referred to as the invisible minority because of their low public profile. Despite the presence of a Chinese community in Britain for more than one hundred years, there has never been a single Chinese Member of Parliament. That record looks even worse when one considers that scores of Afro-Caribbean and South Asian MPs have been elected in recent decades. The situation in the US is just as disappointing, where less than a handful of Chinese-heritage members of Congress have ever been elected. It's an extraordinarily poor showing for a community of 3.8 million people. Gloria Chan, of the Asian Pacific Institute for Congressional Studies, says that perceptions have helped to hold them back. 'There's always this stereotype – we're quiet, we don't speak up, we don't fight back when we're made fun of, we're nerds, etc,' she said. 'It's been difficult for Asian Americans to break through those stereotypes.'

However the stereotypes are now being exposed as precisely that. Mee Ling Ng is a political pioneer. She was born in Malaysia and became the first female Chinese-origin local government official to be elected in Britain in 1986 when she won a place on Lewisham Borough Council. Ng, a jolly woman who overflows with enthusiasm to get more young Chinese people involved in politics, explained to me that it's not culture but memories of political repression that explain why the Chinese in Britain have made less of a mark on public life than other ethnic minorities. 'The majority of Chinese in Britain are used to a single-party state, where trade unions are banned,' she noted. 'Some are from Malaysia and Singapore, but those still are oppressive regimes. The mentality is: "We mustn't raise our head above the parapet. We are here to make a living." In China you would have got your head shot off if you raised it above the parapet. Political reticence is in our psyche, not our DNA.'

That psyche is changing. In 2009 Judy Chu became the first Chinese woman to be elected to Congress, as a representative of California. She hasn't been quiet. In 2012 Chu secured a historic apology from the House of Representatives for the 1882 Chinese Exclusion Act, which prevented any immigration from China to the US for six decades (we will hear more about that noxious article of legislation in a future chapter). And anyone who thinks that the Chinese diaspora don't care about politics should visit one of the regular meetings of the Chinese wings of UK political parties, which are all working tirelessly to get the first Chinese British MP into Parliament. What is most refreshing about these gatherings is that younger Chinese have absolutely none of the 'keep your head down' attitude that was prevalent in their parents' generation.

We sometimes cite Hong Kong as an example of the Chinese people's lack of burning concern for democracy and civil liberties. After all, didn't the Chinese there meekly return to the illiberal embrace of China after the transfer of the territory from British to Chinese control in 1997? Chris Patten, the final colonial governor of Hong Kong, recalls hearing from advisers that 'no one in Hong Kong [is] really interested in politics'.[48] Certainly, before Patten's five-minutes-to-midnight reforms, none of the previous British administrators had seen fit to introduce democratic elections in the territory.

But those who claim the Hong Kong Chinese are 'not really interested in politics' have not been paying attention. In 2003 the legislative council that runs the territory, at the behest of Beijing, attempted to clamp down on the territory's guarantees of free speech and freedom of association. The response was extraordinary. Some 500,000 people, around 7 per cent of Hong Kong's entire population, demonstrated in opposition. They filled the streets and overpasses of Hong Kong Island in a tide of humanity, forcing the authorities to back down.

And demonstrations are starting to become a habit in the former colony. In 2009 there were large protests against plans to build a high-speed rail link to the mainland. There were more mass demonstrations in 2012, forcing the legislative council to drop a Beijing-promoted plan for mandatory 'national education classes' in all schools in the territory. As in mainland China, a younger generation has been in the vanguard of these demonstrations. And as in China the opposition have used modern telecommunications to project their message as widely as possible. My friends in Hong Kong tell me that they fear more attempts by Beijing to dismantle the territory's freedoms will come, but they are resolute they will not surrender their liberties meekly.

And they will have political support in that fight. There is no more vigorous defender of civil rights in Hong Kong than the legislative council member, Leung Kwok Hung. With his waist-length black hair and his Che Guevara T-shirt, Leung looks more like a left-wing biker than a politician. But when Jackie Chan suggested that Chinese people 'need to be controlled' Leung spoke for the majority of Hong Kong people in his response: 'He has insulted the Chinese people. Chinese people are not pets.'

MUSEUM OF LIES

The Shenzhen Museum is an image of sleek modernity. Its monumental cantilevered roof resembles a giant samurai sword resting on the world's largest stand. In the museum's plush, air-conditioned galleries one can learn about the history of Shenzhen, from its origins as a Neolithic fishing settlement to its prosperous present as southern China's most spectacular boomtown. But like almost all of China's museums it's not the place to go for an unbiased account of China's history in the twentieth century. The wall texts are full of bombastic denunciations of China's backwardness under the emperors and the nation's glorious transformation by the Communist Party.

One plaque relates how the Communists mustered the anti-Japanese resistance in the province of Guangdong during the Second World War. 'The Shenzhen people, led by the CCP [The Chinese Communist Party], quickly organized armed forces to resist against the Japanese forces,' it relates. I was with a Chinese friend, a graphic designer in his late twenties, and we read the text together. There was an unexpected response. My friend shook his head sucked his teeth and muttered: 'That's incorrect, it was the nationalists, not the Communists who fought the Japanese in Guangdong.' This surprised me because up until that point I'd never heard him say anything about politics and I'd assumed that he had no interest in history either.

Appearances can be deceiving in China. It may seem on the surface that everyone is apolitical, but dig deeper and one can often find profound passions. Ordinary Chinese people can complain for hours about the corruption of officials, the heavy hand of the police and the gilded life of the 'princeling' offspring of senior Party leaders. But they have to trust you first. What always strikes me when I try to engage Chinese friends for the first time in discussions about the prospect of political reform in the country is the fear that exists. The dark cloud of Tiananmen Square and the crackdown ordered by Deng Xiaoping in 1989 still hangs heavy. Most people know what savagery the regime is prepared to sanction in order to survive. And many Chinese have learned to keep their heads down. They have a deep understanding that the regime is capable of taking everything they have and leaving them with no redress whatsoever. So, notwithstanding the bullishness of netizens, they are ultra cautious. They have learned to be discreet. And it seems to me that outsiders often misinterpret that discretion as contentment or apathy. The Chinese might not be in the streets demonstrating for full political rights like the people of the Middle East, but that does not mean they do not care about freedom. If someone asks for something and they are beaten viciously as a result, the fact that they no longer ask for it does not mean they have stopped wanting it.

One can understand why Communist Party hardliners pump out the message that Western-style democracy is antithetical to traditional Chinese culture. Political reform would be a threat to their fragile networks of power and wealth. There is nothing unusual about this. It is the same story in every autocratic regime around the world from Russia to Saudi Arabia. And in all such places one hears the same justifications for repression, such as 'cultural differences' and scaremongering about something even uglier and more dangerous to the world replacing the present regime.

How then to explain the persistence of the idea of Chinese indifference to democracy in our minds? Why are there so many apologists for the Chinese Communist Party, whereas defenders of autocrats such as Vladimir Putin or Robert Mugabe are relatively thin on the ground? I suspect part of the answer is simple ignorance. Some of those who make the defence appear to have been sucked into the orbit of Party chiefs and sympathetic business leaders so long that they genuinely believe the technocratic Communist Party embodies the will of the people. China's impressive economic record might be another reason. We tend to associate growth with free societies, not autocracies, so if China is growing, it can't be a true dictatorship, can it? Perhaps the explanation must also find room for the old prejudice about the passivity and servility of the Chinese nature, underpinned by the supposed immutability of Chinese political culture.

So what sort of democracy would the Chinese choose if they were ever given a choice? You will find many ordinary people in China who genuinely fear that granting full voting rights and introducing a multi-party system overnight would plunge the country into chaos. Some intellectuals such as Yu Keping of Peking University advocate a gradualist approach.[49] They argue that the reform process should start with the democratization of the Communist Party itself before moving on to innovations such as independence for the courts. Framed like this, China's democratization would be a stealthy affair, akin to its economic liberalization since 1978.

This sounds attractive to many. People are understandably terrified of turmoil and, besides, gradualism has a good track record. China is indisputably a freer place thanks to the economic reforms initiated by Deng Xiaoping. Since the 1980s Chinese farmers have been given the freedom to sell their surplus produce, the freedom to travel to the city to work in factories, the freedom to move factories once they arrive. Urbanites have won the freedom to set up businesses, the freedom to travel abroad for tourism, and the freedom to send their children to study in foreign countries. It is an incomplete liberty compared to what exists in the West, for sure, but few Chinese would argue that they are less free than they were thirty years ago. So could a similar process of liberalization follow in the political sphere?

THE CHOICE

Song Jiaoren was shot in the kidney by an assassin at a Shanghai train station at 10.40 p.m. on 20 March 1913. He died in hospital two days later. And with him died the young dream of Chinese democracy. Song, just thirty years old but already a veteran of revolutionary republicanism, was on the verge of power. A senior lieutenant in Sun Yat Sen's Nationalist Party, which had just prevailed in China's first national elections, Song had been expected to become the first democratically elected prime minister of the new republic.

After only one month in office, Sun had voluntarily surrendered the Chinese presidency to the head of the former Qing army, a tubby survivor with a cannonball-shaped head called Yuan Shikai, as the price for keeping the young republic from sliding into civil war. But Song was determined to shackle Yuan with constitutional government and a strong parliament in order to prevent the nascent republic morphing into a dictatorship. The young man's assassination (widely believed but never proven to have been ordered by Yuan) thus cleared all obstacles from the general's path to complete power. Yuan quickly moved to ban the Nationalist Party, dissolve parliament and drive Sun out of the country, in fear for his life.

Later that year, a celebrity American political scientist called Frank Goodnow travelled to China to dispense advice on what constitution the new republic should adopt. Goodnow concluded, rather like many Chinese and others do today, that the Chinese people were, regrettably, simply not ready for full democracy. He recommended, instead, the establishment of authoritarian constitutional monarchy until such time as China had matured politically. 'China's lack of discipline,' he explained, 'and her disregard of individual rights make it probable that a form of government which has many of the earmarks of absolutism must continue until she develops greater submission to political authority, greater powers of social cooperation and greater regard for private rights.' No one was more pleased by this verdict than Yuan. The president, brandishing this conclusion by an esteemed American expert, crowned himself emperor in 1915 by what he said was 'popular acclamation'. The vain old despot shed his Western-style military garb for the ornate robes of his old Qing bosses.

Yet the Chinese people turned out to be less than enthusiastic to find themselves back under the jurisdiction of an empire, still less an emperor like Yuan. One by one, provinces declared independence. It turned out that the people were not yearning for Goodnow's constitutional monarchy with 'earmarks of absolutism' after all. Yuan scrambled backwards, dying in 1916 a humiliated and reviled figure. But by then it was too late for democracy. The country had splintered into the dominion of a diverse selection of military strongmen.

Chinese democrats today face a difficult choice. Should they place their hopes in gradual reform, accepting the continued dominance of the Communist Party, just as some once pragmatically acquiesced in the continuation of the Qing empire? Or should they hold out for their full democratic rights, knowing that gradualism could, as so often before, give the reactionaries opportunities to slam the lid down on freedom's escape? The only good news is that China should this time be able to reach its answer free from the influence of patronizing outsiders' views about what kind of liberty, if any, the Chinese are fit for.

CHINA HAS THE WORLD'S FINEST EDUCATION SYSTEM

Every year on 7 June an unfamiliar stillness descends on China's deafening megacities. The angle grinders and piledrivers of the construction sites fall silent. Roads are blocked off. Police officers decommission their car sirens. Even taxi drivers refrain from bashing their horns for a day. A force has tamed these urban jungles, something even more powerful than the restless spirit of Chinese capitalism: education. This is the day of the nationwide college entrance exam, known as the Gao Kao. And absolutely nothing must be allowed to interrupt the concentration of the millions of eighteen-year-old students packed into school halls across the country.

The Gao Kao, literally the 'tall exam', is aptly named. The test looms intimidatingly large in the lives of families across China. Students spend their evenings after the long school day cramming more information into their fatigued brains. Parents have been known to rent apartments nearer their child's school in the run-up to the exam in order to reduce the daily commute and to free up more precious hours for revision. After-school coaching classes do a thriving trade.

The authorities take the integrity of the exam just as seriously. The exam authors are held in secret compounds to prevent them leaking the questions. Prison inmates are given the job of printing the papers for the same reason. And pity the child caught cheating in the exam room. They face the prospect of not only being disqualified, but also prevented from ever taking the test again. Their name will be entered on a national blacklist, perusable by prospective employers.

The extremes of behaviour to which the exam drives children, parents and their teachers grow more astonishing by the year. Pictures emerged a few years ago of students in a classroom in Hubei province being fed energy-boosting amino acids from intravenous drips while they hunched over their books. There have also been reports of girls in the city of Tianjin taking contraception pills to delay their periods out of fear that their concentration could be impaired at Gao Kao time. Shanghai schools were forced to put a limit on homework hours to prevent overexertion. We tend to assume that this mass worship at the altar of education, this obsession with formal examinations, this overwhelming parental pressure, is the Chinese way. It seems to be a tradition that extends back to Confucius, a big part of the explanation for the country's economic resurgence.

Travellers have long been astonished by the tendency for the Chinese to drive their children hard in pursuit of learning. In the seventeenth century the Spanish missionary Domingo Navarrete noted that the school children in the country enjoyed just eight days of play a year and had 'no vacations at all'.[1] China, as we have seen, invented the ultra-high-stakes, competitive, standardized test. For hundreds of years imperial rulers selected scholars to form the class of officials, described as 'mandarins' by outsiders, based on their performance in a series of academic exams, which tested their recall of the Confucian classic texts. This exam planted seeds of respect for scholarship deep in the soil of Chinese civilization, seeds that have since grown into mighty trees.

The rigours of today's Gao Kao seem to owe something to the imperial examination system. In the old days, candidates would be shut up in small brick cells containing just a bench and table. They would then be given a question at 10 a.m. and required to compose a 2,000-character essay by sunset. This went on for three days. Standards were punishingly high, with candidates expected to have perfect recall of a corpus of work some 430,000 characters in length. The pass rate was a mere 1 per cent, rising to 2 per cent in generous years. Many retook the tests year after year without passing. There were cases of long-bearded geriatrics sitting the exam, ever hopeful that their excruciatingly formalistic 'eight-legged essay' would finally prove satisfactory. But despair was the more common emotion. Young men went mad under the pressure of breaking into the literary bureaucracy, not least Hong Xiuquan, the man who led the Taiping Rebellion, whom we met in the first chapter. Hong failed the Gao Kao of his day four times before he concluded that he was the younger brother of Jesus Christ and raised the standard of revolt against the Qing Dynasty.

But for all its torturous asperity, the exam seemed to be a motor of social mobility. A poor unconnected lad from the provinces could study hard and become an official by doing well in the test. To be appointed a mandarin meant impregnable economic security, thus learning and education became the key that could unlock a better life. For centuries, joining this scholarcracy constituted the 'Chinese dream'. Communities pooled their resources for the sake of it. Villages worked 'book lamp fields', so named because the crop was sold to pay for lamps that would be used to light the nocturnal studies of promising local children. Lin Zexu, who became a hero of Chinese nationalism for defying the imperial British in the nineteenth century, described such a scene of rural aspiration. He wrote: 'Through freezing days and endless nights, in a broken down three-roomed apartment, with the north wind howling angrily, one lamp on the wall, young and old would sit next to each other, doing our reading and our needlework ... until the night was out.'[2]

The exam was perfectly impartial to boot, meaning that the rich could not bribe their way to success. In a harbinger of today's anti-corruption safeguards, every script was rendered anonymous, with scribes employed to copy out each completed paper before marking to ensure examiners could not recognize the handwriting of individual candidates.

Outsiders like Voltaire were impressed with the system, especially the fact that the officials were selected purely on the basis of academic merit rather than family lineage or wealth. Ralph Waldo Emerson praised the fact that in China education was an 'indispensible passport' to social advancement.[3] And in 1847 a British diplomat in Canton, Thomas Taylor Meadows, went so far as to argue that the extraordinary longevity of the Chinese empire was a consequence of its examination system. As he put it: 'The long duration of the Chinese empire is solely and altogether owing to the operation of a principle ... that good government consists in the advancement of men of talent and merit only, to the rank and power conferred by official posts.'[4]

Meadows suggested that the British government should adopt a similar system for selecting public servants. He did not have to wait too long. In 1855 the Civil Service Commission was established. At the heart of its recommendations was a standardized exam, independently marked and open to all. A little piece of China was now at the heart of the mighty British Empire.

Some Britons are still mesmerized by the Oriental academic example. In 2010 Michael Gove, the UK Education Secretary, wrote a newspaper article in which he positively gurgled with enthusiasm about the quality of the school system he had witnessed on a research trip:

> In one Beijing school I was handed a thick book with screeds of Chinese characters and the odd paragraph in English. 'Is this a textbook,' I asked? No, I was told, it was a compendium of research papers published in academic journals by people at the school. 'Gosh,' I replied. 'Your teachers must be well qualified if they are regularly publishing new work in university journals.' The papers were not, I was told, the professional work of the teachers. They were the homework of the pupils.

Gove returned home with the conclusion that 'schools in the Far East are turning out students who are working at an altogether higher level than our own'.[5]

The British Education Secretary is not alone in reaching that view. Sarah Gashi, an Oxford undergraduate who had taught English in China summed up her impressions in a student newspaper in 2011, writing that 'Chinese students have a work ethic of dedication, resilience and self discipline, which quite frankly puts us – not only British students but also Oxford undergraduates – to shame.'[6]

The same academic inferiority complex can be heard in America too. Margot Landman, the director of a teacher exchange programme for the National Committee on US–China Relations, was one of the first Americans to teach in China in the late 1970s. The Chinese children she encountered were 'extraordinarily motivated to learn in ways that our kids aren't'.[7] Not only are China's students hungrier for self-improvement, but the teachers are better at feeding them too. Sarah Nisbet, a former head of the UK exams regulator, Ofqual, relates that 'for us the logical consequence of discovering that a pupil "can't do maths" is often for him/her to drop it. In the

East it would be for teachers and friends to provide more help and for the student not to give up.'

It seems that just about every Western education specialist who visits China is destined to return as a believer in the superiority of the Chinese way of learning.

IMPORTING THE CULTURAL REVOLUTION

The results of that way seem to speak for themselves. Every few years the Paris-based think tank, the Organisation for Economics Co-operation and Development (OECD), performs its Programme for International Student Assessment, known as 'PISA'. This is a stand-ardized test of pupils' skills in maths, reading and science. In 2009 fifteen-year-old children from Shanghai came top in all three dis-ciplines, considerably outperforming children from richer nations such as the US, Britain and Germany.

This superior academic performance is apparently manifested in higher education too. A report by America's National Academy of Sciences in 2010 noted the 'excellent facilities and abundance of talented graduate students in China'.[8] In 2011 the UK's Royal So-ciety released a study showing a seven-fold increase in the number of scientific research papers published by Chinese universities be-tween 1996 and 2008.[9] That puts China on course to overtake the US in the volume of scientific research published by the end of this decade. The Royal Society report also noted that China has been increasing its public outlays on research and development by 20 per cent a year since the turn of the Millennium, making it the second biggest spender in the world after America.

'Get ready for China's domination of science' proclaimed a headline in the *New Scientist*.[10] 'The country that invented the com-pass, gunpowder, paper and printing is set for a globally important comeback' was the verdict of David Shukman, the BBC's science correspondent.[11]

It's about values. We assume the Chinese education system is overtaking our own because Chinese society respects learning more. Andreas Schleicher is the German statistician who oversees PISA. One American news magazine described the white-haired, mous-tachioed, stern-looking Schleicher as 'the world's schoolmaster' and 'the most influential education expert you've never heard of'.[12] And the world's headmaster likes the look of the industrious Chinese pupil in the front row of the class. Schleicher said that in Europe and America students tend to put their success or otherwise down to luck or their background. Not in China, though. 'They take responsibility. They can overcome obstacles and say "I'm the owner of my own success" rather than blaming it on the system.'[13]

Some Chinese friends of mine with experience of education in both China and the US have noted the difference in the attitudes of students to high academic achievement. 'The best student in China might be the class monitor, or really active in other activities. But in the US, students who excel at studies are pictured as nerds,' one of them informed me.

Now we are increasingly being urged to adopt some of those Chinese educational values. Michael Gove says he wants a Chinese-style 'cultural revolution' in learning at home. The authors of *Britannia Unchained*, a group of Conservative British politicians, agree. 'International league tables show that British pupils are falling behind their peers in South Korea or China,' they warn. 'We have to stop lowering the bar in our schools, choose more academic subjects and work longer hours.'[14] Americans say that we have something to learn from China too. 'Can we become just a wee bit more Confucian ourselves, at least in terms of elevating education in our priorities?' pleaded Nicholas Kristof in the *New York Times*.[15]

But the example goes deeper than public policy; it's about how we raise our children. In 2010 Amy Chua, a Yale law professor and daughter of Chinese immigrants, published the bestselling *Battle Hymn of the Tiger Mother*. Chua sniffed at what she described as our soft approach, suggesting that 'many Chinese secretly believe that they care more about their children and are willing to sacrifice much more for them than Westerners, who seem perfectly content to let their children turn out badly.'[16] Chua claimed she was merely writing a jokey and self-deprecating personal memoir rather than a parenting handbook, but that didn't stop many commentators arguing that, yes, what our coddled, system-blaming and under-achieving children need is a good dose of Chinese-style 'Tiger parenting'.

And if we don't embrace the educational philosophy of Confucius and imitate the action of the Tiger Mother? Well, we nurse the fear that the decline and fall of our civilization will inevitably follow. American think tanks have warned that we are on course to see two hundred million Chinese graduates by 2030, a legion of brainiacs equal in size to the entire US workforce.[17] Furthermore, they note, these Chinese graduates are mostly trained in 'hard' subjects such as engineering, maths and sciences, unlike Western students who increasingly study 'soft' social sciences and humanities.

Trepidation at the prospect of super-intelligent and hyper-motivated Chinese graduates walking all over our decadent and ignorant youngsters in the globalized twenty-first-century jobs market have taken hold. Thomas Friedman, author of 2005's influential *The World is Flat*, writes: 'When I was growing up, my parents told me, "Finish your dinner. People in China and India are starving." I tell my daughters, "Finish your homework. People in India and China are starving for your job."'[18]

Barack Obama himself has argued that the nation which 'out-educates us today will out-compete us tomorrow'.[19] No prizes for guessing which nation he was talking about. Meanwhile, Allison Pearson, a British pundit, saw Chua's Tiger Mother parenting as a reflection of the changing of the guard of global power. She writes: 'Along comes a Chinese woman who writes about how Western parents are setting their kids up for mediocrity and decline. It reads like an allegory of a nation that's losing its superpower to another.'[20]

But the irony is that our panic over a nascent educational superpower in the East, a nation powered by thousands of years of Confucian meritocracy, would provoke a hollow laugh from many Chinese.

THE UNATTAINABLE CHINESE DREAM

Let's start with the history. The imperial education system that fed the meritocratic scholarcracy was never the incorruptible engine of social mobility that visitors took it to be. Despite the Confucian emphasis on learning, there was no universal state provision of free education in imperial China. That meant families had to dip into their own pockets to prepare their sons (and it was, of course, only sons who were given the opportunity) for the imperial exams. This inevitably favoured the well-off, mainly the landed gentry. The son of the typical farmer would be unlikely to sit even for the lowest level provincial tests. The 'Chinese dream' was only for those with some money.

And even for those who made it through, the playing field was not level. The historian John Chaffee has shown that during the Song Dynasty, when the imperial exam system settled into its classic form, it was progressively corrupted. 'The meritocratic aims of the founding emperors were largely subverted,' he argues. 'People learned to work the system in order to improve their chances of passing and gaining official status.' Chaffee describes how some candidates moved to prefectures where quotas were less stringent, and relatives of officials took special examinations that had been created to reduce the likelihood that they would be unfairly favoured by the examiners but which in fact gave them a competitive advantage. Others simply cheated or paid bribes.[21]

The Manchu warriors of the northeast who founded the Qing Dynasty in 1644 helped to undermine the meritocratic integrity of the system too. Their sons, having been trained as nomadic hunters and warriors, were highly unlikely to become proficient in regurgitating the ancient texts of Confucian scholars. So new routes for 'academic' distinction were created which, happily, included good horsemanship and archery skills.[22]

The Communists who took control of China's education system, along with everything else, in 1949, did not fall for the myth of the enlightened imperial exam system. The whole thing had been, according to Mao Zedong, nothing more than an institutional aide to feudal repression. Yet Maoist educational innovation produced something far worse. The Cultural Revolution Mao launched in 1966, a nationwide ideological frenzy designed primarily to take revenge on what he regarded as his disloyal party, was one of the most philistine popular movements in history. Books by politically suspect authors were destroyed, as were supposedly reactionary works of classical literature and poetry. Students were encouraged to victimize their 'class enemy' teachers. Many scholars were tormented until they committed suicide. For three years universities and high schools admitted no new students while youths known as Red Guards ran wild, assaulting anyone they deemed insufficiently loyal to the revolution. When even Mao realized the violence had spilled out of hand, tens of thousands of teenage urban Red Guards were sent to perform manual labour in the countryside for 're-education'. Millions of ordinary Chinese had their schooling interrupted for more than a decade, creating a lost generation. It is hard to know whether to laugh or weep at Michael Gove's statement that he wants a cultural revolution in British education 'just like the one they've had in China'.

The history of Chinese education has often been less than glorious. And so, when one scratches the glossy surface, is the present. Far from being the purring Rolls-Royce of our imagination, the vehicle actually looks close to breakdown. Chinese higher education is expanding as fast as the wider economy. In 1998 around 830,000 people graduated from Chinese universities. In 2012 more than 6,000,000 did so. These are the astonishing numbers that transfix think tanks. The Chinese government is proud of them too. The education ministry has declared that 'higher education in China has achieved the shift from elite to widespread education, completing a process that other countries have needed forty or fifty years – or even longer – to complete.'[23]

The problem is that the higher education sector is not coping with the expansion. There is a shortage of decent teachers in China. One of the baleful legacies of the Cultural Revolution is that only around a third of the present cohort of Chinese professors have doctorates. And with salaries far lower than in Western universities the sharpest tend to migrate to teaching jobs abroad. Almost none of the Chinese students who received a doctorate at American universities in 2002 had returned home five years later.[24]

There are not enough high-quality institutions either. In Scandinavia there exists one world-class university for every million inhabitants.[25] Yet China, a nation of 1.3 billion people, has just seven colleges in the top 200 of the Times Higher Education World University Rankings 2011–12. The highest-ranked institution in mainland China is Peking University in 49th spot. According to another respected higher education ranking body, China was well down the international league table in terms of resources, environment, connectivity and output. This reputed educational superpower was outperformed in 2012 by, among others, Slovakia and Malaysia.[26]

The result is that huge swathes of China's army of graduates are simply not educated to a decent standard. Nor are they trained in the kind of skills that the Chinese economy is crying out for. Despite China's reputation as a country that churns out scientists and engineers, many employers complain that graduates are not equipped with the practical skills they need, whether that is the ability to wire a circuit or to weld a pipe. 'Our universities encourage research and theory and there are relatively few vocational schools,' according to Pan Chenguang, who compiles an annual report on national skills for the Chinese Academy of Social Sciences. He adds: 'Most students feel that the social status of attending a vocational school is lower, so they don't want to go.'

All this means that China has an ant problem. On the monotonous outskirts of most major Chinese cities there exist large communities of graduates in their twenties living in overcrowded and crumbling accommodation. Often their dwellings are single rooms carved out of basements, with a communal bathroom. They have been priced out of the city centre by soaring rents and inflated property values. These graduates travel crazily long distances on public transport into the city, where they work as shop assistants, data-entry clerks, receptionists and cashiers. Many of these luckless youngsters grew up in the countryside or in provincial towns. They worked hard in school and managed to get into decent universities to study subjects such as accounting and computer science. But now they are stuck in dead-end and low-status jobs for which they are, on paper at least, hugely over qualified. They are China's 'ant tribe'.

The term was coined by Professor Lian Si of Peking University. He did not mean it to be insulting. As he puts it: 'They share every similarity with ants. They live in colonies in cramped areas. They're intelligent and hardworking, yet anonymous and underpaid.' Professor Lian estimates that there are around one million ants across the country, with a hundred thousand in Beijing alone.

STILL MARXIST AFTER ALL THESE YEARS

The Royal Society has a claim to be considered the cradle of the modern physical sciences. The academy, founded in the reign of King Charles II, is the most venerable extant scientific organization in the world. Former fellows include such giants as Isaac Newton,

Charles Darwin and Ernest Rutherford. So when the Society released its report showing an explosion in published science research from Chinese universities it understandably made quite an impact. But what the Royal Society, bizarrely, failed to stress was the low quality of much of this Chinese research in recent years.

Relatively few of the tens of thousands of papers pumped out by Chinese scientists every year are cited by other professionals in the same fields in universities around the world. The work of American and British scientists is far more influential. Between 2004 and 2008 American scientists accounted for 30 per cent of global citations and British scientists 8 per cent. German scientists were responsible for 7 per cent of citations. By contrast, China's share of global citations was a mere 4 per cent, despite the explosion of publications in those years.[27]

It is also telling that China has failed to translate this massive increase in scientific publication into new technologies. In 2009 China registered 1,600 patents in the US. Japan, by contrast, registered more than 35,000, Germany 9,000 and Spain 6,500.[28] An explanation for the gulf between quantity and quality lies in the fact that there is huge financial pressure on Chinese researchers to publish. Average scientist salaries are low and university superiors tie the bonuses and promotions of faculty staff to how much work they get printed in journals.

This crude pressure is a symptom of the underlying sickness in Chinese higher education: a lack of independence. Marxist–Leninist doctrine says that educational institutions must be tightly controlled by the state to ensure ideological orthodoxy. And China's Communist leaders, for all their talk of creating a modern and dynamic higher education sector, have stuck to that command and control model. Universities are still very much part of the machinery of state power in China. The presidents of academic institutions are appointed by the Communist Party, and political interference in university affairs is routine. Professor Yang Rui, a higher education specialist at the University of Hong Kong, puts it like this: 'The Chinese model is that education is there to serve the government. Education is to help the government to govern. To put it another way, to control.'[29]

Visitors who are used to seeing and experiencing universities as independent institutions find this difficult to believe. After all, from the outside, Chinese universities look rather like our own colleges. They have lecture halls, libraries, halls of residence and so on – everything one would expect to find in Britain or America. Yet appearances are deceiving. Until recently all students had to spend 15 per cent of their time attending compulsory classes on Marxist dialectical philosophy. While that requirement has now been dropped, it has been replaced with mandatory history lessons, where students are force fed the line that the Communist Party saved China from a century of humiliation and weakness.

Just as corruption riddles the Chinese state, it is common too in Chinese academia. In 2009 two university researchers from Jinggangshan University in Jiangxi were found to have faked data in seventy crystallography papers.[30] The fraud was uncovered by the journal that published them, not the university itself. And there are few signs of the academic authorities taking their policing duties seriously. According to Cong Cao, an expert in China's education system based at Nottingham University, these kinds of misdemeanours, if uncovered, often get swept under the carpet, especially if someone senior in the university is involved. 'When someone is guilty of misconduct – plagiarism, falsification of data – they are less likely to be punished than in Western universities,' he says. 'If you are small potatoes, probably you will get punished. But in many cases eminent professors are implicated and it's difficult. Some of these professors become eminent with the help of the Party. Now if those people are guilty of some form of misconduct, how do you explain that you made them eminent? A leading author's more likely to get off.'[31]

Cao concludes that the fraud that has been uncovered so far is merely the tip of an iceberg of academic corruption. A 2009 survey of scientists by the Chinese Association of Science and Technology showing that 55 per cent of respondents knew of misconduct by their peers seems to support that depressing conclusion.[32]

TOO POOR TO GO TO SCHOOL

Ma Yan was an apple-cheeked thirteen-year-old who desperately wanted to stay in school. But one tragic day her parents told her that they no longer had the money to continue sending her. In her diary Ma Yan, a Hui Muslim from rural Ningxia province, recorded how she was given the bad news:

> We have a week of vacation. Mother takes me aside. 'My child. There's something I have to tell you.' I answer: 'mother if you have something to tell me, do it quickly'. But her words are like a death sentence. 'I'm afraid you may have been to school for the last time. Your brothers and you add up to three children to be sent to school. Your father is the only one earning money, and it's not enough ... I'm back in the house and I work the land for my brothers' education. How I want to study! But my family can't afford it.[33]

Ma Yan got lucky. Her mother relented, taking on extra back-breaking agricultural work (picking a rare herb popular with rich city dwellers) in order to scrape together the money to keep her daughter in lessons. And the world found out about the plight of Ma Yan because her mother gave her daughter's diary to a foreigner who was passing through their village. The foreigner published the text as *The Diary of Ma Yan: the struggles and hopes of a Chinese schoolgirl.*

The tale of Ma Yan's difficulties in getting an education in rural China (at one stage she describes how she lacked the money even to buy a pen for her studies) became a bestseller. But perhaps the most astonishing aspect of the whole affair is that the struggles Ma Yan chronicled took place not when China was on its knees during the crumbling final days of the Qing empire, not in the midst of the Communist/Nationalist civil war of the late 1940s, not during the madness of the Cultural Revolution, but in 2000 and 2001, at the dawn of a century that we are told China will bestride like an economic colossus.

What the story of Ma Yan demonstrates is that problems in Chinese education go much further than skulduggery in a few universities. They start at the grass roots. Primary and secondary school fees have now been abolished, but the gulf between China's top urban schools and its rural institutions – schools like that of Ma Yan – is wide and getting wider. A report by Unesco in 2010 found that public expenditure per student in the cities of Beijing and Shanghai was eighteen times higher than in the poorest provinces. For cash-strapped and corrupt local governments education is very far from a priority. This means it is getting progressively harder for rural children to get to university. The World Bank has warned that many are dropping out long before their state-mandated nine years of learning are over. This has contributed to an increase in nationwide illiteracy rates, which went up from 7 per cent in 2000 to 11 per cent in 2005, an astonishing trend in an industrializing nation like China.[34]

Even in the fast-growing urban centres educational inequality is growing. The children of China's migrant workers who have accompanied their parents on the journey to the city, twenty-five million by some estimates, get funnelled into special schools staffed with unqualified teachers. Despairing of the poor quality of these institutions, some migrant workers in Beijing have even set up their own schools, pooling their resources to hire buildings and to pay teachers. The city authorities ordered some two dozen of these prefabricated institutions to be shut down in 2012, cutting off the water to ensure compliance in typically brutal fashion. The bureaucrats promised that all the migrant children would be given places at proper state schools, but the parents suspected that officials, concerned at the ballooning urban population, were actually trying to bully them into sending their children back to their home villages to be looked after by grandparents. They dug in their heels.

Can all this really be happening in the same China that studies show to be producing the best-educated children in the world? It turns out that the single PISA study, which showed Shanghai youngsters outperforming everyone else in the world, is doing an awful lot of work in sustaining this rosy impression. The exercise is akin to judging British and American educational standards by testing students from top fee-paying preparatory schools.

The PISA tests were actually performed not just in Shanghai but in nine provinces across China. Andreas Schleicher says that the academic performance of Chinese students in the countryside was also 'remarkable'. But the Chinese government has not allowed the OECD to publish the figures, which seems a very odd decision if the results are really so impressive. Nor should PISA be treated as infallible. One study has credibly argued that the PISA tables underestimate the relative performance of British school children.[35] The relative performance of other nations, including China, might well be correspondingly overstated.

China's massive state investment drive in education and research has been a favoured topic of the media since it fits the popular narrative of China as a rising superpower. Spending is certainly up. Annual Chinese expenditure on research and development has risen 20 per cent in real terms over the past decade. However, some wider context is also important when digesting these sorts of figures. China's total public spending on all levels of education is around 4.5 per cent of GDP, but the share in wealthy countries is 5.5 per cent to 6 per cent, while Brazil, another fast-growing poor economy, spends 5.1 per cent.[36] The fact is that China still lags not only behind the world's high-income economies, but also some of its international developing world peers in terms of the raw financial resources that the country devotes to education. And for all the talk about China's impending dominance of the university sector, we should also remember that in 2009 less than 5 per cent of working age adults in China had been through some form of higher education, versus 27 per cent in Europe and 41 per cent in America.[37] This is a country that has a daunting amount of catching up to do.

'LIKE A USED CONDOM'

We might think that China's systems of tuition have always reflected classic Confucian philosophy, but the great sage himself would surely recoil at what has been done in his name to generations of Chinese students. Confucius made it quite clear he believed understanding, not just the acquisition of knowledge, ought to be at the heart of scholarship. 'Those who think but do not learn are in danger,' he warned, 'but those who learn but do not think are lost.'[38] It is a warning the architects of the imperial exam, which tested an ability to recall massive chunks of classic text, ignored. And the results were pretty dire. That old exam is now commonly identified as one of the intellectual constraints that prevented China, despite its head start as a great innovator, from making the scientific breakthroughs that enabled the West to industrialize in the eighteenth century.[39]

The designers of the Gao Kao have also ignored the Confucian warning. The skill that the Gao Kao rewards above all is memorization. Creativity and critical thinking are pretty much an irrelevance. One professor I spoke to lamented the contrast between the Western sceptical tradition of learning and China's emphasis on the transmission of an unchanging body of wisdom. 'In ancient Greece they said challenge authority, challenge ideas, challenge anything,' he told me. 'The Confucian system always provided a cage. If you are creative enough they give you a slightly larger cage. But you are never allowed to go beyond the cage.' This is no stereotype. In a restaurant in London's Soho, a middle-aged Chinese business consultant described to me the difficulties he faced in adapting to the Western style of education when he was asked to write his first essay after arriving in the 1990s at a British university to study for an MBA. 'I reproduced a chunk of text from a book,' he said. 'But my professor said, "No, no I want to know what *you* think." It was the first time anyone had said that to me.'

It's a common experience for Chinese students when they leave the Chinese educational environment. The Beijing-based journalist, Helen Gao, describes something similar when she came to a Western university. 'The analytical essays on my history tests felt dauntingly, even impossibly amorphous compared to the straightforward multiple-choice questions that had long characterized my exams,' she recalls. 'I was used to strictly formatted Chinese argumentative essay topics, for which I had memorized hundreds of paragraphs that I could organize like jigsaw puzzles. Western-education-style papers on, for example, the significance of symbols in a novel was not the sort of expressive, creative thinking for which my Chinese teachers had prepared me.'[40]

But is the Chinese system designed to equip Chinese students for work in the domestic economy and to make a contribution to a Chinese society that runs by different rules than those that govern the West? The problem is that the Gao Kao method of teaching does not even seem to be effective in a Chinese environment. Of the top students in Chinese high school exams almost none go on to excel in later life. A study of a thousand top scorers in the Gao Kao between 1997 and 2008 discovered that 'none of them stood out in the fields of academics, business or politics'.[41]

Other problems spring from Gao Kaoism. Because the test is so all-important, schools tie the remuneration of teachers to how well students do in the test. The more students the teacher manages to squeeze into a good university, the higher their bonus. This incentive-driven aspect of the Chinese education system, which owes more to the free-market fundamentalism of Milton Friedman than Mao, has malign side effects, with teachers engaging in endless rounds of drilling, rather than ensuring students' actual comprehension of a topic.

Student complaints about their teachers can be heard the world over, but in China the level of alienation has reached extreme levels. Eric Mu, a Chinese graduate and journalist, has vividly described his contempt for a system in which teachers are routinely abusive and crudely driven by league tables. After taking the Gao Kao, Mu says that he 'walked out of the room feeling like an abandoned condom, used and hollow'.[42] Han Han, a glamorous young racing driver and the country's most popular blogger, describes the feeling of passing through China's schools as akin to taking a shower while wearing a coat. 'The education system tries to create homogeneous personalities, just like making chopsticks,' he says. 'For chopsticks to work properly, you have to make them all exactly the same length.'[43]

There are rumblings of rebellion from higher education too. In 2012 an anonymous third-year student published a polemic titled 'I don't forgive the education I receive'. In a familiar analogy, the author compared the country's education system to a dehumanizing and demotivating assembly line.

One of the differences between Chinese educational culture and that of the West is supposed to be that in China pupils help their peers to learn. Sarah Nisbet, formerly of Ofqual, has noted that the coffee bars of Singapore, which has a majority ethnic Chinese population, 'are often filled with small groups of students discussing their lessons with the more able helping the others'. Yet Eric Mu paints a starkly contrasting picture of primal competition. 'When you feel that the guy sitting beside you is your potential enemy who may rob you of a lifetime of happiness, altruism is not going to be your guide,' he says. While it may be true that top students are heroes in China, the other side of that coin is that underachievers can sometimes find themselves ostracized.

Sometimes art speaks more eloquently than personal testimony. Anyone tempted to believe the myth of China's uniformly brilliant, motivated and happy young learners should watch the online satirical cartoon *Kuang Kuang's Diary* (which is the country's equivalent of *South Park*) on YouTube. An episode from 2009 called 'Blowing up the School' featured Kuang Kuang's pet chicken launching a suicide attack on the school after her master was beaten to death by sadistic teachers for daring to speak the truth in lessons. The episode attracted a million hits on the day it was released.

WEST IS BEST

Everyone in China has heard of *Harvard Girl*. It was the title of a book written in 2000 by two parents outlining how they managed to get their daughter, Liu Yiting, accepted on a scholarship by the American Ivy League university. The book was a terrific success, shifting more than 1.5 million copies in China and making Liu a household name. The 'character-building' pedagogical techniques the parents described, such as getting the toddler Yiting to hold ice until her hands turned purple, made for a lively read. But what made the book so popular was that Liu Yiting's parents had achieved what every Chinese parent wants: an overseas education for their child.

The massive popularity of a US higher education among Chinese parents shows that they are well aware of the deficiencies of the domestic system. In 2011 157,000 Chinese students studied in the United States, up fourfold on a decade ago.[44] And there are plenty more youngsters lining up to make the trip across the Pacific. Universities across Europe are popular too, including elite British universities such as Oxford and Cambridge. In 2010 there were 90,000 Chinese youngsters at UK higher education colleges. Of all the world's overseas students combined, the majority are now Chinese.

A 2012 survey by the Chinese magazine *Hurun Report* found that around 9 out of 10 wealthy Chinese, defined as people with assets of US$1 million or more, intend to send their children to universities abroad. A third also want to send their children abroad for high school. The *Hurun Report* looked at the preferences of the rich because they are the only ones who have the means to acquire a wildly expensive foreign education. A small number of overseas Chinese students get scholarships, but 93 per cent are self-funded, meaning that their parents pay. The annual tuition fees at Harvard are around $40,000 a year. To put this in context, the average annual disposable income in urban China in 2012 was just $3,900. An overseas education is an option only for the well-off. However, other survey evidence suggests that the lower middle classes aspire to precisely the same thing.

The Hurun Report poll made it clear that a foreign education is no mere status symbol like a luxury watch or branded handbag; rather it is regarded as superior to what is available at home. Of the respondents, 46 per cent praised the well-rounded education available abroad, 23 per cent were attracted by the greater creativity, 17 per cent liked the open-mindedness and 14 per cent appreciated the more personalized tuition on offer.[45]

A foreign education even has tacit political backing. The daughter of the most senior Communist Party leader Xi Jinping enrolled at Harvard in 2010, albeit under a pseudonym. The son of the now purged regional boss of Chongqing, Bo Xilai, is another. Bo Guagua studied first at Oxford and has since enrolled at Harvard. A host of other political 'princelings' have also made the trip to Western academia, including the grandson of the former senior leader Jiang Zemin.

There are, it is true, some dissenting voices. Zhou Qifeng, the president of Peking University, said in 2011 the American education system could not be very high quality because of the calibre of political leaders it produced. The US education system, he concluded, 'is a complete mess'. China's universities, by contrast, he said, were progressing well. However, an online debate provoked by these comments indicated little support for Zhou's views. Of 40,000 people who volunteered their opinion, a mere 5 per cent agreed with him about the state of the US system, while only 8 per cent felt that the Chinese education system had improved. Many also accused Zhou of hypocrisy, noting that he himself had studied at the University of Massachusetts.

ENDANGERED TIGERS

Can anything be salvaged from the rubble of Chinese education? It might not have been intended as a parenting guidebook, but Amy

Chua's *Battle Hymn of the Tiger Mother* bore some similarities to *Harvard Girl*. Like Liu Yiting's parents, Amy Chua put her daughters on a rigid academic regimen from an early age. 'By the time Sophia was three,' Chua writes of her elder child, 'she was reading Sartre, doing simple set theory, and she could write one hundred Chinese characters.'

China's schools and colleges might be stultifying warehouses of rote learning, but won't these sorts of parenting techniques ensure that, ultimately, Chinese children come out on top? The performance of the children of Chinese immigrants seems to support this thesis. In the UK, girls from the poorest Chinese families get better results at GCSE exams, generally taken at age sixteen, than any other ethnic group, even Chinese girls from wealthier families. As one report noted, they not only compensate for the disadvantage of their home circumstances, they seem to do better because of it.[46] There's stellar over-achievement from Chinese students in US schools too. The Chinese are, in the parlance of sociology, the 'model minority'.

Yet Chua's claim that this success is due to Tiger parenting, or that the methods she chose to deploy with her own children are representative of the behaviour of all Chinese parents, looks overdrawn. The kind of obsessive and domineering approach she described undoubtedly takes place in some homes, as *Harvard Girl* shows, but my impression from speaking to many Chinese families is that it is increasingly a minority pursuit. And to the extent that parents do put pressure on their children to work hard, Chua's characterization of this as an aggressive process seems well off target. 'If your next time's not perfect I'm going to take all your stuffed animals and burn them,' was Chua's most notorious threat.

I've spoken to many Chinese people both in China and elsewhere who are repulsed by the idea of motivating children in this manner. The Tiger Mother stereotype also helps conceal the ways in which attitudes to parenting have evolved in China. One can find just as many urban parents in China who are endlessly indulgent of their children, spoiling them with generous allowances and gifts. In Taiwan there has been a government attempt to reform parenting, with the promotion of a programme called 'education of love' designed to discourage physical chastisement.

The dominant impression left by Chua's book is actually not so much a strict parent, but of a woman who lives in a snobbish world where the strong-willed dominate the weak, the less intelligent rightly end up at the bottom of the social pile, and the violin and piano are the only civilized musical instruments. 'Even in third grade, classmates made fun of me,' she tells one of her daughters in frustration. 'Do you know where those people are now? They're janitors, that's where.'47 God forbid that the precocious child of a Tiger Mother should end up in such a distastefully low occupation. Chua is fully entitled to her sour view of human relations and her fetish for the 'subtle, exquisite' shape of the violin, but is she entitled to project her own ugly motivations and rather tiresome preoccupations on to 1.3 billion Chinese people?

Let us be clear. Education is indeed highly socially valued in China. One can recognize that from the amount that parents are willing to spend on getting their children schooled abroad. My own relatives have spent ridiculous amounts to ensure that their daughters are properly educated. One travelled to New York for a master's degree in modern art, another went to Hong Kong for management studies. The sums their parents spent relative to their incomes were truly staggering, making UK and US college tuition fees look like chicken feed. Children are brought up to value education too. I've seen my cousin's seven-year-old son being literally spoon fed from a bowl of soup by his grandmother while he writes Chinese characters into his exercise book. And there's no doubt that students do push themselves to the threshold of a nervous breakdown at exam time.

But rather than assuming this behaviour to be the manifestation of an immutable Chinese character, we ought to think a little more deeply about *why* it happens. Massive competition is one reason. Some 9.15 million children sat the Gao Kao exam in 2012. Yet there were only 6.5 million university places available. Because colleges tend to funnel students into specific industries, a good university means the chance of reasonably paid white-collar work. A lesser college raises the risk of turning into an 'ant' graduate. And failing to get in to any higher education college means a life of hard manual work. Children in the provinces have to be especially high scorers in the exam to get into China's two top universities in Beijing, since a large number of places are reserved for local youngsters. The tectonic plates of Chinese urban society are moving apart frighteningly quickly. People have to move fast to get on the comfortable side. If such a shift were taking place in our own countries, public exams here would probably be treated with obsessive seriousness too by both students and parents.

The one-child policy raises the stakes higher still. There is one grandchild for every four grandparents now. If those grandparents are relying on their family to help them financially in their old age the pressure on the child to get a good job ratchets up considerably. These financial pressures are even stronger in the countryside. Here the diary of Ma Yan spells it out:

> I suddenly realize why mother hasn't gotten medical help before. It's so that we can keep going to school. School costs tens of yuan all at once. Where does this money come from? It comes from the sweat and hard labour of my parents. Father and Mother are ready to sacrifice everything so that we can go to school. I must work really hard in order to go to university later. Then I'll get a good job, and Mother and Father will at last have a happy life.[48]

We are told that the Chinese are obsessed with education because of their Confucian esteem for learning, but the Cambridge-based Korean economist Ha-Joon Chang argues that the education mania in his own home country, which sees similar pressure put on students, has a more materialist explanation. Chang thinks it is driven by employment insecurity and a meagre welfare state. 'Pupils study hard, thinking that better educational qualifications may give them a layer of protection in an unforgiving labour market,' he has argued. And that leads to a vicious circle. 'Since everyone is studying hard, they have to run faster to stay in the same place,' he says. 'The result is the combination of long study hours (double that of Finnish children, who do equally well in international tests) and enormous mental stress.'[49] The same forces are at work in China, which, as we will see later, has an even smaller welfare state, with lousy provision for pensions, health care in old age and scant unemployment benefits.

Wherever it springs from, all this academic pressure is as much a curse as a blessing for the Chinese economy. It produces workers who are diligent but ultra risk averse, competent but uncreative. Diligence and competence were the skills that China needed in the first phase of its economic comeback. What it needs to advance further are graduates who are capable of innovating. The funny thing is that just as angst in our own nations is growing about the inadequacy of our education systems in the face of this threat from the East, Chinese families are also increasingly fretting about their own children's ability to compete in the global market for talent.

GOODBYE GAO KAO?

There are undeniable qualities in Chinese education and parenting. The Confucian exam system might have often been rigged, but it did provide a modicum of upward social mobility for those lucky enough to be born into the gentry – probably more so than existed in Europe during the Middle Ages. And the Communist government does deserve some credit for its mass education drive. National literacy rates have risen from 67 per cent in 1980 to around 90 per cent today. Even allowing for a fudge of the definition of literacy, the performance has still been impressive. China compares well with other emerging economies such as Turkey and Mexico in terms of the proportion of students who finish high school (65 per cent versus 45 per cent).[50] The average number of years that Indian children spend in school is 4.4 years, compared with 7.5 years in China.

Gao Kaoism also seems to be effective at imparting the core skill of numeracy. A Chinese friend working in a public relations firm in London notes that she seems to be better at mental arithmetic than her Western peers, thanks to the rote learning of her youth. 'I'm amazed that they need to use a calculator for the most simple sums,' she observed. Nevertheless the Chinese education system is undeniably in need of major reform. It is not something to be feared in the West – and certainly not emulated.

As the US commentator Robert Samuelson has noted, our alarm at the educational and scientific resurgence of China has echoes of the panic provoked when the Soviet Union unexpectedly put a satellite into orbit in 1957.[51] Then, as now, there was angst among politicians and pundits over how we were losing our scientific edge to dynamic Communist academia. We now see how foolish the 'Sputnik scare' was. Our open scientific institutions were far superior to those of our Soviet counterparts, where researchers could be purged if they held heretical views on innocuous subjects such as plant genetics. We have not woken up to the fact that the Chinese higher education sector still has more in common with the centralized and politicized institutions of the Soviet Union than the liberated world of Princeton and Oxbridge.

The good news for China is that faint rumblings of change can already be heard. There are some signs that the ferocious culture of cramming is waning as children begin to understand that the rewards on offer often do not justify the effort involved. 'People still work hard at secondary school, but they mostly stop when they get into university,' one Chinese friend admitted to me. It is also interesting that fewer high school students are bothering to take the Gao Kao now. The numbers who squeezed into exam halls on 7 June in 2012 were a million down from the 2008 peak of ten million. Gao Kaoism may be declining.

And the top universities are improving in the quality of their tuition. The more enlightened faculty members are encouraging critical thinking, rather than just knowledge absorption. Another Chinese friend of mine who works at a US think tank told me proudly: 'When I was at Beijing University, the teacher told us that our first reaction should be to question, no matter what anyone else tells you.' The brain drain might be slowing too. Some overseas-trained scientists are coming back to work in Chinese institutions. There are hopes that more returnees – 'sea turtles' as they are known in China – will follow.

The government proposed a series of higher education reforms in 2010, including allowing greater autonomy for universities. The private sector could help provide a push too. Chen Weiming, a businessman and Harvard graduate, has founded a private university outside of Shanghai. Entrance to Xing Wei College will be determined not just by Gao Kao scores, but also essays and interviews.[52]

At a lower level there are interesting educational innovations. In her book *Factory Girls*, Leslie Chang describes how private night schools have been established in one industrial megacity, Dongguan, serving migrant workers who have been spat out unqualified by the existing state education system.[53] These institutions ignore all the traditional paraphernalia of competitive testing and rote learning and instead focus on coaching public speaking, English language and other practical skills that enable blue-collar migrants to move to office jobs.

We are asking the wrong question. What matters is not whether the Chinese education system is about to overtake our own. That is a paranoid fantasy. The question that matters is: can China reform its systems of learning in time to drive its economy onwards? Professor Zhuan Minxuan, a former deputy director general of the Shanghai Education Commission, says it will take time. 'We have more than two thousand years of rote learning, so you cannot say in one night all the people have to change their behaviour,' he points out. And vested interests in universities can be expected to fight reform if it undermines the power and status of their politically appointed managers. Some also fear that reform could be socially regressive too. Yang Rui of the University of Hong Kong warns that reducing the importance of the Gao Kao could open the door to corruption, with pupils using their personal connections, or '*guanxi*', to get into the best universities.

Yet China is likely to modernize in the end. It has long been more adaptable and practical on matters of education than it often appears from the outside. As we saw, even the wool-dyed reactionaries of the Qing Dynasty ditched the Confucian exam system after 1905. The republican government that followed grasped the need to push the 'new learning' of science from the West. And they enacted a host of radical structural university reforms in the 1930s. Recognition is growing among today's leaders that education reform is an economic imperative.

It is possible to imagine that one year in the not too distant future 7 June will come round and the roads in China's cities will not need to be blocked. Construction sites will be able to carry on their work as usual and taxi drivers will be able to lean on their horns as if it were any other day of the year. And the millions of Chinese students taking their exams will surely be better off for it.

THE CHINESE LIVE TO WORK

The golden spike was hammered into some dirt near the scrubby mountain town of Promontory, Utah. To the west of the expensive yellow pin stretched a ladder of metal tracks that ended in the great metropolis of New York. To the east snaked a newly built iron highway that terminated in California. It was 10 May 1869 and the two coasts of the United States of America were now connected, for the first time, by a continuous railroad.

Before then, a journey between the west and east coasts of America had taken months along the bumpy Oregon wagon trail. To make the voyage by sea was even more of a slog, with travellers forced to sail around Cape Horn, the southernmost tip of the Americas. On the First Transcontinental Railroad, however, the trip from one end of the country to the other took just seven days. An economic revolution for America, still bleeding from the wounds of its shattering Civil War, could now begin.

One would not guess it from the many official portraits commissioned to commemorate this ceremony, nor from the scores of photographs that were taken and published in endless popular newspapers, but the new railway that united America ought to have come with a giant 'made in China' stamp. The rail company that had built the eastern section of the line, the Central Pacific, had a labour force that was 90 per cent Chinese. This crew had hacked and blasted its way through the 7,000-foot-high Sierra Nevada mountain range, enduring six brutal winters and frequent lethal avalanches. Some two thousand Chinese labourers are estimated to have died on the job, most of them buried in shallow graves at the side of the track.

One man, though, remembered their efforts. On the same day that the golden spike was hammered down, Edwin Crocker, the Central Pacific's legal counsel and brother of the line's big boss,

Charles Crocker, gave a speech in Sacramento, in which he paid special tribute to the eleven thousand Chinese who had worked on the line. 'I wish to call to your minds that the early completion of this railroad we have built has been in large measure due to that poor, despised class of labourers called the Chinese, to the fidelity and industry they have shown,' he declared.[1]

Some railway managers had been sceptical of the Crockers' plan to recruit Chinese labour to work on the railway. A common view was that the 'Orientals' would prove too physically slight to cope with the physical rigours of railroad construction. But Charles Crocker never had any doubts. 'Make masons out of Chinamen? Did they not build the Chinese wall, the biggest piece of masonry in the world?' he asked.

And it wasn't just the Chinese workers' industry that the Crocker brothers liked. A few years earlier Charles had written to Cornelius Cole, a California congressman, to note another outstanding quality in his new labour force. 'They prove nearly equal to white men, in the amount of labour they perform, and are far more reliable,' he observed. 'No danger of strikes among them.'[2] Indeed, so docile were the Chinese that they became known among the other navvies as 'Crocker's pets'.

Hard working and docile – such was the image of the Chinese in the High Sierras in those pioneering days of the 1860s. And such is the image of the Chinese that continues to dominate today, a century and a half later.

THE LAND OF UNREMITTING INDUSTRY

Our perception of the Chinese as an unusually diligent people was formed long before the Crockers began recruiting. As usual, it was the Catholic missionaries to China who first sketched the portrait. The eighteenth-century French Jesuit, Joseph de Prémare, sent back this observation in a letter:

It cannot be said in China, as in Europe, that the poor are idle, and might gain a subsistence, if they would work. The labours and efforts of these poor people are beyond conception. A Chinese will pass whole days in digging the earth, sometimes up to his knees in water, and in the evening is happy to eat a little spoonful of rice, and to drink the insipid water in which it was boiled.[3]

Prémare's near contemporary, David Hume absorbed this impression. The Scottish philosopher commented on the Chinese's 'industriousness'. In a remarkably accurate vision of the 'made in China' future, Hume observed: 'were he as near us as France or Spain everything we use would be Chinese'.[4]

The view strengthened in the nineteenth century. William Napier was an irascible Scot, given the job of supervising trade in Canton on behalf of the British Crown in the 1830s. Napier was a useless diplomat and detested Chinese officialdom. But he nevertheless took his hat off to the 'hardworking and industrious people' of Canton that he encountered.[5]

Mark Twain, who witnessed Chinese laundrymen in Virginia, was of the same mind. 'The disorderly Chinaman is rare, and a lazy one does not exist,' he wrote. Twain drew an unfavourable contrast with his fellow Americans, noting that 'white men often complain of want of work, but a Chinaman offers no such complaint; he always manages to find something to do.'[6]

Protestant missionaries in China were just as effusive about the native work ethic as their Catholic counterparts had been. Arthur Henderson Smith saw it as a characteristic that ran right through Chinese society, from top to bottom. The wealthy, he noted, 'do not retire from businesses, but devote themselves to it with the same kind of degree of attention as when they were poor'. Smith witnessed scholars pushing themselves beyond exhaustion in preparation for examinations. Farmers were equally diligent. Smith saw them bestow 'the most painstaking thought and care upon every stalk of cabbage, picking off carefully every minute insect'.[7] When Rudyard Kipling visited Hong Kong in 1900 he was impressed by the work ethic of the Chinese he witnessed scurrying around the entrepôt. 'Neither at Penang, Singapore, nor this place have I seen a single Chinaman asleep while daylight lasted,' he wrote. 'Nor have I seen twenty men who were obviously loafing. All were going to some definite end.' There was a metallic quality to the Chinese worker, felt Kipling, who mused on 'where he hides his love of Art, the Heaven that made him out of the yellow earth that holds so much iron only knows.'[8]

The perception was persistent. In the 1930s Carl Crow, the American journalist and entrepreneur, described China as a 'land of unremitting industry' where 'that a man should work is accepted as one of the laws of nature'. There was something saintly about this. 'If it is true that the devil can only find work for idle hands, then China must be a place of very limited Satanic opportunities,' mused Crow.[9]

Other visitors were similarly inspired. Evans Carlson, a United States marine serving in China, was impressed by the industriousness of the Chinese Industrial Co-operatives of the 1930s and 40s formed to supply the anti-Japanese occupation effort. From their Chinese name, '*gongye hezuoshe*', Carlson plucked the term 'gung ho'. In a 1943 interview he said, 'I was trying to build up the same sort of working spirit I had seen in China when all the soldiers dedicated themselves to one idea and worked together to put that idea over.'

Yet not every outsider has seen something admirable in the Chinese work ethic. Max Weber, the German sociologist best known for his theory of the Protestant work ethic, discerned a similar industrious quality in the Chinese. However, in the case of the Chinese, the ethic was tempered by what sounds like a kind of mental retardation. Weber described 'the unlimited patience and controlled politeness; the strong attachment to the habitual; the absolute insensitivity to monotony; the capacity for uninterrupted work and the slowness in reacting to unusual stimuli, especially in the intellectual sphere.'[10]

Others developed this theme into something more likely to provoke fear. Jack London saw the Chinese appetite for labour as an almost inhuman characteristic. He wrote in a 1904 essay:

The Chinese is the perfect type of industry. For sheer work no worker in the world can compare with him. Work is the breath of his nostrils. It is his solution of existence. It is to him what wandering and fighting in far lands and spiritual adventure have been to other peoples. Liberty to him epitomizes itself in access to the means of toil. To till the soil and labour interminably with rude implements and utensils is all he asks of life and of the powers that be. Work is what he desires above all things, and he will work at anything for anybody.[11]

This characterization proved a potent influence on writers. In George Orwell's *1984* the mysterious empire of 'Eastasia' could never be conquered because of 'the fecundity and industriousness of its inhabitants'. It is not hard to trace Orwell's literary inspiration.

The Chinese work ethic is still a wonder to us today. Sir Martin Sorrell, the head of WPP, the world's largest advertising conglomerate, experienced an epiphany while riding a train from Hong Kong to Guangzhou in 1989. He recalls that he 'looked out of the window and saw thousands of Chinese working on a Sunday. I thought, "what are the British doing at this time?" Watching football at the pub. I decided we had no choice. The future was here.'[12]

Visitors to Shanghai are often astonished to see construction crews working through the night on the latest skyscraper or a new road, their labours illuminated by searchlights. Television and newspapers show pictures of workers napping at their positions on the production line during a brief break on an eighteen-hour shift in the southern factory city of Shenzhen. As we saw in the previous chapter, Chinese school children spend their evenings, after the school day is done, in special cramming classes. 'The work ethic animates everyone from the wealthiest entrepreneur to the lowliest factory hand,' concluded the historian Niall Ferguson.[13]

And Chinese women are just as impressive as Chinese men. In 1931 the American author Pearl Buck won a Pulitzer Prize for her novel *The Good Earth*, a tale of peasant life set in the late Qing Dynasty. Buck depicted her heroine, O-Lan, taking up the scythe within minutes of giving birth.[14] Buck's novel, and a 1937 film of the same story, were influential in shaping American attitudes to China between the wars. And we are still impressed by the work ethic of Chinese women. John Gapper, a *Financial Times* columnist, has noted that 'Chinese women tend not to take extended breaks during their child-bearing years, instead putting offspring in day care and continuing with their careers.'[15] From the field to the factory, the setting changes but the work ethic endures. This Chinese capacity for hard work seems to touch our lives indirectly every day. We take it for granted that when a product is made in China it will be less expensive than if it were manufactured elsewhere. Why? Because we tend to assume that workers in China are simply content to work harder and for less money.

The Chinese diaspora seems to have carried this ferocious appetite for labour with them from the mother country, just as they did in Mark Twain's day. 'People in these groups have an awesome commitment to work. By most measures these groups value industriousness more than whites,' noted David Brooks of the *New York Times*.[16]

And this notion that the Chinese are incorrigible hard workers is by no means confined to outsiders.

EATING BITTERNESS

There is a saying in China, '*chi ku nai lao*', which roughly translates as 'eat bitterness, endure labour'. Such are the ideas that are absorbed by Chinese children with their mother's milk. The Chinese American anthropologist Martin Yang, in a 1945 study, quoted a father in the city of Qingdao imparting values to his family. 'Listen children, there is nothing in this world that can be won easily,' he said. 'A piece of bread must be earned by one day's sweat … The desire for better food, better dress, a good time, or the easy way will lead but to the ruin of our family.'[17]

This emphasis on hard work survived the destruction of the imperial system and was taken to still greater heights in Communist China. Mao Zedong seemed to identify the diligence of the Chinese as the material with which he would construct his new superpower. At the seventh Communist Party Conference in Yan'an in 1945, Mao was named supreme party leader. And in his closing address the Chairman related the struggle for Communism in China to an ancient folk tale of a foolish old man who, with his two sons, set about moving two mountains with their hoes.

Another greybeard, known as the Wise Old Man, saw them and said derisively, 'How silly of you to do this! It is quite impossible for you few to dig up those two huge mountains.' The Foolish Old Man replied, 'When I die, my sons will carry on; when they die, there will be my grandsons, and then their sons and grandsons, and so on to infinity. High as they are, the mountains cannot grow any higher and with every bit we dig, they will be that much lower. Why can't we clear them away?'

Mao told his fellow delegates that two great mountains were now weighing down on China in the shape of imperialism and feudalism, but they would soon be cleared away by the unrelenting labour of the Chinese people.

That was just the beginning of the exhortation. Mao's 'Little Red Book' contained a chapter with the title 'Self-reliance and Arduous Struggle'. One demanded hard labour from the population. 'What is work? Work is struggle!' it said. 'There are difficulties and problems in those places for us to overcome and solve. We go there to work and struggle to overcome these difficulties. A good comrade is one who is more eager to go where the difficulties are greater!'

Like Kipling, Mao sensed 'iron' strength in the Chinese people. Wang Jingxi, the leader of an oil exploration team in Daqing, was turned into an icon for his relentless efforts to discover black gold in the minus 30 °C temperatures of Manchuria. This 'Iron Man of Daqing', as he became known, was invited to a national congress of heroes in 1959 and became the star of a nationwide propaganda campaign.

Nowhere was the ethic of hard work for the cause of transforming China pushed harder than in the slogan 'Learn from Dazhai'. In the 1950s Mao forced the nation's peasantry into collectivized farms. Following the example of the Soviet Union, smallholdings were abolished and the private ownership of land was made illegal. Animals and farm implements were designated as common property. It was a revolutionary shift. But Mao also needed to demonstrate that collectivization was producing better results than the old 'feudal' ways. Dazhai, a small village in Shanxi province, in northern China, seemed to offer that proof. The soil in Shanxi had always been poor, yet the commune there had delivered impressive yields of grain. The peasants reportedly worked on the collectively owned fields with an astonishing keenness. Mao saw his propaganda opportunity. In 1964 the slogan 'In agriculture learn from Dazhai' was suddenly everywhere. It was proclaimed from posters all across the land. The five characters were daubed on bridges and walls the length and breadth of the country. Dazhai's gravel-voiced headman, Chen Yonggui, toured China and, despite being only semi-literate, was appointed to the Politburo. Another propaganda star was Guo Fenglian, a seventeen-year-old peasant, who was hailed by Mao as an 'iron girl' because she relished the tough agricultural work that even many of the men of the village found difficult. Dazhai's propaganda value lay in the fact that it was a collectivized farm that was delivering spectacular results. But the real secret of Dazhai's success was said to be the hard work and ideological fervour of its population. If the rest of the Chinese population demonstrated the same zeal, said Mao, they too could work the miracles. 'Work bitterly, diligently, and with extra energy, and build our village into a Dazhai-like one in three years,' was the peasants' mantra.

Outsiders were impressed by Dazhai. An American journalist, Sheldon Weeks, visited the village in 1976 and came back convinced he had witnessed something remarkable. He marvelled at how the villagers continued to work even through the harsh winter months. 'The lessons of Dazhai are the lessons of struggle, conflict, leadership, commitment, dedication, hard work,' he concluded.[18]

Today's Communist officials might have rejected Maoism, but they seem to retain the belief that the Chinese are a kind of iron people, capable of working harder than other more cosseted populations. In 2011 Jin Liqun, the chairman of China's giant sovereign wealth fund, the China Investment Corporation, held forth on the causes of the eurozone debt crisis. It all came down, he submitted, to a deficient Western work ethic relative to the Chinese. 'The root cause of trouble is the overburdened welfare system, built up since the Second World War in Europe – the sloth-inducing, indolence-inducing labour laws,' he said. 'People need to work a bit harder, they need to work a bit longer, and they should be more innovative. We [the Chinese] work like crazy.'[19]

Other Chinese concur. Lee Kuan Yew, the ethnic Chinese former Singaporean prime minister whom we met in the previous chapter, thinks that the Chinese work ethic has cultural roots. And therein he finds an explanation for China's economic edge over another emerging nation, India. 'The Indians haven't got the Confucian culture,' he has argued. 'Without being imbued in a culture that enjoins you to endure hardship and have the stamina to struggle on in a cohesive society where the individual subsumes himself for the benefit of the family and his society, it's difficult to expect that degree of sacrifice.'[20]

This Chinese ability to endure hardship is part of my own family history. When my grandparents came to Britain to open a laundry in 1960 they toiled for ridiculously long hours. The only days they had off were bank holidays – and that was solely because customers were thin on the ground at such times. That kind of exertion is still going on. The Tuscan city of Prato, Italy's historic centre of clothing production, is now home to some twenty thousand Chinese garment workers. The journalist James Kynge interviewed some of them for his 2006 book, *China Shakes the World*. A man from Shenyang, in northern China, described working eighteen hours a day, to which his friend responded, 'Eighteen hours? More like twenty. Then four hours sleep. Then twenty hours again, and then again … It is exhausting. Mostly what you dream of all day is being able to sleep.' A punishing routine. But then Kynge describes the response of another Chinese migrant worker present: 'a small man with a southern accent, said something in an almost inaudible voice. "People from the northeast are lazy."'[21]

Put it all together and an irresistible image forms of Chinese people who seem to be culturally programmed to work hard and, what is more, to relish the labour. That seems to be true whether they are in the motherland itself, or making a living overseas. So did Jack London speak the truth when he said that, for the Chinese, freedom is to be found 'in access to the means of toil'? Can it be that the Chinese live solely to work?

'ALL THE SAME GOOD FOR CHINAMEN'

Our historical memory can be selective. Many Americans know that the Chinese played a titanic role in the construction of the early railroads, but it would probably come as a surprise to discover that those labourers tried to rebel. In 1867, two years before the line was complete, two thousand Chinese on the Central Pacific went on strike in the mountains. Their demands were for equal pay with white workers. They wanted $40 a month, up from $35. They also demanded a working day in the open limited to ten hours, rather than the dawn-to-dusk shifts they had been required to put in. Furthermore, they said the maximum working day in the fetid tunnels cut through the mountains should be limited to eight hours. The Chinese had noticed that white workers were not required to work such long shifts. As a spokesman for the Chinese put it: 'Eight hours a day good for white man, all the same good for Chinamen.' On top of that, the workers demanded an end to the right of overseers to whip them, or to prevent them from leaving for other employment.

The Sierras strike did not end well. The Chinese won no support from the minority of white workers and the bosses soon cut off the supply of camp food to the strikers. If they exercised their right to leave the railroad they would risk starvation. The strike collapsed after just one week and the Chinese went back to work. Yet the revolt by Crocker's pets did sufficiently concern the railroad bosses that they made plans to call up several thousand black workers as a potential replacement.

American railroad barons were not the only foreigners to harness the strength of the Chinese worker in the nineteenth century. From the early 1800s the British East India Company, which then held a monopoly over Oriental trade, began hiring Chinese, mainly from the southern provinces, to work on its ships. Like the workers on the California railroads, these crews were seen as cheap and docile labour. It was believed that, unlike obstreperous British sailors, there was no chance of the Chinese going on strike for better pay or conditions.

When the monopoly ended in 1833, successor firms, such as Liverpool's Blue Funnel Line, picked up where the East India Company had left off, hiring crews in Hong Kong and putting them to work as greasers in the sweltering engine rooms. The liner chiefs of the merchant navy were pleased with their new labour force. By 1914 there were some six thousand Chinese seamen working on British-registered merchant ships. And during the Second World War their numbers rose to twenty thousand as more labour was recruited from Singapore and Shanghai.[22] By 1945 they represented 15 per cent of the manpower of the merchant fleet. Alfred Holt, the boss of the Blue Funnel Line, is reported to have said on his deathbed in 1911: 'Keep my funnels tall and blue, and always look after my Chinese crew.' Like the Crockers, Holt understood how much of his success he owed to the industry and dedication of his Chinese labour force.

Yet despite the perception of British merchant naval recruiters that the Chinese were more compliant than white sailors, they too had their difficulties with their workforce. In 1922 thirty thousand Chinese seamen from Guangzhou and Hong Kong went on strike, demanding higher wages from the shipping companies. Chinese sailors also withdrew their labour in Liverpool in 1942, at the height of the Second World War. They were being paid a fifth of the rate of white seamen and they demanded parity. The strike lasted for four months and, like the revolt of Crocker's pets, ultimately collapsed. The Chinese were forbidden shore jobs and threatened with deportation to China if they refused to return to work. The point is not whether the Chinese workers overseas won or lost their industrial battles, but that, contrary to the common perception, they were not ready to bear any burden for the privilege of a job. History clearly records that the Chinese stood up for what they regarded as their legitimate rights.

Chinese history also belies the common image of the native work ethic. Dazhai, Mao's favourite village, has been exposed as a fraud. The commune there was given special help from the state that other collectives were denied. The army lent a bulldozer to level the hillsides to create the commune's impressive terraced fields. And Dazhai's land reclamation was achieved with forced labour, rather than peasants willing to work through the winter for the glory of Communist China.[23] Far from representing a shining example of what could be achieved through socialist agricultural production principles, Dazhai was the Potemkin Village of Mao's China. Its primary purpose was to fool the Chinese, and outsiders – people like Sheldon Weeks, quoted above – into believing that agricultural collectivization was working.

In fact, it proved almost impossible to motivate peasants on China's giant communal farms, where all land belonged to the state and grain was requisitioned at a price well below the cost of production. Huge increases in agricultural productivity followed Deng Xiaoping's liberalization in the late 1970s and early 1980s, when peasants were allowed to break up the communes and return to farming smaller household plots.[24] The fact that in 1985 China became a net grain exporter for the first time in a quarter of a century, after decades of famine and near starvation, discredits the notion that the Chinese work ethic was strong enough to force the barren soil of Communist economics to yield a bountiful harvest.

And what of China today? To look at this vast nation and to assume that its entire population is content with the gift of hard work that has been created by China's economic liberalization is to repeat the mistake of Sheldon Weeks in the 1970s. Strikes and protests are illegal, but their number has nevertheless been creeping up in China's factory belt in recent years. As pleased as the Chinese are to have new jobs in the industrializing economy, that is by no means the only thing that matters to them. Like workers the world over, they too value dignity and fairness.

THE LAZY YOUTH

My relatives in Guangzhou have a problem. Its name is the '*ba ling hou*' – the 'after eighties generation', youngsters born in the era of Beijing's post-1979 one-child policy. They are China's little emperors and empresses, spoiled rotten by their doting parents. My cousin, who works in a hotel in Guangzhou, is scathing about that generation's lackadaisical and unmotivated attitude. 'It is very hard to get those born after 1980 to give good service,' she tells me. 'They do not want to work hard.' My aunt, who runs a PR business in the city, has similar frustrations when it comes to hiring new graphic designers. Few, apparently, are prepared to put in extra hours in the office, even when the deadline of an important project is looming. When I raise the indomitable Chinese work ethic with my relatives, I get confused looks.

At least those members of the *ba ling ho* are actually working. The Chinese media has identified a growing phenomenon it terms '*ken lao zu*', which translates as 'bite the old folks'. This refers to youngsters in their early twenties who are not actively looking for work, but seem content to sponge off their parents forever. This perception of a generational shift in outlook on work is not restricted to the Chinese mainland. Something similar is taking place in Taiwan, where commentators fret about the 'strawberry generation' of young people who are, it is said, easily bruised, like the fruit, and unable to cope with hard graft. A life of relative sweetness, it is said, means that these youngsters don't have a taste for 'eating bitterness'.

Another common phrase in China is '*fu er dai*' or 'second generation rich', which refers to the flashy and good-for-nothing offspring of those who have made vast fortunes on the back of the nation's breakneck economic expansion. An unknown twenty-year-old called Guo Meimei provoked widespread disgust a few years ago when she posted pictures of herself online posing with her white Maserati sports car (which she described as her 'little horse') and a collection of designer handbags. I asked a Chinese friend who works for the Shanghai municipal government what would happen if the *fu er dai* grew in number. He gave me a horrified look and said: 'The country will fail.' As with all media caricatures, there is an element of exaggeration here, but the existence of these stereotypes in China does somewhat undermine the notion of an eternal indomitable Chinese work ethic. Moreover, it remains true that the new generation has a different outlook and more relaxed perspective on life than their parents.

Too often we forget that China is still a developing country. Though it is now the world's second largest economy, China's per capita GDP remains a fifth of that of the US and a quarter of Britain's. As poverty and hunger fade as a memory for most people, attitudes to work are likely to move closer to those in the West. Indeed, the angst over the *ba ling hou* indicates that this is already happening. As the Cambridge development economist Ha-Joon Chang has pointed out, culture does not mechanistically determine economic outcomes. It is a two-way process. Often economic outcomes determine culture too. Such changes can be revolutionary. A century and a half ago the Japanese were sometimes considered lazy by Europeans. That impression shifted after the country's industrialization.[25] It could shift with regard to China too in the coming decades, albeit in the other direction.

There are lessons from the experience of other nations that industrialized long before China. In the early decades of the nineteenth century, children as young as six would work in the deafening and dangerous cotton factories of Lancashire for up to twelve hours a day, cleaning bobbins and unclogging looms. Others child apprentices in Britain were sent up residential chimneys to clear out soot.

The Factory Acts, those grand landmarks in British social legislation, reduced the hours that children were allowed to work in textile mills in northern towns. A series of laws also put a stop to child chimney sweeping. No one would today suggest that these laws were an attempt to curb the work ethic of Victorian children. Their willingness to endure such conditions was a reflection of their poverty, a minimal welfare system and the dominant market power of factory owners in early industrial Britain. Those were the realities faced by unskilled adult workers in the era too. Those workers were willing to put in brutally long hours because the alternative – a life sweating in the fields or begging in the cities – was deemed even more hopeless. The same conditions of widespread poverty and inflated employer power are not so different from those that exist in China today.

There is other evidence too of a cultural shift. Since 1994 the polling company Gallup has been asking Chinese people to choose from a series of statements the one that comes closest to describing their own values. These range from 'work hard and get rich' at one end to 'don't think about money or fame, just live a life that suits your own tastes' at the other extreme. In 1994 68 per cent of respondents chose 'work hard get rich'. In 2005 the proportion had fallen to 53 per cent. There has been a shift at the other end too. In 1994 only 11 per cent chose 'just live a life that suits your own tastes'. By 2005, 26 per cent subscribed to that Western-sounding philosophy.

Relative wealth influences attitudes. Among those earning annual household incomes of more than 30,000 RMB, which is a middling income in urban China, one-third of respondents chose 'work hard and get rich' as their credo. Among residents of the cosmopolitan centres Beijing and Shanghai only a quarter subscribed to that view. Around half of respondents from those cities wanted to live a life that suited their tastes. Among Chinese with incomes below 3,000 RMB ($500), however, 71 per cent identified with the austere philosophy of hard work. Rural China seems heavily skewed towards this outlook too. Among county dwellers, 65 per cent chose 'work hard get rich', while 19 per cent opted for 'just live a life that suits your own tastes'.[26] The poorer the person, it would appear, the stronger the work appetite. This implies that as wealth increases, the appetite for spine-jarring work will diminish.

There are other stirrings that indicate a cultural evolution in attitudes to toil. Chinese newspapers now feature articles on the 'work–life balance' of Scandinavian countries. Contrary to the image of Chinese women valuing a career over their children, increasing numbers are choosing to stay at home, provided their husband has a decent salary. A communications manager in a Guangzhou hotel told me that if she had children she would give up her job. 'It's not good that parents hand over their children to their grandparents and go off to work,' she said. A trend is coming into focus. As China has become richer and more urbanized, the ferocious appetite for work is already eroding. And as the country's level of economic development increases, we should expect this to continue. The popular twenty-seven-year-old Beijing blogger, Zhao Xing, sums up this new philosophy. 'Don't get wrapped up in your title and the words on your business card,' she has written. 'Life is not lived for the sake of those few words. Don't sacrifice your soul and your ideas for anything.'[27]

WORK TO LIVE, NOT LIVE TO WORK

The argument should not be pushed too far. Even if the work appetite wanes as China becomes wealthier, the belief in the virtue of toil is not going to be erased entirely from Chinese society. Nevertheless, it is the grossest of errors to assume that what motivates the Chinese to 'eat bitterness and endure labour' is some sort of masochistic love of work. US anthropologist Stevan Harrell has researched the Chinese work ethic and come to the conclusion that it is more accurately described as an 'entrepreneurship ethic'.[28] Work is purely a means to an end for the Chinese. And that end is, usually, family advancement and an escape from poverty. The Chinese work hard when – and only when – they can see the potential benefits to themselves and those around them from hard graft.

Agricultural productivity shot up in China after the end of Mao's collectivization policy when farmers were allowed to return to the system of family-owned plots and earn profits from any surplus crops they produced. This was not because Chinese peasants were secret counter-revolutionaries, determined to block the creation of a modern Chinese state (as Mao ranted), but because in order to function effectively collective farms required levels of supervision that were impossible to implement. The system hinged on supervisors rewarding those farmers who were the most productive by issuing them extra 'work points', credits that could be turned into food and clothing coupons; but there were not enough officials to judge accurately who was working harder. So the system degenerated into corruption and, in the end, no one had any incentive to put in any effort at all.[29] Farmers would work while the cadres watched, but down tools as soon as they were out of sight. During the Great Leap Forward some famished peasants put networks of lookouts in place and slept through the afternoons.[30] The point is that even illiterate peasants were able to recognize when working hard would bring them no direct benefit. If work was the breath in their nostrils, China's farmers managed to avoid inhaling.

One must think about the Chinese work ethic in the context of the family too. Professor Wei Shangjin of Columbia University in New York, and Zhang Xiaobo of the International Food Policy Research Institute, argue that the modern Chinese appetite for work is, to a large degree, a consequence of the imbalance in the ratio between young men and women. When Beijing imposed the one-child policy in 1979 in order to curb China's population growth, millions of families were determined that their one child would be a son rather than a daughter. As so often in poor countries, a male child was considered much more valuable than a female. Historically, a son was an economic asset, whereas a daughter was a liability. A son also held out the promise of the continuance of the family name. Ultrasound-screening technologies now allow families to determine the gender of the foetus early in the pregnancy. The consequence has been a surge in abortions of females. Selective abortions have caused China's gender balance to collapse. In 1980 there were 1.07 boys for every girl. By 2000 the ratio was 1.18. And by 2007 it was 1.22. What this imbalance means is that 1 in 9 boys in China, mathematically, has no hope of marriage. On a national level, that translates into some thirty-two million young men.

Wei and Zhang argue that this has created intense competition in the marriage market among young males and, by extension, their families. Mothers and fathers attempt to improve their son's chances in this market by accumulating as large a pot of savings as possible, something that makes their son more attractive to potential brides.

And the Chinese attempt to reach this goal, according to Wei and Zhang, by working extremely long hours. The two academics also say this is supported by evidence they have collected showing men from villages in which there is a severe shortage of young women tend to be more likely to do unpleasant and arduous jobs in the construction and mining industries in pursuit of higher pay.[31]

No matter how convincing one finds this particular theory – and not everyone buys it – there is ample evidence that the key to understanding the Chinese work ethic lies in economic incentives. A lust for hard work is not some biological feature of the Chinese character. James Kynge befriended one of the twenty-hour-a-day Chinese garment workers that he interviewed in the Italian city of Prato. The labourer admitted to the journalist that he had earned more than enough money to pay for his passage back home, but that he stayed in Italy, doing arduous sweatshop labour, for one reason: in order to pay the school fees of his son who lived with his mother back in China. 'It's all for my son,' he admitted.[32] I recognize this impulse of self-sacrifice for the sake of the family. My grandmother and grandfather did not work seven days a week in a laundry in Sheffield because they enjoyed boiling sheets and ironing collars into the small hours. They did it in order to improve the lives of their children. But this is, in fact, a commonplace immigrant tendency. There is nothing particularly Chinese about the first-generation migrant slogging their guts out. When one considers that there are some two hundred million internal migrants in China the native work ethic surely becomes a little more understandable.

Chinese hard work is driven by a host of influences, but none is more important than a desire for a higher standard of living. The Gallup survey cited above indicated that the majority of Chinese desire to 'get rich'. To us those words imply luxury, but for many inhabitants of rural China, 'rich' often means being able to feed one's family and educate one's children.

'THE MEANEST SLAVE ON EARTH'

The belief that Chinese people work hard for no other reason than that they enjoy toil, that they derive fulfilment from the act of labour itself, is one of the great myths of China. One might be tempted to assume that it is a rather benign myth. When Mark Twain noted the work ethic of Chinese immigrants in America he was trying to pay a compliment. As he put it: 'They are a kindly disposed, well-meaning race.' After all, who would object to being thought of as hard working by nature? Better surely than to be considered lazy. But no matter how well meaning some of the propagators of the idea might have been, the myth of the Chinese attitude to work has historically been the facilitator of great injustice and cruelty.

The origins of the word 'coolie' are unclear. One theory is that it comes from a Portuguese word for an Indian slave. Another is that it derives from the Mandarin words 'ku li', meaning 'bitter strength'. The word is more associated with the Chinese than Indians, but the association with slavery, from the Portuguese, is pertinent too.

After the African slave trade was stamped out by the British navy in the 1830s a labour shortage emerged in the colonies and former dependencies of Latin America. Chinese peasants filled the gap. In the middle of the nineteenth century some 95,000 were conscripted to work the sugar plantations, cotton fields and guano islands of Peru, which was then newly free of its submission to the Spanish crown. Chinese peasants were recruited by local compradors who promised them a chance to make decent money overseas. They signed contracts selling their labour for a fixed period, usually eight years, and were transported to the Portuguese colony of Macao where European fleets waited for their human cargo to the New World. While nominally free, the existence of these labourers once they arrived in Peru was little better than the African slaves whose places they were taking. They were forced to toil for seven days a week. Any surplus cash they accumulated was often sucked up by their employer in the form of charges for food and board. Those who sought to escape were flogged and exposed in the burning sun as punishment. Many attempted suicide, and in 1870 five hundred coolies revolted, butchering white Peruvians in the Pativilca valley, north of Lima.[33]

Chinese labourers – some 125,000 of them – were transported to Cuba too in these decades. Again, their lot was little better than slavery. Some were volunteers, but many were recruited by force or deception by their own countrymen. These Chinese procurers were called 'corredores' by the Cuban plantation owners, the same term that had been used to describe the Africans who had sold other Africans. The similarities did not end there. The Chinese were transported in the same ships previously used to ferry African slaves and with the same captains. These were known as 'floating coffins' for their fearfully high mortality rate. Of every hundred men who made the trip only seventy survived. Those Chinese who did make it were housed in the same quarters as slaves on arrival. They were subjected to the same cruel punishments, being placed in stocks and leg chains for disobedience. They could even legally be executed for breaking their contracts. The Chinese in Cuba worked alongside black slaves doing the same tasks. When their eight-year term of indenture was over, they were often forced to sign a new contract. For most it made little difference because they had been unable to save enough to pay their passage home. The Chinese in Cuba, like their counterparts in Peru, fled when they got the chance. The 1872 census on the island recorded that of the 35,000 coolies nominally under contract, 7,000 were runaways.[34] Some 2,000 Chinese fought with the rebels in the Cuban struggle for independence from Spain. A monument in Havana honours the Cuban Chinese who fell in the war. It is inscribed: 'There was not one Cuban Chinese deserter, not one Cuban Chinese traitor.' Once more the Chinese had demonstrated that they were not as docile as their reputation suggested.

While this exploitation was taking place, remember, Victorian intellectuals were gushing with tributes to the inspiring work ethic of the Chinese. They were entertaining fantasies too: in 1873 Sir Francis Galton, the Victorian polymath and cousin of Charles Darwin, proposed a bold scheme to colonize the African continent using Chinese labour

> in the belief that the Chinese immigrants would not only maintain their position, but that they would multiply and their descendants supplant the inferior Negro race. I should expect that the African seaboard, now sparsely occupied by lazy, palavering savages, might in a few years be tenanted by industrious, order-loving Chinese, living either as a semidetached dependency of China, or else in perfect freedom under their own law.[35]

Rudyard Kipling also drew a contrast between the industriousness of the Chinese and 'that great big lazy land' of India. The poet, from the balcony of his Hong Kong hotel room, mused that 'if we had control over as many Chinese as we have natives of India and had given them one tithe of the cosseting, the painful pushing forward, and studious, even nervous regard of their interests and aspirations that we have given India, we should long ago have been expelled from, or have reaped the reward of, the richest land on the face of the earth.'[36]

The mid-nineteenth-century Liberal British Prime Minister, Lord Russell, made harnessing Chinese labour sound like a Christian duty. 'By judiciously promoting emigration from China and the same time vigorously repressing the infamous traffic in African slaves', he wrote, 'the Christian Governments of Europe and America may confer benefits upon a large portion of the human race, the effects of which it would be difficult to exaggerate.'[37]

The most notorious colonialist of his era, the Belgian King Leopold II, was thinking along similar lines. 'What would it cost to establish five big Chinese villages in the Congo? ... Two thousand Chinese to mark our frontiers, what would it cost?' he enquired of an aide.[38] In an effort to realize his dream, around 540 Chinese labourers from Hong Kong and Macao died in 1892 while building Leopold's railway in the Congo. Of these, around 300 were worked to death, while the rest fled into the bush never to be seen again. Poor Leopold must have wondered what had happened to their famous work ethic.

The Portuguese shut down Macao as a coolie hub in 1874, which effectively ended the trade. But if some prominent Englishmen – the very intellectual cream of their society – had had their way, it would have continued. Men who congratulated themselves on their enlightened abolition of African slavery rubbed their hands at the thought of exploitative Asian cooliedom expanding.

Even in places where Chinese labour was more free, their lot was often still pitiful. The Chinese call America '*mei gwok*', which means 'beautiful country'. But guided by this fallacy about their appetite for toil, the beautiful land was to show an ugly face to Chinese immigrants. In 1873 the US fell into a prolonged economic slump after a stock market collapse. Agricultural produce prices plummeted, pushing many farmers into hardship. Lower wages decimated the living standards of the working classes. Unemployment ballooned. And, as so often in times of economic stress, people looked for scapegoats. In the Chinese labourers, the immigrants who had been lured first by the California gold rush and then by the railway construction boom, they found them. The Chinese were easy targets. They were visually and culturally distinct, with their pigtails, small stature and incomprehensible language. In a depressing irony, Irish and Russian migrants in California, who had experienced prejudice from nativist mobs on the east coast, now visited the same bigotry on the Chinese. And these European Americans seized on one grievance about their fellow immigrants above all: their work ethic.

A populist movement sprang up that blamed the wealthy robber-baron industrialists for driving down wages by hiring cheap and energetic Chinese labour. But it was the Chinese, rather than the employers, who felt the full force of public anger. Denis Kearney, the owner of a San Francisco carting businesses, who had migrated to America from County Cork, founded a group called the Working-men's Party in California. The group's slogan was unambiguous: 'The Chinese must go'. An extract from a letter written by Kearney that appeared in the *Indianapolis Times* on 28 February 1878 set out his message:

A bloated aristocracy has sent to China, the greatest and oldest despotism in the world, for a cheap working slave. It rakes the slums of Asia to find the meanest slave on earth, the Chinese coolie, and imports him here to meet the free American in the labour market, and still further widen the breach between the rich and the poor, still further to degrade white labour. These cheap slaves fill every place. Their dress is scant and cheap. Their food is rice from China. They hedge twenty in a room, ten by ten. They are whipped curs, abject in docility, mean, contemptible and obedient in all things. They have no wives, children or dependents. They are imported by companies, controlled as serfs, worked like slaves, and at last go back to China with all their earnings. They are in every place, they seem to have no sex. Boys work, girls work; it is all alike to them. The father of a family is met by them at every turn. Would he get work for himself? Ah! A stout Chinaman does it cheaper.[39]

Like all immigrant bashing through history, this was economic nonsense. The hard times were a consequence of a collapse in investor confidence, not a surplus of labour. And as we have seen, the Chinese on the railroads had tried to get pay parity with white workers only to be beaten down by the bosses. Not only were they underpaid, they now found themselves cursed for being underpaid.

Yet the Chinese had few friends willing to point out this gross injustice. During the 1870s, anyone with an Oriental appearance on the West coast was liable to suffer abuse and violence. In Los Angeles in 1871 seventeen Chinese were hanged by a five-hundred-strong mob. It was the largest lynching in American history. Among the victims, according to one eyewitnesses, was a boy 'not much more than twelve'. As the innocent Chinese were strung up, one white man danced on a roof with glee shouting, 'Come on boys, patronize home trade!' Eight men were jailed for manslaughter in the following weeks, but their sentences were soon overturned on a suspicious technicality.[40] The shameful truth was that anti-Chinese pogroms were tolerated by the city authorities. Policemen and even a city councillor are believed to have been among the Los Angeles lynch mob that day. The media was of one mind too; in those years, local newspapers competed to outdo each other in racial slurs against the Chinese.

But the disease was much more than an outbreak of localized bigotry. In one of the great stains on America's democratic history, this demagoguery bore legislative fruit. In 1882 Congress passed the Chinese Exclusion Act, a transparently racist piece of legislation that barred any immigration by individuals of Chinese origin. The preamble said: 'In the opinion of the Government of the United States the coming of Chinese labourers to this country endangers the good order of certain localities within the territory.' The US legislature had bowed before the grotesque arguments of Kearney.

The period between the end of the Civil War and the Great Depression is usually presented as the era when America opened its doors to the world. Between 1870 and 1930 some twenty-five million Europeans are estimated to have travelled to America to make a new life. The US celebrates the poem of Emma Lazarus, inscribed on the Statue of Liberty, as the American philosophy on immigration. It reads: 'Give me your tired, your poor, your huddled masses yearning to breathe free, the wretched refuse of your teeming shore. Send these, the homeless, tempest-tost to me, I lift my lamp beside the golden door!' Yet how many Americans today are aware that the golden door in this era of immigration was slammed in the face of the Chinese? The Chinese Exclusion Act was not repealed until 1943, when Chiang Kai Shek's China became an ally of the United States during the Second World War. Even then, only around one hundred migrants a year were permitted to enter. It was not until 1965 that official discrimination on the grounds of national origin was finally abolished. For eighty-three years, the United States' policy towards Chinese immigration was shaped by unconcealed racial prejudice.

Jack London was one of the finest American authors of his era, a literary revolutionary and a source of inspiration for Ernest Hemmingway and John Steinbeck. Yet when he wrote about China he dipped his pen in the same bigoted ink as the demagogic leaders of the California mobs. London's characterization of the Chinese work ethic was almost indistinguishable from that of Kearney. If anything, London's vision was even more offensive. 'The Unparalleled Invasion', London's 1910 short story, imagined the Chinese nation expanding through exponential population growth and colonizing the rest of Asia. The response of the rest of the world, of which the author of *White Fang* offers not a hint of condemnation, is a genocidal attack on China using chemical weapons.[41]

Anti-Chinese bigotry, fired by fears of the Chinese work ethic, was not limited to America. Australia and Canada had their own equivalents of the Chinese Exclusion Act in these years, and there was a similar panic amongst the British working classes about the prospect of being 'swamped' by cheap and docile Chinese labour in the early twentieth century. The expansion of coolie labour became a rallying cause for working-class labourers in the early twentieth century. British labourers were furious that some fifty thousand Chinese had been recruited after the end of the Boer War in 1902 by British firms to work in the South African gold mines of the Witwatersrand. The Trade Union Congress passed a motion arguing that this use of Chinese workers represented the 'degradation' of the British Empire. Around eighty thousand people turned out at a Hyde Park protest against 'Chinese slavery' in March 1904 and the issue was still salient in the 1906 election that swept the Conservatives from office and installed the Liberals. The derisive cry of 'pigtail' could be heard in political debates across the country. It did not seem to occur to protestors that the Chinese themselves were not willing slaves but the primary victims of this practice. Of the 935 Chinese deaths in the mines in the first year alone, almost half were due to homicide, suicide and various accidents.[42] The labourers were kept in virtual prison camps for the duration of their three-year contracts, and lashed with rhinoceros-hide whips if they sought to escape.

Political pressure from Britain meant that the coolies' South African mining contracts were not renewed, probably mercifully. But Chinese continued to work on board imperial ships, where conditions were better. As the merchant navy took on ever larger Chinese crews, white seafarers began to agitate. In 1916 the British Seafarers' Union and the National Sailors' and Firemen's Union lobbied Parliament on the matter. And as with the US Congress, the response of the British government to this racist lobbying should be a source of abiding national shame.

The British government could not legally deport the Chinese, since they had broken no law, but it arbitrarily tightened the terms of the crews' leave to remain, requiring them to ship out by a specified date. The result was that, after the First World War, hundreds of Chinese sailors who had settled in the port of Liverpool, many with British wives and children, were forced to leave. The same thing happened, but on an even larger scale, in the wake of the Second World War. By 1946 Home Office figures show that 1,362 Chinese sailors had been repatriated, most of them unwillingly. Around 300 half-British and half-Chinese families were broken up for good, leaving scores of children to grow up without contact with their fathers. Alfred Holt's plea for the Blue Funnel Line to look after his Chinese crew had been ignored.

What did the Chinese themselves feel about this kind of treatment in the West? One unnamed Chinese worker in America gave this testimony: 'In order to make a living here, we have to endure all year around drudgery and all kinds of hardship. We are in a state of seeking shelter under another person's face, at the threat of being driven away at any moment. We have to swallow down the insults hurled at us.'[43] Huie Kin, who founded New York City's first Chinese Christian Church, wrote an account of his experiences in San Francisco's Chinatown during the 1870s. 'We were simply terrified,' he recounted. 'We kept indoors after dark for a fear of being shot in the back. Children spit upon us as we passed by and called us rats.'[44] It makes for quite a contrast with the portrait of an inhuman, unfeeling, drone painted by the likes of Kearney and London. Like any victim of abuse and discrimination, the Chinese worker burned inside.

As we have seen, Chinese that worked abroad, on the US railroads, on British ships, or on Peruvian guano islands, were prepared to stand up for their rights – but transparently discriminatory labour practices were imposed nonetheless. It is worth asking why railroad bosses, shipping line owners and others felt justified in paying Chinese labourers and sailors less than white workers who were doing the same job. Part of the explanation was cynical exploitation by greedy men. By bringing in a low-paid foreign labour force, they were intimidating native workers. Mark Hopkins was one of the Central Pacific's executives who advocated hiring black labourers when the Chinese went on strike in the Sierra Nevadas. Hopkins described a form of ethnic divide and rule: 'A Negro labour force would tend to keep the Chinese steady, as the Chinese have kept the Irishmen quiet.' But could the myth of the Chinese love of work also have played a facilitating role? If a labourer is culturally programmed to work hard, why would an employer needlessly diminish his own profits by paying equal rates? If labour is the 'solution of existence' for the Chinese, as Jack London put it, why waste money on furnishing them with tolerable conditions?

But it is not just non-Chinese who have exploited the myth. As described, the supposed Chinese appetite for toil and tolerance of hardship has been promoted just as energetically by the Chinese themselves. Mao used it as a propaganda tool in the Dazhai campaign and it was also at the fore of the Great Leap Forward of the late 1950s, when farmers were instructed to neglect their fields and devote their energies to steel production. The result was that harvests failed and famine descended. Some experts put the resulting number of deaths as high as forty-five million.[45] Nor were these deaths merely a tragic accident resulting from a misguided policy.

The China scholar Frank Dikötter has shown that during the Great Leap Forward cadres ordered the withdrawal of food as a weapon to punish those deemed not to have worked hard enough.[46] Millions were deliberately starved to death. Pregnant women were made to work in the fields, often bringing on miscarriages. Maoist propaganda had set the standard for the Chinese work ethic – and those who failed to live up to it had to be made to suffer.

NO SUICIDES PLEASE

At Foxconn's Apple plant in Shenzhen sleeping workers in their communal dormitories are roused if an urgent new order comes in during the night from the technology giant's US headquarters in Cupertino, California. One former Apple executive described to the *New York Times* in 2012 how 'each employee was given a biscuit and a cup of tea, guided to a workstation and within half an hour started a 12-hour shift fitting glass screens into bevelled frames. Within 96 hours, the plant was producing over 10,000 iPhones a day.'[47]

Conditions for workers in the factories that cover China's southern and coastal provinces are tough. Hours are punishingly long and the pay is low. The working week is often six full days, excluding overtime. Workers, most of them migrants from the countryside, live in cramped dormitories. They are typically only able to visit their families just once every twelve months, at Chinese New Year.

The Foxconn plant in Shenzhen – which also handles orders for technology firms Dell, HP, Motorola, Nintendo and Sony – came to the attention of the world's media in 2010 after a number of workers committed suicide by throwing themselves off the factory's roof. The Taiwan-owned Foxconn responded by erecting giant nets to catch falling employees. It also required its 450,000-strong workforce to sign 'no suicide' pledges.[48] HEG Electronics in Guangzhou, which manufactures for Samsung, has been accused of employing child labour in its plants.[49]

The Hong Kong-based organization China Labour Bulletin, which campaigns against exploitation in Chinese factories, has chronicled cases of Chinese who have died from overwork, a phenomenon known as 'guo lao si'. The CLB estimates that at least one million people in China currently die in this way each year.[50]

Manufacturers operating in China provide the most Spartan conditions and pay the lowest wages that they can get away with. And with a vast impoverished workforce, and a ban on free trade unions in China, they can get away with an awful lot.

But the Western dimension to this exploitation story is not to be overlooked. Jin Liqun of the China Investment Corporation boasts that China lacks Europe's 'sloth-inducing labour laws' – and that is precisely how the Western companies that have incorporated Chinese labour into their global supply chains like it. There is very little pressure on Chinese factories from Western clients to improve conditions for workers or to raise wages. The American executive who described Foxconn workers being woken in the night to put together iPhones sounded pleased rather than disturbed. 'The speed and flexibility is breath-taking,' he gushed. 'There's no American plant that can match that.'

Companies that would never get away with imposing such severe working conditions on Western workers happily allow people in their Chinese feeder factories to suffer them. Cynicism and hypocrisy are doubtless part of the explanation. 'We've known about labour abuses in some factories for four years, and they're still going on,' one anonymous former Apple executive said last year. 'Why? Because the system works for us. Suppliers would change everything tomorrow if Apple told them they didn't have another choice.'[51] As with the old railroad bosses and naval chiefs, the myth of the Chinese appetite for work is likely to play an enabling role. It is much easier for Western executives to turn a blind eye to inhumane conditions if they can tell themselves that the Chinese don't really mind back-breaking toil.

Indeed, these Western firms have, over the past decade, put pressure on Chinese suppliers to tighten the screws on their work forces still more. In 2007, the Chinese government introduced a consultation for a new law that included several initiatives to improve the rights of workers. This prompted objections from Western corporations and investors, led by the US Chamber of Commerce in China, which argued: 'We believe it [the new law] might have negative effects on China's investment environment.' It even warned, in a veiled threat, that the law may 'reduce employment opportunities for PRC [People's Republic of China] workers'.[52]

Not everyone regards Western multinationals in China as ex-
ploiters. The Chinese American author Leslie Chang, who wrote
a penetrating study of Chinese female factory workers, points out
that these young women can – and often do – switch employers, in
contradiction of the notion that they have no market power. She
says young Chinese often want to work overtime to increase their
wages, and are not forced to do so by their bosses. Chang urges us
not to judge Chinese working conditions by our own standards.
What might seem inhumane conditions to Europeans and Americans are not so bad viewed in a Chinese context. Life in a factory
dormitory offers more hope and independence for a young girl than
a life in the countryside.[53]

There is some truth in this. A report by the independent Fair
Labor Association (FLA) in 2012 on three Foxconn plants found
that 44 per cent of workers wanted to put in *more* hours, rather than
less, in order to earn extra money.[54] But this is not the full picture. Li
Qiang, founder of the New York-based China Labour Watch group,
which chronicles strikes and protests in Chinese factories, points
out that one of the reasons workers are often keen for overtime is because their wages are insufficient to live on, or to build their savings
to the desired level. The FLA report found that 65 per cent of workers believed their basic salary was not enough to meet their needs.
And it is hard to interpret the growing number of riots at Chinese
factories – including one at Foxconn's Taiyuan plant in 2012, which
seems to have resulted from pressures to complete massive orders
very quickly – as evidence of a contented workforce. One also has
to consider the impact of the *hu kou* registration system, designed
to tie Chinese to their place of birth. This restriction makes rural
workers who travel to urban areas in search of employment semi-
clandestine, thus significantly weakening their bargaining power in
relation to their bosses. Employers often take full advantage by imposing low wages and demanding long hours.

Qiang emphatically rejects the notion that there is some inherent
Chinese work ethic that enables them to tolerate more hardship
than Westerners. 'It's been forced by the system, it's not their character or their culture,' he told me. 'There's no unions in China, there's
no representation of the workers, they can't fight for their rights.
There's no choice. If they want to make some money they have to

work these really long hours under bad conditions. There are no other jobs. It's not their natural predisposition to be hard working. They're being forced.'[55]

Many millions of rural Chinese prefer urban factory work to agricultural labour. That is why they have chosen to travel to cities. It would be patronizing to suggest that they do not know what conditions are like before they arrive; they have friends and personal networks that inform them. But the existence of this willing supply of labour cannot reasonably be used to justify, or ignore, the many malign aspects of Chinese industry. There is no inconsistency in supporting China's industrial development while at the same time putting pressure on Western corporations to demand higher safety standards and better general conditions for workers in their Chinese supply chains.

Those who profess concerns that such improvements will ultimately make Chinese workers worse off can be safely ignored. In the British debates on the nineteenth-century Factory Acts many Victorian industrialists, in their efforts to preserve the profitable status quo, offered the spurious argument that legislation to improve working conditions would result in mass unemployment. It did no such thing. Nor would similar reforms to improve the lot of industrial workers in China.

Chinese menial workers in the West suffer from a similar malign neglect as their counterparts at home. Many migrants here find themselves effectively forced by people smugglers, known as snakeheads, to work in near slave-like conditions across the black economy, in restaurant kitchens, secret garment factories and vegetable farms. Twenty-three inexperienced Chinese cockle pickers, bossed by a callous gang, drowned in the sands of Morecambe Bay in 2004 after their group was caught out by the lethal incoming tide. In the wake of that tragedy, the British government legislated to rein in the gangmasters who organize this kind of ad hoc labour. But the legislation is only patchily enforced. The assumption of the UK authorities, all too often, appears to be that when Chinese migrants are found working in harsh and unsafe conditions they are doing so willingly.

STILL HUNGRY FOR WORK

Last year Douglas McWilliams, the founder of the UK's Centre for Economics and Business Research, delivered a lecture in London that made uneasy listening for his audience. McWilliams's thesis was that Western societies such as Britain are becoming steadily less competitive in the rapidly expanding global economy. To support his argument, McWilliams pointed to the fact that, if one adds up the hours, the residents of wealthy ethnic Chinese societies such as Hong Kong and Singapore work for five more months every year than Westerners. 'They behave with the hunger of societies that are poor even though they are becoming rich,' he said. 'They don't take prosperity for granted. In Singapore, GDP per head is already 30 per cent higher than in the UK. In Hong Kong it is 50 per cent higher. Yet they both work just as many hours per year as they did when they were poor.'[56] Unless we recognize the scale of this 'challenge' from the East, said McWilliams, countries like the UK will end up drifting into stagnation and, ultimately, experience a collapse in living standards.

As we have seen, it was once the labour unions that presented the Chinese work ethic as an economic threat. Today it is the champions of capitalism who seem to be ringing the alarm bells. Right-leaning politicians and commentators warn us that our societies are losing ground against highly motivated Asian competitors.

A group of neophyte Conservative Party politicians last year published a tract titled *Britannia Unchained* in which they lamented the deficient UK work ethic. 'Once they enter the workplace, the British are among the worst idlers in the world,' they complained. 'We work among the lowest hours, we retire early and our productivity is poor.' Like McWilliams, these politicians drew a contrast with hard-working majority ethnic Chinese cities such as Singapore and Hong Kong. Britons, they said, need to emulate the Oriental working culture and 'rediscover the lost virtue of hard work'.[57]

One hears similar alarums concerning intimidating Chinese labour market competition in America. 'If all US jobs were moved to China, there would still be surplus labour in China,' Sandra Polaski, a former State Department special representative for international labour affairs, has warned.[58] The implication of such statements is usually that jobs will haemorrhage abroad as multinational firms outsource their manufacturing to the cheaper East. Some Western intellectuals even suggest we will soon have no choice but to buck up our ideas. 'As the Chinese come to dominate the global economy, they'll expect everyone to work as hard as they do,' asserted Niall Ferguson in his 2012 television documentary on China.[59]

There are overlapping confusions and distortions to be dealt with here. Comparable surveys are hard to come by, but it does seem to be true that average working hours in China are longer than in Europe and America. According to the OECD, the Chinese work for 340 minutes per day in paid work; the British, by contrast, put in 261 minutes and the Americans 289.[60] However, working hours in China are nothing remarkable by the standards of other developing nations. The same OECD figures show that Mexicans, for instance, do slightly more paid minutes of work per day than the Chinese. Other data suggests the Chinese work fewer hours than Bangladeshis, Thais, and Indonesians.[61] Moreover, working hours in themselves tell us almost nothing about an economy's prospects. Greeks work significantly longer hours than other Europeans, but that has not stopped their economy plunging into chaos in recent years.

It may come as a surprise to many, not least Conservative politicians, but the fact is that workers in developed nations are still vastly more productive than the Chinese. What this means is that the typical worker in Europe or America delivers more output for each hour worked. Indeed, this is why we have higher incomes than the Chinese. We are more productive because we are better 'capitalized' than the average Chinese worker – we have more physical capital (machinery), human capital (education) and technological capital (computers). A labourer with a tractor ploughs more fields in a day than a farmer with a hoe, even if the two work the same number of hours. A literate sales manager will win more business than one who did not finish high school. A firm with a digital database will tend to be more efficient than one that still relies solely on metal filing cabinets. These advantages enable Westerners to exert themselves more efficiently.

But aren't the Chinese rapidly catching up in their acquisition of capital? And if they keep working more hours won't they, in the end, be richer? This is what Douglas McWilliams implied when he noted that the ethnic Chinese inhabitants of Singapore and Hong Kong still work longer hours than us, despite having successfully closed the income gap.[62] Where these 'little dragons' lead, won't the great dragon of China herself follow? And don't we risk finding ourselves less wealthy than the Chinese?

Not necessarily. The residents of Hong Kong and Singapore, and also Taiwan, despite having levels of capital per worker similar to advanced nations, are still not as productive as Americans, Britons and northern Europeans.[63] Those extra working hours only make their average incomes roughly the same level as Americans, not significantly higher. They are richer, per capita, than Britons, but this is solely due to the extra hours, not greater productivity. There is a lesson here. Presuming China retains its long-hours culture as its people grow richer (which as we have seen is a highly questionable assumption), that will not in itself push Chinese incomes above those in the rich world. That will only happen if they also manage to work as efficiently as us.

This leads to another crucial point: what pushes up living standards in the long run is productivity growth, or the ability of workers to produce ever more output for every hour worked. China has seen its average living standards soar over the past three decades, not so much because its population has been putting in longer hours but because it has been successful in raising workers' efficiency year after year. The shift from agriculture to factory work has elevated the productivity of millions of Chinese workers. Agricultural work is mainly subsistence labour. The farmer makes a small surplus, but generally eats what the family plot produces. These workers contribute more national output working on an assembly line, using modern industrial technology, than they do ploughing a field or raising pigs. The country has also benefited from absorbing advanced world technology. It is these simple productive realities, not some awesome national work ethic, that have propelled China forward. To put it another way, labour conservation, not heroic labour exertion, has pushed up incomes in China.

But can they keep it up? The monumental challenge for China is to continue to grow productivity per worker at the same rate as it has in recent decades. There remains plenty of scope for further 'catch-up' growth. As the country imports more technology from the West, educates a larger share of its workforce and shifts more of its population from agriculture to industry, the productivity of its labourers should carry on growing. And at some point in the coming century China's population could attain advanced world living standards.

Yet uninterrupted progress is by no means a given. A number of states in the Middle East and Latin America industrialized quickly in the 1960s and 1970s but failed to grow incomes beyond around $15,000 per capita. Having exhausted their supply of excess cheap rural labour and reaped the easy gains of importing the latest Western technology, they got stuck in what has been termed a 'middle-income trap'. Their productivity growth stalled as their ability to increase labour efficiency dried up. No domestic innovation took the place of imported Western technology as a source of productivity growth. China, with its $9,000 per capita income, is not at this danger zone yet, but is closing in fast on this threshold of stickiness.

Another way of thinking about China's challenge is to consider the nature of the country's output. At the moment, the economy is dominated by the construction sector and labour-intensive manufacturing. China will not reach Western living standards simply by building ever more roads, or forever assembling foreign-designed technology in its factories. In order to get rich, China needs to design popular branded consumer goods itself. It also needs high-end domestic manufacturing and service sector jobs that add value and thus command higher wages. In this context, working hours are a red herring and Jin Liqun's boast about the Chinese 'working like crazy' is the pinnacle of irrelevance. It is inspiration, not endless buckets of perspiration, that China requires over the coming decades.

These are not new or abstruse arguments. The basic principles of what economists term 'growth accounting' can be found in any undergraduate textbook. So what, then, to make of the ubiquitous praise for long Chinese hours, or the bizarre warnings that the Eastern work ethic is set to result in a downward economic spiral of doom for the rest of us? Some of it is ignorance, a naïve belief that there is a connection between long working hours and long-term growth. But more often than not this is a political tactic designed to scare our workers and intimidate domestic trade unions into accepting lower pay and worse conditions. It says more about us than it does about China.

THE COOLIE MENTALITY

There is no rest on Sunday in the smoggy town of Kaiping in Guangdong. I visited an old friend of my grandmother's on that day and found the small courtyard in the middle of a doughnut of residential blocks dotted with large piles of bright crimson jeans. Next to each pile, upon a small stool, sat an elderly woman diligently sewing. They were earning their families a little extra income by accepting piecework from a local exporter. The fact that this meant stitching for hours at the weekend did not seem to perturb these women. They looked up briefly as we pulled up in our four-by-four. But their eyes soon fell again to their needlework. When we emerged from our family friend's home an hour later, one of the nearest piles of clothes had grown so large that we were boxed in. We had to clear a path so the vehicle could depart. Surveying such scenes of quiet industry it's very easy to fall for the myth of the eternal Chinese work ethic. These women might have been the farm workers Arthur Henderson Smith encountered a century or so earlier, diligently picking insects from stalks of cabbage.

But appearances can deceive. Things are changing fast in China. The first generation of Chinese migrant workers, who experienced famine and the turmoil of the Cultural Revolution in their youth, were conditioned to embrace hard labour when China embarked on its long-delayed industrialization. But their children increasingly have a different attitude. Many fail to see why they should sweat every hour of the day for scant rewards. Today's production-line workers – most of whom left the farm before ever tasting the rigours of agricultural work – are better educated and are beginning to demand higher wages.

They are getting them too. Foxconn, which employs more than one million workers across China, has granted double-digit pay awards in recent years, albeit from a miserably low base. These workers have demographics on their side too. The working population, thanks to the low birth rate brought about by the one-child policy, will soon peak at around one billion, and thereafter start to contract in size. This means the labour market will continue to tighten in coming years, putting upward pressure on wages. Manufacturers have been moving their factories to the interior of the country, where labour is more abundant and wages lower, but wages are going up inland too for the same demographic and cultural reasons. Those economists and politicians who issue warnings about the indomitable 'competitiveness' challenge from China are increasingly out of date. Chinese manual labour is now more expensive than other developing nations such as Mexico and Sri Lanka. The age of 'cheap China' is drawing to a close.

We have seen how the Chinese Whisper of the native work ethic has historically been used to justify exploitation. Mercifully, the scope for that has diminished. Chinese workers are beginning to assert themselves. But a soft bigotry still lingers. A British right-wing pundit once told me that it was a terrible shame the people of Hong Kong had been denied full British citizenship when control of the colony reverted to Beijing in 1997. Britain, he said, should have transplanted the entire hard-working population of Hong Kong to Liverpool and swapped them with the lazy natives of Merseyside. 'We would get a population who have a work ethic and the benefit scroungers of Liverpool could try their luck with the Communist Party,' he informed me, delighted by his Swiftian proposal. Little did he know, however, that he was merely articulating an updated version of Sir Francis Galton's dream of colonizing Africa with hard-working Chinese and displacing the lazy and 'palavering' black natives.

Just as Victorian bigotry still lingers in our countries, the ghost of Maoist dogma on work continues to haunt modern China. Dissidents can still be sentenced to 'reform through labour', as they were in the 1950s. In 2008 Liu Shaokun, a teacher who campaigned for justice for children crushed to death by 'tofu' buildings in the Sichuan earthquake of that year, received just such a sentence. There remains a secret network of prison camps known as '*lao gai*' where dissidents are forced to produce cheap manufactures for exports.[64] Work is still used as a punishment in China, a form of mental re-programming.

There can be no denying that the Chinese do, often, work

ferociously hard. But our tendency to link this behaviour to some sort of coolie mentality has gone unchallenged for too long. Chinese people, by and large, work hard in order to escape poverty and in-security. They are not mindless drones, or willing slaves. They make a rational calculation over when to, and when not to, work. Nor are the Chinese a breed of iron people, capable of astonishing feats of endurance and sacrifice on behalf of the motherland, as Chair-man Mao once asserted to suit his own ends. No Chinese dreams of working himself or herself to the point of death. And when it comes to working conditions and productivity – that crucial key to future prosperity – it turns out to be China that needs to catch up with us, not the other way around.

THE CHINESE HAVE RE-INVENTED CAPITALISM

The ballroom of the Dorchester was packed with business executives, bankers and politicians. The Chinese ambassador to the Court of St James, Liu Xiaoming, was in attendance. So was his American counterpart, Louis Susman. It was a black-tie dinner at the celebrated Park Lane Hotel to celebrate the 2011 Chinese New Year. Our hosts were the 48 Group, an organization devoted to fostering Chinese–British trade. Stephen Perry, the 48 Group's chairman, sprang to the podium. He had come to praise the Chinese economy. And he did the job with gusto. The country's leaders were the wisest of economic stewards, Perry told the audience. The people were the most industrious on the planet. Perry praised the Chinese economy until his encomiums were ricocheting off the mirrored walls of the ornate ballroom. Then his voice dropped and his features turned grave. 'Now,' he said, 'we enter the era of China *the leader*.' All across the room heads were nodding. Everyone knew it was true. The Chinese were now the pioneers of capitalism.

What a difference a century makes. A hundred years ago the Chinese were reckoned to make pretty hopeless capitalists. In 1915, Max Weber, the father of sociology, concluded that the 'Chinese ethos', by which he meant their cultural esteem for scholarship and officialdom, was soil too inhospitable to allow the germination of 'rational entrepreneurial capitalism'.[1] To put it bluntly, the Chinese cared more about becoming bureaucrats than starting businesses. They lacked the mental disposition to invest for the future, to adopt new technologies and to embrace new ways of doing things. It all made sense. How else to explain the fact that China, at the turn of the twentieth century, was an empire of poor peasants while the West had attained new heights of industrial and commercial sophistication? It had to be something to do with the culture.

In identifying culture as the source of China's developmental backwardness, Weber was elaborating an older theory. As far back as the eighteenth century the Scottish philosopher David Hume, never a Sinophile like his contemporary Voltaire, had identified the homogeneity of China – 'one vast empire, speaking one language, governed by one law, and sympathizing in the same manners' – as the reason the country had not made scientific breakthroughs comparable to those of Europe. Hume hypothesized that in China 'none had courage to resist the torrent of popular opinion. And posterity was not bold enough to dispute what had been universally received by their ancestors.'[2]

Yet Weber's theory of Chinese culture being inhospitable to capitalism and progress, which once seemed so self-evidently true, has been turned on its head. It's now common to hear our scholars and politicians assert that Confucian values – family loyalty, a reverence for education, a strong sense of personal responsibility – have been a tremendous benefit for the Chinese capitalists, helping them to, yes, invest for the future, adopt new technologies and embrace new ways of doing things. We assume that those values explain the fabulous success of Chinese merchant communities in South Asia, from Thailand to Singapore.[3] They explain the commercial vibrancy of Hong Kong. And now, of course, they explain the formidable economic expansion of China itself. It has to be something to do with the native culture.

Indeed, nowadays the Chinese are often reckoned to be better capitalists than those of us who once scoffed at them. Business gurus write about how Westerners can learn from the dynamism of Chinese entrepreneurs.[4] Politicians have lessons to learn too. According to Stephen Roach, a former Asia chairman of the Wall Street banking giant Morgan Stanley, China succeeds because its policy makers take a long-term view. 'China is cut from a very different cloth from the advanced economies of the West,' he says. 'Long focused on stability, it is more than willing to accept the short-term costs of a growth sacrifice to keep its development strategy on track.'[5] Shades perhaps of the 'patience of Asia'?

Gary Becker, a Nobel prize-winning economist from the University of Chicago, says that China's authoritarian political system gives it an advantage. 'Visionary leaders can accomplish more in autocratic than democratic governments because they need not heed legislative, judicial, or media constraints in promoting their agenda,' he claims.[6] Anthony Bolton, the fêted British investment fund manager, agrees. He has lauded the fact that in China 'things get done where often in other economies they get bogged down in politics'.[7]

The Chinese seem to understand what businesses need. John Hamre, a former US deputy secretary of defence under Bill Clinton, related a sobering tale of two Western executives he happened to get chatting to in Heathrow Airport to illustrate how the Chinese authorities help enterprises, rather than getting in the way, as their counterparts in the developed world do:

> One businessman was on his way home from China. He had just spent a week working out the details to build a major manufacturing facility at a booming Chinese industrial park ... The mayor said they will provide free transportation services from downtown to the factory for employees for two years. The local university promised an intern program for engineering students. And on it went. The other businessman relayed the challenges he faced with his factory in America. He wanted to double the size of the factory, but was informed he needed a new environmental impact study before he could approach zoning authorities. He sought a meeting with federal officials who were managing 'stimulus' funds that he hoped would help finance the expansion. But he was informed he could not meet with the assistant secretary because it would possibly suggest a 'conflict of interest'.[8]

The idea that the Chinese do capitalism better than us has gained in popularity since the near meltdown of the American financial system in 2008. 'China is proving particularly adept at reaping globalization's benefits while limiting its liabilities,' according to Charles Kupchan of the Council on Foreign Relations.[9] Dani Rodrik of Harvard University says that China is prospering because its leaders have had 'the self-confidence to defy external blueprints'.[10]

Enthusiasm for the Chinese way seems to extend across the political spectrum. Free trade unions may be banned in China, but some Western labour organizations nevertheless admire the Chinese model. Andy Stern, a former president of the Service Employees

International Union, hails China's state capitalism as 'superior' and has argued that the US needs to learn from the East: 'America needs to do what a once-dominant business or sports team would do when the tide turns: study the ingredients of its competitors' success.'[11]

The Chinese are hailed as excellent crisis managers. The country emerged from the global financial crash unscathed, thanks to the deft management of its leaders, who pushed through a massive stimulus package at exactly the right time. While the West slumped into the worst downturn since the Great Depression of the 1930s, China's annual growth rate never dipped below 9 per cent. 'The Chinese government's economic management has been absolutely brilliant, it's a supremely competent state,' enthuses British journalist Martin Jacques. It's a common view. David Pilling, Asia editor of the *Financial Times*, praises China's 'highly competent leaders' who 'for all their faults have steered the economy through 30 years of spectacular growth'.[12]

China has stealthily annexed the future too, we're told. Of the world's major economies only China has had the foresight to ensure that it will have a steady supply of the world's increasingly scarce commodities, according to Zambian economist and former banker Dambisa Moyo.[13] The former International Monetary Fund official Arvind Subramanian believes that China's renminbi could replace the dollar as the premier global currency by the end of the decade. We could see a 'redback' to replace the mighty American greenback.[14]

Not so long ago we used to scoff at the 'five-year plans' produced by Communist states, regarding them as a byword for wasteful investment and fiddled statistics, but now Beijing's multi-year development blueprints are treated with the highest seriousness. 'It's always right to follow what the [Chinese] government does, so look at the five-year plan to see where the government's sympathy lies,' is the sage advice from respected US investor Jim Rogers.[15] And why? Because in stark contrast to the corrupt old Soviet Union, Chinese five-year plans actually get delivered.

They're impressive green capitalists too. According to the British environmental campaigner, Jonathon Porritt, China has set tough energy and water conservation targets and has done some 'serious legwork' in measuring GDP in a way that takes account of the cost to the environment. Porritt suggests big technological breakthroughs in the development of green technologies such as photovoltaics or hydrogen-powered cars could be achieved by China in the coming years. Unlike their Western counterparts, China's leaders 'absolutely get' the seriousness of the climate change threat, he tells us.[16]

Once there was a 'Washington consensus', which involved the US and international financial stewards such as the International Monetary Fund telling poor nations that they needed to privatize industries, liberate their financial systems and open up their markets to foreign competition if they wanted to develop. But China has shown that it is possible to grow without doing those things. Some now speak of a rival 'Beijing consensus'.[17] Mark Leonard, head of the European Council on Foreign Relations, argues that Chinese state capitalism, rather than the Western free market variety, has been the big winner from the era of globalization. 'For the first time since the end of the Cold War,' he says, 'Europe and America face a formidable alternative: the Chinese model.'[18]

ENDLESS SUPERLATIVES

In some ways the enthusiasm of the cheerleaders for Chinese capitalism is understandable. The story of Chinese growth over the past three decades is indeed awe-inspiring. In 1979 the economy was smaller than Britain's, despite having a population twenty times larger. Since then the Chinese economy has doubled in size roughly every eight years and is now twenty-two times larger than when it began its reforms. In 2009 China overtook Japan to become the second biggest economy in the world. It is expected to surpass the United States in 2017.[19] China has undergone the most spectacular expansion in history. Britain's industrialization took a hundred years. China has accomplished it in just thirty.

The country has played host to the largest migration in history too. Around 200 million Chinese farm workers have travelled to the cities since Deng Xiaoping relaxed China's tight residency controls in the early 1980s, many to work in the kind of factories we saw in the last chapter. The pace of urbanization has been astonishingly fast. At the beginning of the reform period 80 per cent of Chinese lived in the countryside. Now more than half of China's 1,340 million people reside in cities. In 1989 China had less than 160 kilometres of motorways. Now the country has the second largest road network in the world, second only to America.

China has transformed itself into the planet's workshop. A fifth of all global manufacturing takes place within its borders. Computers, microwave ovens, televisions, mobile phones, furniture: all of them are 'made in China'. The city of Wenzhou is responsible for the production of 80 per cent of all the world's cigarette lighters and other plastic 'stuff'. A Christmas town churns out almost half of the world's winter decorations. China makes 70 per cent of all children's toys. China clothes us all too. A town in Zhejiang province made a pair of socks for every person on Earth in 2011. There's another town that stitches virtually all of the world's jeans. The superlatives seem to be endless. China is the world's biggest producer of steel, the world's biggest market for car purchases, the world's biggest exporter, the world's biggest consumer of luxury goods.

All this economic activity has had a profoundly positive impact on the lives of the Chinese people. Average per capita incomes have risen more than tenfold. The World Bank estimates that China's economic expansion since the late 1970s has pulled some 500 million people out of poverty.[20] That's more than one and a half times the present population of the United States. China's modernization has been the most successful poverty alleviation programme ever.

I've seen the good this has done at first hand. When I first visited Guangzhou back in 1986 the worldly possessions of my great-uncle's family could be squeezed into a tatty sideboard. White goods were still very difficult to acquire, often requiring help from overseas relatives.

The previous year my father had received a letter from his eldest cousin, written on paper as thin as crêpe, with an urgent request:

Dear cousin. I am in pressing need of an icebox. A 150–170 litre two-door Japan-made Mitsubishi, Toshiba or Hitachi of common type. According to the Chinese customs tariff every overseas Chinese, when entering China, is permitted to bring in [an] icebox, duty-free, every year. So please go to a Chinese emporium in Hong Kong and buy the model of icebox mentioned. With the certificate and invoice I will pick up the box in Guangzhou. As to the expense and fees required I will surely pay them back in full in foreign currency.

In 1986 came another plea:

> Dear cousin. The China Travel Service Guangdong has opened a
> free bazaar solely for overseas Chinese, ethnic Chinese of foreign
> nationality, and the like. I wonder if you can take us there and
> buy a washing machine? Could you spare even a day's time and
> come back for it?

Today my great-uncle has a giant plasma television and a larger
sofa than the one I have at home in London. If he wants to buy an
icebox, a washing machine – or any other modern piece of technology – he doesn't need to get relatives to import it; he simply goes to
the department store in the fancy Tian He shopping district. 'You
can see that life is so much better,' my cousin told me proudly on
my last visit when we fell to talking about the old days.

My relatives left Jung Wo Lei to live in the city. But rural living
conditions have improved out of all recognition too. Access to
vaccines, clean drinking water and basic health care is better than
it was. Many children who would once have died in childbirth
stand a chance of survival; the infant mortality has fallen by three-
quarters since the late 1970s.[21] Mothers' deaths in childbirth are
down impressively too. China's economic boom has literally been
a lifesaver.

The Party seems to be delivering for the Chinese people. A 2011
Gallup Poll found that 80 per cent of the population saw their economy getting better, while just 5 per cent saw it declining. By contrast
the same poll in the US showed 48 per cent of Americans envisaging
an improvement in their own circumstances and 43 per cent expect-
ing a deterioration.

By some measures the Chinese economy seems to be increasing
in sophistication too. China now boasts 73 firms in the Fortune
Global 500 list of the world's largest companies by revenues, from
telecoms firms, to insurance companies to car manufacturers. The
Industrial & Commercial Bank of China has a larger market capitalization than any financial institution in America.

China has progressed so much in just three decades, it's been an
economic success story on an unprecedented scale. So what is to
prevent the country carrying on at the same giddy clip indefinitely?

Aren't the cheerleaders for China's model of capitalism right when they say that we have a lot to learn from the East?

Well, to see why such ideas are overblown, let's start by taking a look at some of the things China has to show for all that stellar growth.

NOT IN SWITZERLAND

The pretty gabled roofs of the Swiss town of Interlaken emerge from the mist. But the mist is not a fog bank rolling off an Alpine slope. Rather it's the pollution on the hills above the city of Shenzhen on China's south coast. A Chinese company has built a replica of the picturesque Swiss town there. It's a luxury retreat complete with a hotel and spa, designed to appeal to Chinese holidaymakers who don't have the time or money to fly halfway across the world to experience the delights of the Swiss mountains. They can even buy chalets in the Chinese Interlaken. The trouble is that very few of the chalets have been sold since the resort opened in 2007. They cling forlornly to the hillsides, curtains permanently open. The hotel, too, is eerily quiet. When I visited in 2012 the streets of the resort were almost deserted.

It's not the only European clone town in the area. Hallstatt, further inland in Guangdong province, is an exact replica of an Austrian village. And then there's Thames Town on the outskirts of Shanghai. With bright red post boxes and Tudor mansions, it's a chocolate-box image of perfect Englishness. Shanghai is also the home of Anting German Town, a cluster of Bauhaus-style architecture. Like Interlaken these theme towns were intended to furnish the Chinese wealthy with holiday homes. But, again, no one is buying. Someone, somewhere, is losing money.

Someone is losing money too on the world's largest shopping mall. Most of the 1,500 units in the New South China Mall in Dongguan have been empty since it opened in 2005. Not even the replica Arc de Triomphe and the mock-up of the Bell Tower in Venice have managed to attract visitors. Which probably has something to do with the fact that the mall is in the middle of nowhere and virtually impossible for most of Dongguan's ten million residents – most of them poor migrant workers – to reach.

China's developers have adopted the philosophy of 'build it and they will come', but all too often they don't come. The coal city of Ordos, thrown up in the wastes of Inner Mongolia, has space for one million residents; fewer than fifty thousand people have actually moved in. Street after street is as barren as the surrounding desert. The sun beats down on clusters of hollow apartment blocks. At the other end of the country, in subtropical Yunnan province, the new town of Chenggong also stands empty, its schools, offices and homes all gathering dust. There is space for one hundred thousand inhabitants. They have yet to arrive.

It's not just property that is underused in China. The suspension bridge that stretches across Jiazhou Bay on the northeast coast is the longest in the world. At twenty-six kilometres the mighty concrete structure could span the English Channel. But its six lanes, which connect the city of Qingdao to one of its outlying districts, are quiet. It was designed to cope with 30,000 cars a day, but has been carrying just 10,000.[22] That is probably because when the bridge opened in 2011, there was already a perfectly good tunnel serving the same route. The newly built Shi Huang highway in Hebei and the Tai Jing highway in Jiangxi have a similar problem. They are so bereft of traffic that sarcastic netizens have suggested China should apply to stage a Formula One Grand Prix on them.

To some these unproductive investments are nothing to worry about. When economists want to estimate a country's developmental potential they add up the total value of its factories, ports, power lines, offices, roads, homes and machinery – things known as 'fixed capital' – and work out how much there is per head of population. In 2012 China's capital stock per person was only a tenth of the level of the United States and just 15 per cent of South Korea's.[23] By this measure China has acres of room for investment growth, even if the occasional unwise construction project gets approved. As we saw in the previous chapter, China needs more capital to become more productive.

Yet what is striking about modern China is how little investment is flowing into areas where it is genuinely needed. There is no doubt that China requires more housing, for example. In Chengdu, the capital of the western province of Sichuan, people wear hats and coats indoors during winter because their old Communist-era housing blocks have no central heating. Many public buildings are also unheated. At dusk in the old city of Shanghai migrant workers wash their faces at street corner standpipes because their slum homes have no indoor plumbing. Tens of thousands of badly paid graduates rent damp bedsits carved out of the basements of high-rise blocks on the outskirts of Beijing. It is estimated that a third of city dwellers live in low-quality collective housing. Homes are also terribly cramped. Per capita living space in major cities is just 76.4 square feet. My great-uncle got lucky with his spacious apartment.

Instead of building homes that would improve the living conditions of poor or middle income Chinese, the developers are busy putting up luxury apartments, or fancy new hotels aimed at attracting business travellers. And the situation has worsened over the last decade: in 2002 low-income housing accounted for 16 per cent of total housing construction; by 2012 it had fallen to 3 per cent.[24]

China needs more roads. To get to Jung Wo Lei, where my grandmother was born, deep in the Guangdong countryside, you have to turn off the battered highway and drive down a lumpy earth track. The yellow mud will still be clinging to your car tyres when you get back to the city of Guangzhou two hours later. It's the same story across rural China. Some 40 per cent of villages lack paved roads providing access to the nearest town. This makes it more difficult for the farmers to take their surplus produce to market. But rather than building roads in underdeveloped rural areas, local governments are commissioning smooth intercity expressways for which there is, at the moment at least, scant demand.

China needs more transport infrastructure across the board. The roads in major cities are gridlocked nightmares. Subway trains are crammed to bursting point during morning commutes. Yet party chiefs have devoted most of their resources in recent years to constructing the world's largest high-speed rail network. This is despite the fact that, even with a hefty state subsidy, fast intercity ticket prices are beyond the means of most Chinese people.

Walk through the streets of China's cities and you can often see people spilling out of public buildings onto the street. This will usually be a clinic. The people are trying to get to a row of counters to describe their medical symptoms and, with luck, get prescribed some pharmaceutical treatment. China urgently needs more health centres and more hospitals. That's even more true of the country-side where some people still don't have any modern public medical facilities. But it's the same old story: the construction work is always taking place somewhere else.

It all points to a colossal misallocation of resources. Local government officials prefer to commission eye-catching building projects – a new airport, a new expressway, a skyscraper, a public square, a sports stadium – rather than the kind of mundane construction work that will actually improve people's lives. And because the promotion prospects of regional officials are determined by their area's annual output figures, there is no incentive for them to give much thought to the long-term profitability of the projects they approve. They will (they hope) have moved on by the time any losses show up. Far from being the 'long-term thinkers' of our imagination, China's capitalist politicians are dangerously preoccupied with the here and now.

China's unproductive investment boom is not only something to worry about because of the waste; it also stokes the risk of a financial crisis. The building boom of recent years has been financed almost entirely by credit. The vast economic stimulus that the government unleashed in the global financial crisis was mostly made up of new bank lending. The total value of all the loans made by Chinese banks more than doubled between 2009 and 2012. Outstanding loans are now equivalent to more than 170 per cent of the entire value of the Chinese economy.[25] Those numbers mean a significant rise in defaults could bring down much of the financial sector.

This vast lending boom did indeed help China ride out the global downturn, but the signs are growing that the pain was delayed, not avoided. In February 2012 the central government felt it necessary to order the banks to roll over a colossal $1.7 trillion in loans made to local governments that were due to be repaid. This suggests that, despite the banks officially reporting very low levels of impaired loans, many borrowers are struggling to repay. Economists talk about 'business cycles', by which they mean the historic tendency of all economies to experience investment booms followed by busts, as poor investments are finally recognized and confidence collapses. China seems to be approaching the end of one mammoth cycle.

THE PARTY IS EVERYWHERE

Shanghai's Xintiandi district is as slick an advert for cosmopolitan capitalism as one could find anywhere on the planet. Amid the elegant restored stone town houses one can find a branch of Starbucks, a Haagen-Dazs ice-cream parlour and a host of luxury boutiques selling expensive handbags and other trophies of conspicuous consumption. Wealthy Shanghainese sip lattes in the cool shade of the interlinked courtyards. The visitor who strolls through the pedestrianized streets of Xintiandi would probably come away with the impression that China is now every inch the sophisticated market economy. But Xintiandi conceals a surprise. In this same complex lies the set of rooms in which the first congress of the Chinese Communist Party was held in 1921. In the heart of this hub of capitalism one finds the Party. And so it is with China itself.

The hardest thing for many outsiders to grasp about modern China is how much the government dominates the nominally private economy. The state is everywhere, even if it is often superficially disguised. The lobby of the Garden Hotel, one of the first Western hotels in Guangzhou, is spectacular. A magnificent golden frieze depicting scenes from the eighteenth-century novel *Dream of the Red Chamber* is suspended behind a long black marble check-in counter. The service in the 'Platinum 5-Star hotel' is the equal of anything you might find in Paris or Dubai. Yet the Garden is owned by the Lingnan Group, which is controlled by the Chinese state. It is as if the Ritz in London or the Waldorf-Astoria in New York had been nationalized.

This is a ubiquitous story. So-called 'state-owned enterprises' are the biggest players in the banking, telecoms, energy and construction sectors. At least 30 per cent of the Chinese economy is directly or indirectly in the hands of government-controlled entities. Some estimates put the figure at more than 50 per cent.[26] The majority of the firms listed on the Chinese stock market are still state-controlled. Of China's one hundred largest firms by market capitalization only four are not government controlled. And since foreign competition is banned in many markets, many of these companies are monopolies.

State-owned enterprises were, unsurprisingly, given their ubiquity, the major beneficiaries of the 2009 stimulus package, scooping up an estimated 85 per cent of the new lending. State-controlled banks were instructed by local government officials to make loans to state-controlled companies whose senior staff are often relatives of those same local government officials. In this incestuous world corruption has inevitably flourished. Cheng Li, of the Brookings Institute in Washington, says that the amount of graft taking place is 'unprecedented in the history of China and unparalleled in the world'.[27]

Analysts have been struggling to come up with a description for China's post-Mao economic arrangements. The Communist Party used to favour 'Socialism with Chinese characteristics', although there is very little about modern China that could be described as socialist, except perhaps a disregard for civil liberties. Some have described it as 'managed capitalism' or 'state capitalism', to reflect the dominant role that state-owned firms play in the economy. 'Market Leninism' is another phrase one hears. Yet given the prevalence of personal networks between business executives and political officials, 'crony capitalism' is probably the most accurate description. Carl Walter and Fraser Howie, two Westerners with long experience of working within the Chinese financial system, argue that 'the state-owned economy, nominally "owned by the whole people", is being carved up by China's rulers, their families, relations and retainers, who are all in business for themselves and only themselves.'[28]

We often hear about the dynamism of China's scrappy entrepreneurs, and there are indeed a number of impressive individuals who have started out with nothing and built vast business empires. Lu Guanqiu, for example, turned a bicycle repair shop into a giant manufacturing conglomerate; Shen Wenrong transformed a village steel works into China's largest privately owned company. However, these success stories come from the first phase of China's opening up in the 1980s, before the state reasserted itself into the economy. The reality is that in today's crony capitalist environment small private companies find themselves at an extreme disadvantage. Start-up businesses in China often find they cannot get loans from state-owned banks to expand. Despite the massive surge in private credit since 2009, they have been crowded out by the state. Many have had to rely on illegal loan sharks who charge outrageous rates of interest.

As for Western businessmen who enthuse about how helpful the Chinese state is to the private sector, they should tell it to Jack. I met him on Shamian Island, a sandbank on the Pearl River in Guangzhou. A small trader with wonky teeth from Henan province, Jack rented out a space in one of the old colonial era warehouses from which he sold traditional Chinese jackets and dresses to tourists. He had dreams of setting up a factory that would affix cheap crystals to trainers and spark a lucrative new fashion craze. 'When you next come,' he promised, 'I will be a big success and I will take you out for dinner.' But at the same time Jack was depressed about the fact that all his profits were being syphoned off by an official extortion racket. 'To open a shop I have to pay the police and local officials. I have to feed everybody. It's very expensive to do business,' he complained.

This kind of predatory corruption from the authorities not only stifles entrepreneurs, it also leads business owners to cut corners to boost profits. After all, if the state is stealing from you, why shouldn't you steal from your customers? Novelist Murong Xuecun describes the mentality thus:

> There is no clear line between the legal and the illegal. Almost every company is cheating on its taxes, and almost everyone does something not completely legal ... Take the owner of a small shop for example. In his striving to run his business, the Commerce Department, the Tax Department, the Police Department, the Fire Safety Department, the Health Department, almost every kind of state power, can force him to close down his shop. Every time he does not follow the wills of these powers, he faces the possibility of complete disaster for him and his family. Due to this kind of insecurity, most people do not keep long-term plans, but rather focus only on instant profits. In government, business, and people's personal lives, we see too many who people care only about profits and not a bit about ethics.[29]

This is particularly true in food production, where managers have a record of bulking out their produce with dangerous chemicals in order to cut costs. In 2007 pet food made in China was found to be responsible for the deaths of hundreds of animals in America.

The same year a spate of deaths of people in Panama was linked to a Chinese-manufactured chemical mixed into cough medicine. In March 2013 the diseased carcases of hundreds of thousands of pigs were found floating in the Huangpu River, which provides tap water for the city of Shanghai. Their origin was a mystery, but one theory was that a disruption in the illegal, but widespread, trade in sickly animals for meat had prompted farmers to dump the swine upstream.

The greatest food scandal so far came in 2008 when the manufacturer of a popular brand of baby milk formula was discovered to be adulterating its product with a chemical called melamine to cut costs. Some 300,000 babies were taken ill, 860 were hospitalized and 6 died. The initial response of the authorities, before a public outcry ripped the lid off the scandal, was to attempt to cover the affair up. This kind of behaviour has more or less killed public trust in the ethics of Chinese businesses. Chinese mothers now try to buy imported baby milk formula if they can. Concern about food safety is a national neurosis.

Construction companies aren't trusted either. Tales proliferate in China of buildings constructed with substandard cement by cost-cutting firms. When an earthquake hit Sichuan province in 2008, killing 68,000 people, there was a widespread assumption that such corner-cutting was the reason a number of schools collapsed so easily.

Public trust is especially weak when it comes to environmental protection. If the Beijing authorities 'absolutely get' the importance of preserving the environment, as Jonathon Porritt claims, their record hardly reflects this. Though the Party has been pledging to impose tighter controls on polluting businesses for years, local governments, in league with rapacious developers, have continued to wave through hundreds of dirty new factories and coal-fired power stations. It might have increased its investment in clean energy technology research, but central government has made the immediate pollution problem far worse by capping consumer energy prices. This has encouraged producers to use the cheapest and most polluting coal to generate power. The results are lethal and unmistakable. In the northern coal-mining city of Datong in Shanxi province the rivers run black with soot and the air is so bad that cars often have to drive with their lights on in the middle of the day. My friends in Guangzhou joke that it's a good day if they can see the 600-metre tall Canton Tower, so bad is the visibility in the city thanks to the pollution. In the Guangdong countryside peasants plant rice in their fields while enveloped in a choking blanket of chemical mist that has been belched out by the thousands of factories across the province. It is no surprise that many of the local 'mass incidents' that break out in China every year are prompted by local authority plans to approve the construction of yet another new factory. One suspects that foreign admirers of Beijing's weak environmental and planning controls would soon change their mind if it was them who had to gulp down China's smog every day.

Sixteen of the twenty most polluted cities in the world are in China and poor air quality causes 300,000 premature deaths and 20,000,000 cases of respiratory illness each year according to the World Bank. Cancer rates in Beijing, where the smog is particularly bad, are up 60 per cent in a decade, even though the proportion of smokers has not changed. Rivers across the country are drying up due to overuse of water by wasteful factories. A study by the ministry of environmental protection in 2011 found that 64 out of 118 cities had 'seriously contaminated' groundwater supplies. Half of China's forests have been destroyed over forty years. The accumulated economic cost of this plethora of natural destruction is staggering. One of China's environment ministers, Pan Yue, put a value on the deterioration of China's air quality and depletion of its other natural resources of between 8 and 13 per cent of the country's GDP each year. This implies that all of China's economic gains over the past three decades have been cancelled out by the despoliation of its environment.

LIFTING THE IRON MAIDEN LID

The idea that the Chinese Communist Party has been an economic steward of rare brilliance is a myth. Hundreds of millions of Chinese have escaped from poverty over the past three decades mainly due to their own efforts, not thanks to the benevolent wisdom of the Party. Deng Xiaoping's contribution in 1978 was to lift the lid of the iron maiden of Maoist autarky and to dismantle the Great Helmsman's lunatic command economy.

Deng, a diminutive Communist veteran, emerged triumphant from the political vortex that opened up after Mao's death. He knew that the late chairman, for all his propaganda about overtaking the West, had set China back by decades. When Mao died in 1976 some 60 per cent of the Chinese population survived on less than $1 a day. 'Poverty is not socialism' was Deng's rebuke to the Maoist legacy.

And Deng wasted no time opening up China both internally and externally. Agricultural productivity shot up because peasants were allowed to sell their surplus produce. Industry boomed because the sons and daughters of Chinese farmers were given tacit permission to move to cities and work in new factories operating in free trade zones. The order books of Chinese factories filled up because foreign investment and expertise was allowed to flow in. People were permitted to open shops and trade foreign goods, resulting in a flowering of entrepreneurship. China's economic take-off was not a 'miracle', as so often described, but a consequence of the return of a measure of freedom to the population; China really boomed because of laissez faire not 'state capitalism'. The myth of the Communist Party's wise management of this great opening up is especially misleading because, in reality, the impact of the Party's interference in the functioning of the economy over the past two decades has been to make China's development lopsided and unstable.

In the 1990s the Chinese government decided to grab more global business for its manufacturers – a practice traditionally known as 'mercantilism' – by holding down the value of its currency. The lower the value of the renminbi against the US dollar, the more successful the country's exporters in world markets. To achieve this currency depreciation the monetary authorities bought up large quantities of dollars, recycling the proceeds into American government debt. And it worked: Chinese exporters boomed and the country registered a large trade surplus. Normally when a country experiences an export boom its currency strengthens as foreign money rushes in, but the Chinese government was not prepared to let that happen. They wanted the export growth to continue. They kept their capital markets closed and persisted with mercantilism. They acquired still more dollars, holding the value of the renminbi down and locking in the exchange rate stimulus for the domestic manufacturing industry. On the eve of the 2008 global financial crash China's current account surplus had reached 10 per cent of the country's output and the state had accumulated around $1.5 trillion of US financial assets. That figure has since grown to $3.4 trillion. Most of those assets are US Treasury bonds, making Beijing the single largest creditor of the United States government.

Some have suggested that these vast holdings of dollar debt put China in a position of geopolitical strength. The argument seems to be that Beijing can assert itself in negotiations with America by threatening to dump its bonds and cause a lethal spike in US interest rates.[30] This is, however, deeply confused. If Beijing were to start off-loading its US debt holdings out of some desire to punish America it would crash the entire market for the securities and inflict massive paper losses on its own portfolio. Moreover, an exchange rate correction is already gradually taking place. The fundamentals of global supply and demand are reasserting themselves. The dollar is falling and the renminbi is gradually rising to reflect America's trade deficit and China's correspondingly stronger position. This means China's accumulated dollar assets are sinking in value. The massive investment that the Chinese government made – equivalent to $2,500 for every man, woman and child in China – looks destined to deliver a significant loss.

The Beijing government also facilitated China's unstable investment boom through its financial repression of China's savers. If you are a Chinese citizen you are prohibited from taking your money out of the country in any great quantity or holding your savings in a foreign currency. You have no choice but to store your money in a state-controlled bank. And these banks have been ordered to pay very low interest rates to domestic savers and to make cheap loans to real estate companies and state-owned infrastructure developers. With the maximum interest rate on bank deposits set below the rate of inflation, savers are losing money every year. Meanwhile, with the inflation rate higher than lending rates, big borrowers have been seeing their debts steadily eroded in real terms. Under these financial conditions it makes sense for any large corporation to borrow and build like there is no tomorrow. Thus China's financial system functions like a reverse Robin Hood, taking from those who have the least and channelling it to those who have the most.

China's financial repression has contributed to other dangerous economic distortions. Driving through the Tian He district of Guangzhou with my aunt one day, she pointed to an anonymous residential building. 'Do you see that?' she asked. 'My flat's in there.' 'Do you live there?' I responded, a little puzzled since we'd just come from her home. 'No, that's my *investment* flat.' It turned out that she'd never lived in the property. She wasn't even renting it out. Investing in property was simply a different way of storing her money.

It's a familiar story across China. Seeing their savings eroded by inflation and low deposit rates, people have ploughed their money into residential property in the hope of better returns. One third of home-owning families in China are estimated to have more than one property. This has, not surprisingly, created an immense bubble. The rich have been the biggest speculators. In Shanghai in 2012 I had lunch in the Pudong commercial district with a friend who works for the city government. Our restaurant had a view out onto the city's skyscrapers. 'Look at that block over there with the golden roof,' he said. 'Those apartments cost about twenty thousand ren-minbi a square metre. It's all sold. But when you look at it at night there's almost no lights on. Why? Because people don't live there. It's just an investment property for them.'

Around half of all the luxury homes in Shanghai are believed to be empty investment flats. Some analysts, basing their estimates on electricity meter readings, say that the number of empty proper-ties around the country could be as high as 65 million.[31] Property speculation has pushed up prices to dizzying heights. A small flat in Beijing cost 20 times annual average disposable incomes in 2010. Compare that with the UK where property values relative to average incomes are at just 4.5 (a ratio close to historic highs for Britain). In 2011 the Chinese government, recognizing that many people are now priced entirely out of the market, felt the need to impose a ban on people owning more than two properties in order to cool the market down.

The one thing worse than a property bubble for the Chinese econ-omy would be a property bust. That would decimate growth, since property construction accounts for around 13 per cent of GDP. It would also bankrupt overextended local governments, which have scant tax-raising powers and have only been able to service their sizeable debts in recent years by requisitioning parcels of communal land and selling them for development. Worse, these public authorities have also used their land holdings as collateral for their bank borrowings. If the property sector were to go into meltdown and land prices were to crash, a large chunk of China's official sector would be dragged down too. The central government might, it is true, have the resources to bail out local authorities thanks to its low national stock of public debt and huge foreign exchange reserves, but a fiscal rescue could still be extremely expensive given that local government debts amount to between a fifth and a half of China's GDP.[32] Moreover, if Beijing had to pay for a large banking bailout on top of that, in a context of rapidly slowing growth, even China's state finances could be stretched to the limits.

The central government thus finds itself caught in an economic trap. If it successfully cools the property market, it risks triggering a financial crisis and a local government financial collapse. But if it carries on stoking the bubble through financial repression, the eventual bust is likely to be even greater. This is a nightmare of the Party's own making. The Chinese government could have avoided such a huge property bubble, had it liberalized its financial system and paid people a decent return on their savings. And government culpability for China's fragile economic state doesn't end there. Had it refrained from using corrupt local governments to channel a lending stimulus to state-owned infrastructure firms, the credit surge would have been more productive. Had Beijing had not pursued a mercantilist trade promotion policy, China's growth would have been less dependent on manufacturing for export and it would not now be sitting on a huge pile of depreciating dollar assets. Tougher environmental controls and a scrapping of energy subsidies would have made for more ecologically sustainable development too.

While restraint in these areas might have cooled China's double-digit growth rates, that would have been a price worth paying for a more sustainable economy. Instead, what we have seen is a catalogue of economic and financial mismanagement by China's leaders in their frenzied dash for growth. Viewed like this, Chinese living standards have improved in recent decades not because of the decisions made by the Party authorities, but in spite of them.

WHERE NEXT?

Much analysis of China's economic future consists of economists drawing straight lines on charts, extrapolating from existing trends. Chinese economic output has grown at an average growth rate of 10 per cent for the past three decades. Assuming expansion at that rate continues, China will be the world's largest economy, in terms of purchasing power parity, well before the end of this decade. Another favoured technique of economists is to assume convergence with Western living standards. The average income per head in China is still only a quarter of the levels in developed countries. This means, apparently, that incomes are set to increase fourfold over the century. Half of the Chinese population now live in cities. Other developed nations have an urbanization ratio of 80 per cent. That means, some say, that China's cities, massive though they might already be, are still only around a little more than half full. This approach is useful up to a point. It outlines a possible destination, but it says nothing about the journey. And it glosses over the more important truth, namely that the present growth path is unsustainable.

The biggest challenge for China will be deflating the twin investment and property bubbles without precipitating a general collapse. The best hope to achieve this is by simultaneously pivoting to a new source of economic growth: consumption.

All economies are sustained by four different types of demand, or spending: fixed capital investment spending, government spending, consumer spending and foreign spending in the form of exports. Before the financial crisis, trade was a significant motor. However, most of China's spectacular growth after 2009 came from fixed capital investment spending, which, as we have seen, is pretty much the same thing as government spending in China. As a share of GDP, combined public and private outlays on infrastructure, construction and industrial capacity building have reached a staggering 50 per cent. To give an illustration of how large this is, in the US and the UK capital investment accounts for just 15 per cent of GDP. Some optimists have argued that rapidly industrializing nations with relatively little physical capital always have huge investment binges and that it's a natural part of the process of catching up with developed nations. This is true. But China's investment rate is crazily high even by historical standards. When Japan and Korea were in the midst of their own frenzied catch-up industrializations in the 1960s and 1970s their investment spending levels never went higher than 40 per cent of GDP. China's has been in excess of that for the best part of a decade. As Barry Eichengreen, Professor of Economics at the University of California, Berkeley, puts it: 'No economy can productively invest such a large share of its national income for any length of time.'[33]

On the other hand, consumer consumption in China is abnormally low. Do not be fooled by all those expensive boutiques in Shanghai's Xintiandi shopping district, nor the proliferation of reports about the burgeoning appetite of the Chinese for Western luxury brands. Frenzied Chinese tourist shoppers may be an increasingly common sight in New York, Paris and London, but consumption in China is only around 35 per cent of GDP, about half the proportion in developed nations.

Happily, this means consumer spending has the potential to take over from investment as a driver of demand. Such a shift would create a virtuous circle. It would stimulate the weak domestic Chinese service economy, under-developed sectors such as retail and healthcare, and also spur more technological development to make the Chinese economy move up the value added chain. Living standards would rise more quickly and people might even be able to afford to live in the luxury apartment blocks that have been thrown up in recent years. In short, the Chinese economy would undergo a much needed rebalancing. How to get there though? How to get the Chinese to spend?

RICH STATE, POOR PEOPLE

If the Chinese people are to spend more, they also have to save less. In big cities more than half of the population currently salt away 25 per cent of their income. A third save more than 35 per cent of what they earn.[34] This is a high level. Even in the most abstemious European nation, Germany, the household savings rate is only around 16 per cent. So why are the Chinese such voracious savers?

'The state is rich but the people are poor' is a popular saying in China, and that reality lies at the heart of the country's economic

dysfunction. The Chinese state has accumulated vast foreign exchange reserves thanks to its mercantilist trade policy, yet its people
have a very meagre social safety net. In the Mao era there was an
'iron rice bowl' that gave workers a guaranteed lifetime income and
offered them free housing, free healthcare, free education for children and a pension upon retirement. These benefits were hardly
generous (consider my great-uncle's tiny old apartment in Guangzhou), but in the context of a deeply poor country they did provide
an element of security. Yet the iron rice bowl was largely smelted
down in the economic reforms of the 1980s and 1990s, and China's
leaders put nothing in its place. People were left to fend more or
less entirely for themselves – especially China's tens of millions of
migrant workers, who enjoy almost no state benefits whatsoever.
Libertarians who fantasize about huge cuts in welfare spending in
their own countries would find China a paradise.

The Chinese state today spends only around 10 per cent of its
GDP on education and health, half the level of most developed
countries. China set up a national social insurance pension fund
in 2000 but coverage could kindly be described as patchy. And the
funds run by local governments are under-resourced and have sometimes failed to pay out. Surveys have found that one of the reasons
people are saving so much is precisely because the state is spending
so little. They are putting money aside to pay for the goods that used
to fill the iron rice bowl: education, retirement, unemployment insurance and health care. The one-child policy has also encouraged
precautionary saving by lumbering most children in China with
not only two parents each to help support financially in their old
age, but also four grandparents. Chinese people understand the
pressure this is exerting on the younger points of these inverted
family pyramids and they save more for their own retirement to
relieve it.

Higher consumption will only follow the creation of a decent
welfare safety net. People will be wary of spending in the shops if
they fear they could be bankrupted by an unexpected medical bill,
or if they worry they are facing an old age of crushing poverty. It
would be more economically efficient for the Chinese government
to provide these public goods than the Chinese people individually.
Higher wages would help the rebalancing too. In wealthy countries

the share of gross national income that goes to wages is commonly between 60 and 80 per cent, and the share that goes to companies in the form of profits and financial surpluses is around 20 per cent. But in China wages account for just 50 per cent of gross national income and company surpluses as much as 45 per cent. The discrepancy is due to the fact that Chinese employers, faced with a large impoverished labour force moving out of the countryside, have for many years been able to get away with paying very low salaries. Yet if the Chinese economy is to rebalance, workers need to be paid more and employers' profits need to come down. This shift needs to happen rapidly to cushion the economic impact of a potential investment plunge and financial crash. If that bubble bursts there is likely to be no source of demand except the Chinese consumer. Exports are unlikely to ride to the rescue with the rest of the world still struggling.

There is another reason not to delay with the demand rebalancing: demographics. China's growth has received a tremendous economic boost in recent decades from the country's young working-age population flowing into cities. China had a massive, willing, workforce at just the time when it needed lots of hands to turn the wheel of industrialization. But fewer children have been born in China since the early 1980s; thanks to the one-child policy, birth rates are down by one third. As a result, the size of the national work force is now likely to start to contract from as early as 2015.

There will be many more elderly people around as a share of the population in the coming decades, which will double the ratio of pensioners to working-age population by 2030. Today 11 per cent of the population is aged over 65; by the middle of this century that proportion is set to reach almost 40 per cent. Paying for the retirement of this cohort will be a growing financial burden on both the state and the workforce. China is hitting this demographic hump at an unusually early stage of its development. Most developing nations continue to have a large working-age population to draw on throughout their industrialization. The fact that China is different has led to fears that the country is destined to 'grow old before it grows rich'. Unless the Chinese economy moves up the value chain, increasing output through technological innovation rather than relying on an increasing supply of cheap unskilled labour, that outcome becomes ever more likely.

CHEATED OUT OF THE FUTURE

We are right to be optimistic about China in a broad sense. The country does have huge potential to grow and develop in a sustainable way. The majority of its people are still living as farmers and surviving on tiny incomes. Many millions more will make the shift from country to town and enjoy higher standards of living in the process. And there are acres of space to accommodate simple catch-up growth that can take the form of the Chinese building comfortable homes, extending transport networks and selling each other the basic services we take for granted. The Chinese economy is staggeringly energy inefficient. Simply by adopting the same power conservation standards as the advanced world, China can significantly reduce its pollution levels. And despite the explosion of copyright piracy in China, the country also had a stellar reputation in the Middle Ages for innovation. There is no reason why China should not be able to tap into that older tradition and power its growth in the coming decades by developing new technologies and other ways of driving up its productivity.

In order to achieve this growth, however, China will need to implement profound structural economic reforms. That means a massive expansion of the public provision of health care and pensions to enable the population to reduce its saving rates. It means central government taking over the provision of these services from underfunded local authorities. It means land reform, to prevent famers being swindled out of their rightful profits from plot sales by local officials. It means a liberalization of the financial sector, allowing people to earn a decent level of interest on their savings. It means higher wages and lower financial surpluses at firms. It means cuts in subsidies for infrastructure expenditure and manufacturing, including ending the practice of covert exchange-rate stimulus. It means a legal system that promotes domestic technological innovation by adequately protecting copyright and intellectual property. It means dismantling crony capitalist networks and encouraging entrepreneurship by privatizing and splitting up the ubiquitous state-owned enterprises.

It also means an end to the one-child policy. Deng Xiaoping introduced this restriction on reproduction out of a fear that a rising population would impede China's growth. That 'cure' now threatens to deliver the very disease itself. It needs to go. As Chinese people get richer they will, in common with other societies, probably choose to have smaller families. But most young women in China I've spoken to would like to have at least two children. Lifting the restriction wouldn't solve China's demographic problem, but it would help relieve it. What China requires, in short, is for the state to get out of the areas of the economy in which it presently interferes to such malign effect, and for the state to get involved in those areas where it has been failing to discharge its responsibilities.

All these structural reforms would be good for China, yet the state is struggling to deliver them. This is because powerful vested interests in corporations, in banks, in industry and in local government do very well out of the unbalanced high investment and export-orientated model. Company owners do not want to pay higher wages to workers precisely because this would diminish their profits. They don't want higher interest rates on their borrowings for the same reason. Bank executives also do not want borrowing rates to rise because some of their customers would likely go bust and they would be forced to recognize massive losses on their own balance sheets. Local authorities do not want cheaper land values and lower property prices because that would compel them to clean up their own precarious finances or, worse, to ask the national government for a bailout. Exporters do not want an end to mercantilism. And so on.

Some in the national leadership of the Party grasp the fact that root-and-branch reform is necessary for sustainable growth in China. Economic rebalancing and consumption-powered growth are part of the present 2011–2015 Five-Year Plan. But many senior party cadres have personally enriched themselves by sitting at the centre of vast national patronage networks that are held together by the present unsustainable model. They do not want the gravy train to hit the buffers. They are supported by security hardliners who reject reforms that would curb their control over business and the population, as these kind of liberalizing reforms inevitably would. Some even believe, like foreign cheerleaders, that the global financial crisis of 2008 showed China has developed a superior economic model and that the country has no reason to change.

There are powerful public and private vested interests in many nations, but in democracies change tends to happen because politicians, in the end, must respond to the broad public interest or lose power. However, in a closed political system like China, leaders are inevitably more beholden to insiders, whether political or commercial, than they are to the public. The mechanism for driving structural economic change is broken. The danger is that China will be cheated out of its prosperous economic future by a backward political system.

Why do we find such vulnerabilities so hard to see? Not everyone is a China cheerleader, of course. There are plenty of economic 'bears' who warn a collapse is likely. But too many of us, dazzled by the headline growth numbers, do not see this threat. We are also trapped in a familiar mode of thinking that holds China as the world's greatest economic prize. From the earliest encounters visitors have been enraptured by the potential to make money from China. Marco Polo caused European mouths to salivate when he described how Kublai Khan had 'a more extensive command of treasure than any other sovereign in the universe'.[35] A British writer observed in the 1840s that 'if we could only persuade every person in China to lengthen his shirt-tail by a foot, we could keep the mills of Lancashire working round the clock'. It is not such a jump from these sentiments to the hyperbolic encomiums at the Dorchester with which we commenced this chapter.

In truth, our enthusiasm for the superior 'China model' of capitalism could not be more misplaced. That model has delivered extreme distortions, which have grown to such proportions that hundreds of millions of livelihoods are now under threat. The existing model is broken. The question is whether China's autocratic rulers are capable of pivoting to a new one in time to prevent the biggest boom in history turning into the biggest bust.

CHINA WILL RULE THE WORLD

It's 2030. In a sleek lecture theatre in Beijing, adorned with a giant portrait of Chairman Mao, a Chinese professor is explaining to his Chinese students why great empires fall. 'Ancient Greece, Rome, the British Empire. America ... They all make the same mistakes – turning their back on the principles that made them great. America tried to tax and spend its way out of a great recession. Of course we owned most of their debt.' The professor emits a cold chuckle. Then his eyes narrow malevolently. 'So now they work for us.' The students roll around in their seats laughing.

This was the scenario presented in an advert produced by American right-wing pressure group, Citizens Against Government Waste, in 2010. 'You *can* change the future, you *have* to' was the concluding message flashed across the screen. 'Join Citizens Against Government Waste to stop the spending that is bankrupting America.' The authors of this propaganda might not have known it, but the buttons of public fear they were pushing to advance their conservative political agenda (the prospect of China ruling the world and the consequent subjugation of the rest of us) have been tapped many, many times before.

We have been experiencing premonitions of a Chinese takeover since the Victorian era. On a visit to Hong Kong in 1899 Rudyard Kipling dined with some of the local colonial commercial bosses. These 'Taipans' were, Kipling discovered, financing railways in mainland China in order to deepen their trade links with the Oriental behemoth. Was it wise, the poet and short story author wondered, to force these 'stimulants of the West' on this vast and dangerous country? 'What will happen,' he asked, 'when China really wakes up, runs a line from Shanghai to Lhassa, starts another line of imperial Yellow Flag immigrant steamers, and really works and controls her own gun-factories and arsenals?'[1]

Such anxious thoughts seemed to haunt eminent Victorians. Field Marshal Garnet Joseph Wolseley was one of the military supermen who were sprinkled over the age. The curriculum vitae of this dashing figure reads like an index of all the dramatic moments of nineteenth-century Britannic imperialism. He was mentioned in dispatches for his valiant conduct in the Crimean War, when Britain and France vied for supremacy over the Black Sea with Russia. He distinguished himself at the relief of Lucknow during the Indian Mutiny. And he was present when British forces burned down the Qing emperor's Summer Palace in 1860. Such was Wolseley's reputation for military efficiency that the phrase 'everything's all Sir Garnet' entered common parlance in Victorian Britain as a kind of shorthand for 'all is well'. In his memoirs in 1904 Wolseley reviewed the various foreigners that he encountered in his career and concluded that it was the Chinese who were the most formidable. '[They] are the most remarkable race on earth and I have always thought, and still believe them to be, the coming rulers of the world,' he wrote. 'They only want a Chinese Peter The Great or Napoleon to make them so.'[2]

Others saw the material of supremacy in the Chinese too. Arthur Henderson Smith, the most famous American Protestant missionary in China at the turn of the twentieth century, held the population he had proselytized in a kind of awe. 'If the time should ever come,' he portentously wrote, 'as come it may, when the far-distant West comes into close and practical competition with the patient Chinese for the right to exist, one or other will be behindhand in the race. And I shall venture the prediction that it will not be the Chinese!'[3]

It was but a short step from awe to fear. The bold colours painted by Smith seem to have bled into Sax Rohmer's ghastly portrait of his fictional Chinese super villain, Fu Manchu, who, we are breathlessly told, 'sought no less a goal than Yellow dominion of the world!'[4]

A coming day of Chinese rule continued to haunt our imagination after the First World War. In 1920, William Somerset Maugham wrote a short story in which a Chinese philosopher with an uncannily impressive grasp of English tells the narrator, in an echo of Kipling's fear, that the West had made a terrible mistake in forcing China into the modern world through violence:

Do you not know that we have a genius for mechanics? Do you not know that there are in this country four hundred millions of the most practical and industrious people in the world? Do you think it will take us long to learn? And what will become of your superiority when the yellow man can make as good guns as the white and fire them straight? You have appealed to the machine gun and by the machine gun shall you be judged.[5]

But could these authors have been merely channelling the words of Wen Hsiang?

When China was forced to open up to European trade in the nineteenth century, the Qing rulers were also compelled to hand over responsibilities for import tax collection to the British. Some of the money went into the imperial treasury, but the bulk was syphoned off to pay for the fines, known as 'indemnities', the foreigners had levied on the Chinese empire for daring to resist their incursions. The European customs officials carried out their duties from grand neo-classical customs buildings in Canton, Hankou and the Shanghai Bund. At the head of this foreign bureaucracy was Sir Robert Hart, an Ulster-born Briton, who was Inspector-General from 1863 to 1908, an astonishingly long posting even by Victorian standards. In his memoirs of 1901, Sir Robert recounted a warning that Wen Hsiang, a senior imperial counsellor at the late Qing court, had issued to the Western states whose militaries had casually opened up China. 'You are all too anxious to awake us and to start us on a new road and you will do it,' said Hsaing. 'But you will all regret it, for once awaked and started we shall go fast and far – farther than you think – much farther than you want.'[6]

Ominous indeed. But did Wen Hsiang really say those words? Or might Hart, one of the early adopters of the term 'the Yellow Peril', have been recycling the most famous prophecy of all regarding China, reportedly expressed by Napoleon Bonaparte? The French emperor, according to legend, one day pointed at a large chunk of Asia on a map of the world and remarked: 'Let China sleep, for when the dragon awakes she shall shake the world.'

Of course, China resembled a beaten dog rather than Napoleon's mighty dragon throughout the first half of the twentieth century, for the country was ravaged by Japanese occupation and then civil war between the Nationalists and Communists. But fears of Chinese world domination soon came flooding back after Mao's forces finally seized power and consolidated their rule. In 1964 the US War Office produced a propaganda video titled *Red Chinese Battle Plan*. Above a soundtrack of menacing martial brass, the narrator tells of Mao's plan to 'divide and encircle, conquer'. The conclusion: 'Thus does militant Communist China and Mao Zedong see the day when Peking becomes the ideological centre of a world enslaved.' From the Yellow Peril to the Red Peril; the colours changed but the message remained the same.

Now we have the Chinese Capitalist Peril. A popular literary theme has emerged in recent years: Western leaders humbled before their Chinese counterparts. In *Super Sad True Love Story* the satirical novelist Gary Shteyngart depicts a future United States that is on the brink of economic collapse with its Chinese creditors weighing up whether to pull the plug or not. The scenario bears a similarity to the fictional opening passage of economist Arvind Subramanian's 2011 book *Eclipse*, which has a US President in 2021 applying for a bailout from the Chinese-run International Monetary Fund. To drive home the point, the book's cover features Barack Obama appearing to bow while shaking the hand of the former Chinese president Hu Jintao.

There's another striking act of imagination in a 2010 publication, *Why the West Rules – for Now* by Stanford historian Ian Morris. Unlike Shteyngart and Subramanian, Morris goes back, rather than forward, in time. He kicks off his ambitious global history of mankind with an imagined 'what-might-have-been' scene that involves Queen Victoria kowtowing before a victorious Chinese general at a London dockside. The historian Niall Ferguson dispensed with all the imaginary tropes and bluntly said what everyone was thinking in his 2012 television series on China: 'We're having to kowtow to new Asian masters.'[7]

'East is East and West is West and never the twain shall meet,' wrote Kipling. But there is a new truism for our own age, a formulation that no serious work of geopolitical punditry can be without: 'Power is shifting from west to east.' Those words, or some variation thereof, turn up in countless newspaper columns, think-tank reports and politicians' speeches. They are a stamp of intellectual seriousness, as seemingly necessary as the 'amen' at the end of a prayer. The same, somewhat elegiac, words grace dinner tables and saloon bars. It's a staple of Internet forums. The idea that the future belongs to China is one of our age's articles of conventional wisdom.

Investors and financial analysts sing from the same hymnbook. 'The nineteenth century belonged to England, the twentieth century belonged to the United States, and the twenty-first century belongs to China. Invest accordingly.' That was the advice of the world's most successful stock picker, Warren Buffett. And bankers and captains of industry, as we saw in the last chapter, have been duly queuing up to sound a fanfare for 'The Chinese Century'.

But it's more than a redistribution of economic power. We're told that China has imperial intentions too. According to the American political theorist Robert Kagan, China has 'a nineteenth-century soul'. This means the country is 'filled with nationalist pride, ambitions, and resentments, consumed with questions of territorial sovereignty.'[8] Stefan Halper, a former adviser at the Reagan White House, on the other hand, sees China's modern imperialism as driven less by ideology than by material considerations. To deliver economic growth sufficiently robust to legitimatize its domestic rule, he argues, the Communist Party has no choice but to 'exploit and co-opt' the rest of the world's natural resources.[9]

Either way, a new age of imperial struggle is envisaged. 'Imagine a rerun of the Anglo-German antagonism of the early 1900s, with America in the role of Britain and China in the role of imperial Germany,' warns Niall Ferguson.[10] Stephen King, chief economist of the bank HSBC, tells us that non-Western nations are 'beginning to enjoy their time in the economic sun',[11] dusting off Kaiser Wilhelm II's 1901 warning that Germany would not be denied its share of Africa's spoils by Europe's other colonial masters.[12] Juan Pablo Cardenal and Heriberto Araujo, two Spanish journalists, see China engaged in an 'unstoppable and silent world conquest'.[13]

Such fears have been legitimized by those at the summit of American politics. In a speech in Zambia in 2011 the former US Secretary of State Hillary Clinton insinuated that the Chinese are the 'new colonizers' of the African continent with their large investment programmes.[14] 'We saw that during colonial times, it is easy to come in, take out natural resources, pay off leaders and leave,' she cautioned.

That same year Human Rights Watch published a report chronicling 'brutally long shifts' imposed on the workers at Chinese-owned
copper mines in the country, which seemed to justify that image of
nineteenth century-style exploitation.

A headline in the *Daily Mail* newspaper spelled out the danger:
'How China's taking over Africa and why the West should be very
worried'. The author of the piece concluded that 'the people of this
bewitching, beautiful continent, where humankind first emerged
from the Great Rift Valley, desperately need progress. The Chinese
are not here for that. They are here for plunder. After centuries of
pain and war, Africa deserves better.'[15]

Just as Britannia sent out its sons to administer the British Empire
150 years ago, some believe China has secretly begun to seed the world
with its inhabitants. According to the *Forbes* writer Joel Kotkin, 'the
rise of China represents the triumph of a race and a culture. Indeed
for most of its history China's most important export was not silk
or porcelain but people. To measure the rise of the Sinosphere, one
has to consider not just China itself but … the "sons of the Yellow
Emperor".'[16] To Kotkin and others the fifty-million-strong Chinese
diaspora are merely the advance guard. It's all happening so fast.
Could it be that we're already part of this modern Chinese impe-
rium and we just haven't realized it yet?

THE NEOCOMMS

Yan Xuetong has a look of contempt in his eyes. 'You obviously
know very little about China' he tells me. My mistake has been to
ask the Dean of the Institute of Modern International Relations at
Beijing's Tsinghua University whether he thinks it conceivable that
China could one day launch a military intervention in Taiwan.

Taiwan, I'm firmly told, is a part of China, so China could no
more 'intervene' on the island than the US could intervene in
Hawaii or Britain could intervene in the Isle of Wight. Having put
me straight on that basic point, Yan, who is sitting next to me at a
dinner at the World Economic Forum in Davos, Switzerland, proceeds to describe to the rest of the table how he expects that, sooner
or later, China will be forced to engage in an overseas military expedition, perhaps in Africa, in order to protect its own citizens

threatened by an outbreak of local civil disorder. The Chinese public will demand it. And the leadership in Beijing, he says, will have the military means to respond. To listen to Yan Xuetong talk is to be left in no doubt that China has 'stood up'.

It was on 21 September 1949 that the world first received notice of this. Mao Zedong rose in front of China's constitutional convention in Beijing. The Nationalist forces of Chiang Kai Shek had fled to Taiwan. The long civil war was over. Now it fell to the preeminent leader of the Communists to articulate the historical significance of the moment. 'The Chinese have always been a great, courageous and industrious nation,' Mao told the delegates. 'It is only in modern times that they have fallen behind. And that was due entirely to oppression and exploitation by foreign imperialism and domestic reactionary governments ... Ours will no longer be a nation subject to insult and humiliation. We have stood up.'[17]

For many decades that boast rang hollow, in spite of Mao's obsession with catapulting China to superpower status. His economic incompetence cut off the country at its knees and plunged China into darkness. Now, after thirty years of spectacular growth in the wake of Mao's death in 1976, the world has started to look at those founding words of modern China in a new light. China really does seem to be rising to its feet at last.

What does this mean for the rest of the world? Nothing good, say many, pointing to an increasingly belligerent intellectual climate in China. In 1996 a group of Chinese academics produced a best-selling collection of polemical essays entitled *China Can Say No*. In its pages they argued that China was sufficiently economically developed to start imposing itself. The same clique followed that in 2008 with *Unhappy China*, which made the case for China to claim its rightful position on the world stage in even starker terms. 'With Chinese national strength growing at an unprecedented rate, China should stop self-debasing and come to recognize the fact that it now has the power to lead the world,' they wrote. In a direct challenge to foreign powers, they added: 'You can start a war if you have the guts, otherwise shut up!' Some have called these authors 'Neocomms' because, unlike the cautious technocrats on the Politburo, they think China should stand tall and proud on the world stage, just as the ultimate Communist strongman, Mao, wanted.

Neocomm pressure certainly appears to have injected some steel into China's foreign policy in recent years. China was blamed by the US for blocking a deal on a new global treaty to reduce carbon emissions at the 2009 United Nations summit in Copenhagen. Many interpreted this disagreement over carbon dioxide emission targets as a proxy battle in the larger struggle between the existing superpower and the 'challenger'.

There are other signs of assertiveness from Beijing. In 2010 Japan arrested the captain of a Chinese fishing boat for ramming a Japanese patrol vessel in the East China Sea. A few months later, China drastically cut its exports of rare earth metals to Japan. These materials are essential to Japan's high technology manufacturing sector and Tokyo accused China of engaging in an illegal act of economic retaliation.

China seems increasingly less concerned with global opinion. Despite a swelling chorus of international objections, Beijing has continued to sponsor some of the most repressive regimes on the planet, from North Korea and Burma to Iran and Zimbabwe. In Central Asia, China's leaders appear to have designs on leading a new axis of autocracy. The Shanghai Cooperation Organisation, which first met in the Chinese commercial capital in 1996, brings together China and a host of other human-rights-abusing states, including Russia, Uzbekistan, Kazakhstan and Tajikistan. In an echo of the days before the Sino-Soviet split of the 1950s, China in 2005 staged joint military exercises with Vladimir Putin's Russia. Beijing has been prepared to block multilateral action against rogue states when it feels Western powers are throwing their weight around. In 2012 China, along with Russia, vetoed a United Nations Security Council resolution to impose sanctions against Bashar Al-Assad's Syria.

China's military capacity is growing too. Defence budgets have been expanding at an average annual rate of 16 per cent each year for the past twenty years and some expect the level of spending to equal America's in cash terms some time in the 2020s. Beijing commands the largest armed force in the world, numbering three million personnel. It boasts modern fighter jets, a fleet of nuclear-powered submarines and long-range missiles. China's first aircraft carrier has entered service and Beijing is investing in stealth technology and probing the possibilities of space military capacity.

There is no shortage of potential local flashpoints. China has unresolved territorial and maritime border disputes with Vietnam, the Philippines, Japan and India. Full reunification with Taiwan, if necessary by force, is still official policy. And China's generals have been sounding increasingly assertive over all of these potential conflict zones in recent years.

Officials talk of the country's 'peaceful rise', but Deng Xiaoping, the man who reversed the country out of the dead end of Maoism, had a more ambiguous phrase: '*Tao guang yang hui*' – 'Hide your light and rise in obscurity'. Could China be biding its time for sinister reasons? Doesn't this pattern of behaviour, these chauvinistic intellectual currents, suggest that Beijing, with its expansionist soul, is secretly set on ruling the world? Aren't we seeing a nascent hegemon?

To give an answer it is first necessary to establish what these emotive phrases – rule the world, new hegemon – actually mean.

THE RISE OF CHANGST

It was the autumn of 2011 and China was being lined up to save the eurozone. European journalists were told that the then French President Nicholas Sarkozy, who was the chair of the G20 meeting of the world's most powerful nations, would soon be making a telephone call to his Chinese counterpart, Hu Jintao. The pliant Hu would, we were informed, agree to pump a hefty portion of Beijing's national savings into a European sovereign debt insurance scheme (which was so complex that not even the finest minds in Brussels were able to explain how it worked). 'Will China rescue the West?' asked the BBC's business editor. 'China to the rescue?' echoed *The Economist*. It never happened, of course. Hu had apparently not been informed of the French script in advance. And Beijing, in the end, decided that if the Europeans were not willing to take the financial risk of propping up their own currency, it wasn't for China to do so.

Aside from demonstrating the staggering chutzpah of Sarkozy and the desperation of the eurocrats, the episode symbolized a global shift in financial might. No one seemed to find anything outlandish in the notion of China bailing out Europe. Why would they? Everyone knows the Chinese are rich now. As a new economic superpower they can afford to extend credit to whichever corner of the planet they desire.

The reality of modern China belies such assumptions. The country is large, but it is also relatively poor. Adjusted for the differences in the purchasing power of the national currency, China could be the world's biggest national economy by 2017, overtaking the United States. But divide that vast economic output by an almost equally vast population and one has a picture of a country in which most of the population survives on relatively little. GDP per head in China was just over $9,000 in 2012. To put that in context, GDP per capita in America was $50,000 and in Britain it was $37,000. Even in the least wealthy eurozone nation, Greece, per capita GDP was $25,000, more than two and a half times larger than in China.[18]

Average annual disposable incomes in urban China in 2012 were just $4,000, and in rural China, where half the population still lives, people scuffled by on $1,300 – the price, roughly, of two and a half iPads in the US. On the United Nations' Human Development Index, which uses metrics such as life expectancy and education, China ranks 101st in the world. States such as Sri Lanka and Algeria, not renowned for their high levels of development, are judged wealthier and healthier. China has come a long way in recent decades, but it has an even greater distance to travel if it is to join the ranks of the 'rich' nations of the earth.

In spite of this, the fear of China's economic rise is palpable. A survey in 2012 found that nearly half of Americans believe China's growth will have a negative impact on the US economy.[19] It is common to hear China's economic growth presented as a 'challenge' to Western prosperity. 'While the world will have more, we will have less of it,' lamented a columnist in the liberal *Guardian* newspaper in 2012 in response to projections of the shape of the global economy in 2060 showing a larger China.[20] Such anxiety, what I earlier referred to as Changst, is rife in popular discourse.

This is misguided. It is generally unhelpful to think about countries as if they were individuals, but in this case such a thought experiment is useful. Imagine you had an unfortunate neighbour who managed to turn his life around and pull himself out of poverty. Does that harm your own standard of living? Does a better life for your neighbour and his family constitute a threat to your own family's prosperity? Most of us would answer in the negative and regard anyone who replied 'yes' as unreasonable and perhaps a little paranoid. Yet when we interpret rising incomes in China as something to be feared we have fallen prey to this peculiar mean-minded logic. Would we really be happier if Chinese living standards were not rising, but falling? Strip away all the clichés about 'power shifting to the East' and that is the rather ugly sentiment that underlies a great deal of our response to China's economic advance.

We were once more far-sighted. Politicians saw the beneficial global economic and security harvest to be reaped from drawing China out of its Maoist seclusion, starting with Richard Nixon in the early 1970s, when the anti-Communist American president stunned the world by visiting the Middle Kingdom. In the 1980s multinational firms from the US and Europe helped integrate China into the global economy by transferring capital, technology and managerial expertise to the country, just as their Victorian forebears had done in the late Qing and republican eras. In the opening-up period American and British universities eagerly trained Chinese students. Governments encouraged trade. Those were wise decisions precisely because they have helped to raise the living standards of the population and have integrated China into the world community. 'Trade freely with China and time is on our side,' said George Bush in 2000, explaining why engagement with a repressive regime can be preferable to isolation. The former president was right on that score. The pity now is that so many of us seem to regret the inevitable consequences of that positive economic engagement.

What about the detrimental impact of greater commercial 'competition' from China that politicians and pundits now frequently refer to? Isn't this one of the clear ways that China's rise really does harm us, as global capital and jobs are ineluctably sucked eastwards? The answer is no. While the supposed rising income threat is based on a perverse mean-mindedness, this idea is based on an economic fallacy. China's growth since its opening up has, it is true, been tremendously boosted by low-cost manufacturing. As a result, some manufacturing jobs in the West have indeed been lost and effectively exported to China (although the largest victims of the 'China price' have been other developing nations which had a niche in low-end manufacturing). But one must also weigh against such costs the considerable economic benefit to us of cheaper manufactured imports. Nations such as Germany, which has a specialism in precision engineering, have seen exports to China surge. Notwithstanding our habitual over-estimation of the size of the China market, there will indeed be plenty of other opportunities for firms to sell into China in the coming years, opportunities that will create jobs. Free trade is today as mutually beneficial as it ever was, even if some of us have lost faith in it.

China's economic catch-up does not constitute a threat to our living standards. In any nation, what drives up wages over the long run is domestic productivity growth, in other words, the amount of output per hour of work. As discussed previously, China can – and indeed must – increase its productivity so its income levels can continue to rise. But nothing that China does will prevent us doing exactly the same. Yes, we are likely to see the gap between our incomes and those of the Chinese fall since we cannot realistically hope to match China's 7 to 10 per cent annual growth rates, but history teaches us that relative economic decline is a far cry from pauperization. The British economy was overtaken in size by America in the 1870s, but Britons today are far wealthier than they were when Queen Victoria was on the throne. Why? Because Britain's economic productivity has risen in that time, enabling incomes and living standards to rise steadily.

But doesn't size matter in other ways? Will not China become the most influential nation state when it attains the status of the world's largest economy? Not necessarily. There is much more to economic leadership than a large GDP. Despite China's stellar growth its economy has produced no world-class technology companies capable of competing with the likes of Apple, Rolls-Royce or Sony. Lenovo and Haier, promising as they may be, are not yet in the same league. Chinese firms are cash rich and the state's sovereign wealth funds are looking to snap up Western firms, but China's home-grown state-owned enterprises are badly managed and grossly inefficient. They have a lamentable record of technological innovation. While the number of patents filed in China has risen, they have yet to bear any substantial fruit. Many filings seem to be attempts to scoop up government subsidies rather than genuine innovative breakthroughs.[21] If Chinese corporations were stripped of their state-protected monopolies, most of them would haemorrhage domestic market share to foreign competitors. This is not a business sector about to conquer the world. As the dissident artist Ai Weiwei has pointed out, the Apple iPad might be assembled in China, but it is impossible yet to imagine the device being designed there.

In any case, the economic shift of weight to China may not be as dramatic as is often assumed. According to the OECD, in 2011 the US made up 28 per cent of global output, China 17 per cent and the euro area 17 per cent. By 2030 it expects China to account for 28 per cent of global output, the US 18 per cent and the euro area 12 per cent. Its vision of 2060 is remarkably similar, with China accounting for 28 per cent of global output, the US 16 per cent and the euro area 9 per cent. If this forecast is accurate, the popular image of a Chinese economic colossus, outweighing the rest of the globe put together, begins to look overblown.[22]

And financial power? It is true that China's leaders have been talking in recent years about creating an alternative global reserve currency to the American dollar, and some large Western banks, sensing a commercial opportunity to profit from a new market, have been promoting the renminbi as that alternative. Yet this is likely to prove another fairy tale. Would global investors be happy to see their assets denominated in the Chinese currency while the workings of the monetary authorities in Beijing are opaque and the country's capital markets are closed to outside investors? To even spell out the question is to draw attention to how ludicrous the idea is. So long as China's financial system remains closed, most investors will keep their money in currencies they understand. In any case, China has floated this idea out of desperation rather than calculation. Beijing would welcome a new reserve currency because it has, as we saw in the last chapter, channelled such a huge amount of its surplus cash into dollar assets that are now slowly depreciating as the US currency falls relative to the renminbi.

WHERE'S THE CHINESE MOTOWN?

The American political scientist Joseph Nye made a lasting contribution to the study of international relations with his coinage 'soft power'. To Nye this is the ability of a nation to get its way in the world not through economic force or military threats (which are classic 'hard power') but through the attractions of its culture to people in every country on the planet. China has very little on this front to offer yet – and Beijing knows it. As the reformist former prime minister Wen Jiabao put it: 'China has a massive trade surplus, but a vast cultural deficit with the world.'

The leadership has been establishing hundreds of Confucius Centres in foreign states to promote Mandarin and export Chinese culture. While such initiatives are not worthless, the inescapable fact is that state-sponsored culture has nothing like the reach of the private variety. Motown and Hollywood are the American towns that have spread American music and film around the world, not Washington. China, of course, has its own domestic entertainment industries, but beyond the cinematic martial arts epics of Zhang Yimou, they have made very few international breakthroughs. And this is unlikely to change while the Chinese government censors its artists.

Beijing's urge to control its culture is as pronounced as ever. In 2012 the film director Lou Ye removed his name from his new film, *Mystery*, after the State Administration of Radio, Film and Television in Beijing took their scissors to the work shortly before release. Lou complained on his website: 'A lot of Chinese film directors avoid making films about the reality of life because of the risk of censorship ... No film is safe, no film investment is safe, no director's creation is safe.' Mo Yan was awarded the Nobel Prize for Literature in 2012, following the success of the French-based émigré Gao Xingjian in 2000, but Chinese novelists are subject to interference too. 'I can clearly feel the impact of censorship when I write,' says Murong Xuecun, the author of dark dissections of life in modern China. 'For example, I'll think of a sentence, and then realize that it will for sure get deleted. Then I won't even write it down. This self-censoring is the worst.'[23] The censorship is often overt too: according to the Independent Chinese Pen Center campaign group there are 143 Chinese authors in prison for dissent. It should scarcely need to be said, but cultural superpowers do not behave in this way.

Soft power also flows from political example. Much of the prestige of the US and Europe stems from the fact that so many people from around the world want to live in those countries. No matter how aggressively or recklessly certain developed states behave in the global arena, the West's open institutions and their relative lack of corruption have a powerful attraction. It is impossible to say the same about China under the Communist Party. Authoritarian government and mass censorship have little global appeal, except perhaps to a handful of tyrants looking for new repressive techniques. My dinner companion, the Neocomm Yan Xuetong, has argued on another occasion that in the twenty-first century 'the country that displays more human authority will win'. If this is the test, then China, under the present human-rights-abusing regime, has already lost and our intellectual fretting over the wider implications of China's belated economic catch-up represents an unwarranted loss of nerve in the power of the values of the open society.

As these pages have noted, we have a tendency to look into Chinese history to interpret the nation's present. But one, pertinent, lesson somehow never seems to be drawn. Before the middle of the nineteenth century China was the largest economy in the world. In 1820 it accounted for 30 per cent of the globe's economic output – more than Europe and the United States combined.[24] And yet in that era China's influence was barely felt outside of East Asia. Instead, it was the far smaller maritime powers of Europe that turned the world of mighty China upside down. Economic size does not automatically translate into hegemony. Unless China reforms, it is perfectly conceivable that the country could, once again, be the world's biggest economy while exerting only limited influence beyond its borders.

THE MINNOW AND THE WHALE

If the trumped-up scare story of an authoritarian China becoming a global hegemon is placed to one side, a narrower question comes into focus: how dangerous is the Beijing regime? Could it menace East Asia and suck the US, which has pledged to protect its allies in the region, into a regional conflict? Again, the alarm seems overdone. Even in its own backyard China is, at the moment, a military minnow compared to the US whale. Despite those double-digit increases in China's military budget in recent decades, American spending on its armed services in 2012 was still eight times larger.

The US budget was $700 billion in that year, against China's $143 billion. Even in relative economics terms, China's outlays were smaller, with the US spending 4.7 per cent of GDP on its military, against 2 per cent in China.

This is only one dimension of America's military superiority. The US has fifty formal military alliances around the globe and 500,000 troops stationed abroad. Washington intends to keep 60 per cent of its navy in the Pacific for the foreseeable future. In addition, Japan, Australia and South Korea all host American troops and bases. China's only formal allies are North Korea and Pakistan. On top of all this America has twenty times more nuclear warheads than China. There is a question mark over the capabilities of the Chinese military too. China might have three million soldiers, but few of its officers or troops have battlefield experience. China has not fought in a war since 1979, when it launched a punitive strike on Vietnam. Contrast that with the US, whose forces have seen action in the Balkans, Afghanistan and Iraq in the last fifteen years alone.

Like all insecure autocracies, the Chinese government is unpredictable. There are some paranoid hardliners close to the centre of power. Some senior military officers, in common with the academic Neocomms, have convinced themselves that the West, in particular America, is attempting to thwart China's economic rise. This is in spite of all the economic assistance China has received from outsiders in recent decades. Colonel Liu Mingfu, a senior officer in the People's Liberation Army, argues that a military conflict with the US is inevitable and says it will be the 'duel of the century'.

There is, however, no evidence that China seeks colonies abroad or that Beijing desires to project its military power to all the corners of the earth. China's conduct in Africa, which triggered Hillary Clinton's lurid warning about neo-colonialism, has been subject to a great deal of misrepresentation. Chinese investment in the African continent has certainly soared, rising from $100 million in 2003 to $12 billion in 2011, and China is suspiciously opaque about both the scale and purpose of its state aid programme. Yet, according to Deborah Brautigam, an American academic who has studied the role of Chinese companies in Africa in depth, these investments are not some kind of concealed territorial grab, but straightforward transactions: the Chinese build roads and factories in return for long-term commodity contracts. They often invest in Africa looking for a simple business return.[25]

In the late nineteenth century some ten million people in the Congo, which was under the control of Belgium's King Leopold II, were done to death through murder, starvation and disease.[26] If Congolese villagers failed to supply sufficient rubber to meet the quotas imposed by their colonial masters, squads of mercenaries were sent to slaughter them. The Belgian authorities demanded that these mercenaries cut off the hands of their victims to prove that their bullets had not been wasted. In German South West Africa, modern-day Namibia, at the start of the twentieth century the Second Reich perpetrated a genocide against the Herero and Nama people, with the rebellious cattle herders left to starve to death in the Omaheke Desert. Survivors were put in concentration camps and forced to perform slave labour.

What is taking place in Africa today, as Chinese investment flows in, cannot credibly be compared with the kind of barbaric treatment that Africans received from European states who insisted on 'a place in the sun' in the nineteenth century. Indeed, many African states have welcomed Chinese investment as a preferable alternative to Western aid. Certainly there is a case for careful scrutiny of Chinese firms' behaviour, and the abuses reported at Chinese-owned copper mines in Zambia should not be ignored. At the same time, it is worth noting that Human Rights Watch, in its report on those abuses of workers rights, censured the Zambian government for failing to enforce its own domestic labour laws. It is also telling that a 2012 BBC poll showed residents of African countries where China has heavily invested tended to be much more favourable to Beijing's economic rise than those of us in the West. Some 89 per cent of Nigerians and 75 per cent of Kenyans felt positively towards China's influence in the world, as compared with 42 per cent of Americans and 57 per cent of Britons. Those nations have trusted their own eyes instead of heeding Chinese whispers.

What China's rising African investment flows really underline is that Beijing's priorities are essentially domestic. Commodity scarcity at home, not an imperial ideology, has compelled China to venture abroad. Indeed, it is this resource poverty that lies, in part, behind Beijing's support for repressive regimes such as Iran and Sudan.

China needs their oil more than it needs the good opinion of our governments. In other words, Beijing's foreign policy can be seen as dictated by weakness, rather than strength.

THE ANGRY YOUTH

Li Jianli was beaten almost to death for driving the wrong sort of car. On 15 September 2012, Li, a fifty-one-year-old factory worker, got into his Toyota Corolla in the city of Xi'an along with his wife and son and set off to look at some apartments they were considering buying. When they reached the city centre the family was engulfed by an angry mob. The crowd surged around the car and some proceeded to smash it with steel bars. Li got out and pleaded with them to stop. In doing so, he made himself a target. One of the thugs battered him about the head with a metal bar, leaving Li slumped against the back of a white van with blood pouring from his skull. By the time he reached hospital, Li was partially paralysed.

Li Jianli was attacked for just one reason: he was driving a Japanese-manufactured car. The attack in Xi'an was merely the foulest of many foul incidents that took place in eighty-five cities across China that month. Mobs rampaged through the streets attacking any 'Japanese' target they could find. Factories were looted, shops trashed and vehicles vandalized. The violence was sparked by a flare-up in a long-running dispute between China and Japan over the sovereignty of some tiny, uninhabited, rocks in the East China Sea known by the Chinese as the Diaoyus and by the Japanese as the Senkakus.

Episodes like the attack on Li Jianli, understandably, raise questions: How nationalistic are the Chinese people? Even if the regime's priority is stability at home rather than expansion abroad, could popular sentiment force the party chiefs of Beijing into a military confrontation with a neighbour? Many point to an ominous trend. Under the rule of Mao Zedong and Deng Xiaoping nationalist demonstrations were rare in China, but such eruptions of popular anger have become increasingly common over the past fifteen years. In 1999 there were hysterical anti-American protests in Beijing after the accidental NATO bombing of the Chinese embassy in Belgrade during the Balkan conflict, which killed three Chinese journalists.

Protestors tried to burn the US consulate in Chengdu. Many foreigners working in China were stunned by the popular rage that
the incident inspired and the conviction of many Chinese that the
bombing must have been deliberate. The sceptical tone of one letter,
published in the *Guangming Daily*, the newspaper which had employed two of the dead journalists, was typical. 'I believe that we
should stop calling NATO's bombing of our embassy a "barbarous
act" – a "terrorist act" would be more appropriate,' it said. 'Something "barbaric" stems from ignorance, but American-led NATO's
despicable act was clearly premeditated ... This was a terrorist attack
through and through.'[27]

There was a further burst of rage two years later when an un-
manned American surveillance plane collided with a Chinese jet
over Hainan Island, killing the Chinese pilot. The Japanese were
targets of popular protests in 2005 when Tokyo approved a school
textbook that downplayed Japanese war crimes in China in the
1930s and 40s. There were yet more outbreaks of anti-foreign resentment when the Olympic torch relay through the streets of Paris and
London before the 2008 Beijing Olympics was disrupted by pro-
Tibet protests. Netizens organized a boycott of Chinese branches of
the French supermarket chain Carrefour in retaliation.

Dissent from outraged nationalism seems to be an invitation to
abuse. That same year, 2008, Wang Qianyuan, a twenty-one-year-old
Chinese girl who was studying at Duke University in North Carolina,
attempted to mediate during a face-off between pro-Tibet protestors
and Chinese students on campus. When footage of her attempted
peace-making was posted on the Internet, Wang was branded a 'race
traitor'. Nationalist netizens published the address of Wang's family
in Qingdao and encouraged others to intimidate them.

The nationalists are getting younger too. Fen Qing or 'angry
youth' are an increasingly common feature of Chinese life. These
young men and women, most of them born after 1990, are intensely
sensitive about perceived slights to China by other nations and tend
to advocate violence as a response. It's frequently said that these
young hotheads scare even the Communist Party, reflected in the
fact that officials have issued public pleas for calm when demonstrations have threatened to get out of hand.

Yet this image of a virulently nationalistic and mindlessly aggressive

Chinese population is one more misleading caricature. There are many people in China who deplored the behaviour of the violent anti-Japanese rioters in 2012. During the disturbances in Xi'an one public-spirited man stood by the roadside holding a homemade placard warning drivers of Japanese-made cars to turn back to avoid being attacked. His action was applauded online. And the assault on Li Jianli unleashed a deluge of condemnation from Chinese netizens. One commentator was keen that the foreign media should not assume the mobs were representative of all Chinese:

> Foreign reporters, when you cover anti-Japanese protests in various cities, can you please give up the use of terms that may hurt many innocent people by mistake, like 'residents in Beijing' and 'citizens of Shanghai'? Can you be more direct and accurate? Like 'hundreds of suspicious people in Beijing,' 'A great batch of dumb-asses in Shanghai,' 'A bunch of nutcases in Shenzhen.'

That netizen had a point. I live in London and would have been intensely irritated if, during the 2011 riots, outsiders had implied that everyone who resided in the British capital was committing arson on the streets, rather than recognizing those acts as the responsibility of a criminal minority.

The attacks on Japanese property by thugs in China in recent years are deplorable, but to interpret them simply as bursts of mindless rage is not especially helpful. There is a context that, while certainly not justification, does offer an explanation. Memories of the atrocities inflicted on the Chinese by the Japanese military during the Second World War are still vivid in China. My great-uncle recalls being close to starvation during the Japanese occupation of Guangdong as civilians were forced to flee the advancing forces of General Hideki Tojo by train. In 1937 the Japanese military slaughtered more than 250,000 people in the city of Nanjing, most of them civilians. Two army officers, Toshiaki Mukai and Tsuyoshi Noda, engaged in a competition to see which of them could behead the most Chinese. There was no attempt to hide this war crime. The headline in the Tokyo *Nichi Nichi Shimbun* newspaper on 13 December 1937 read: 'Incredible record – Mukai 106, Noda 105 – Both 2nd Lieutenants go into extra innings'.

My cousin works in a large Western hotel in Guangzhou where many Japanese business visitors stay. 'Relations are fine, we must be friends,' she told me. But she also added: 'What we cannot accept is if they try to deny what happened in the Second World War.' That does not seem such an unreasonable position. Consider what the reaction would be in Europe if the German government approved textbooks for use in schools that downplayed the atrocities of the Nazis in the Second World War. This is the equivalent of what Tokyo did in 2005. And what would happen if the German Chancellor Angela Merkel attended a memorial service at which Nazi war criminals were honoured, as Junichiro Koizumi did for their Japanese equivalents throughout his premiership in the 2000s when he visited the Yasukuni shrine in Tokyo? One suspects that the outrage of the world would be deafening. And would it not be justified too?

Some perspective is also needed when it comes to evaluating the Fen Qing. Shortly before the 2012 anti-Japanese riots I happened to be in Shanghai. In a noodle house on Nanjing South Road I got into a conversation with some cheerful students who turned out to be from my father's home province of Guangdong. The connection, I was proudly informed, as we slurped beef noodles, made us 'old kinfolk' or '*lao xing*'. But the connection looked in danger of becoming frayed when I mentioned that I couldn't understand all the fuss about the uninhabited Diaoyu islands. Why not, I wondered aloud, simply abandon them? Let neither side have them. Unthinkable, I was told. One girl who had taken the English name Helen told me that it was impossible for China to relinquish its territorial claim: 'It's important that China does not lose face.' Her friend, Cherry, agreed: 'It's as if someone takes over a part of your house. No one would be able to accept that.'

Were these representatives of the angry youth, I wondered? If they were, they didn't seem hugely animated. The Diaoyus weren't a subject that particularly interested the students. They preferred to talk about their desire to study abroad. I think the majority of Chinese young people are more like Helen and Cherry than those who go out to attack Corolla drivers, or the raging Fen Qing who fill Internet message boards with chauvinistic bile. The caricature of the Chinese as proto-Fascists, waiting to throw their support behind some sort of aggressive military adventure, is hard to recognize.

That said, there is no disputing the strength of patriotism in China, but to understand the nature of that patriotism one needs to be informed about China's history in recent centuries. We tend to assume that when China's leaders relinquished Maoism they created an ideological vacuum in the society, which they have desperately filled with aggressive nationalism. It's sometimes argued that Chinese anti-colonial sentiment is a product of a successful party propaganda campaign that began in the late 1980s, with school children being raised on the 'wolf's milk' of belligerently nationalistic history textbooks.

Those textbooks are certainly unhelpfully emotive when it comes to the nineteenth-century Opium Wars. As Yuan Weishi, a professor at Guangzhou's Zhongshan University, has pointed out, they paint China as a passive victim of imperial aggression, ignoring cases of Chinese collaboration with Europeans. Even so, it may be a mistake to interpret Chinese anti-colonial feeling as merely the consequence of state brainwashing.

In 1839 a Chinese official called Lin Zexu, whom we met briefly in the education chapter, destroyed stocks of Indian-grown opium that the British had imported into China in contravention of imperial law. The British navy, in response, undertook a punitive strike on old Canton. The Chinese forces were swiftly routed and the Daoguang emperor was compelled to allow Britain to import opium at will. The British also seized control of the island of Hong Kong. In 1840 the future British Prime Minister, William Gladstone (a man presumably uninfluenced by modern Chinese textbooks), put the case against his own country:

> A war more unjust in its origin, a war more calculated in its progress to cover this country with permanent disgrace, I do not know, and I have not read of ... [our] flag is hoisted to protect an infamous contraband traffic, and if it were never to be hoisted except as it is now hoisted on the coast of China, we should recoil from its sight with horror, and should never again feel our hearts thrill, as they now thrill with emotion, when it floats proudly and magnificently on the breeze.[28]

The Qing rulers of China had banned the sale of opium in their territory out of concern over its harmful social effects. The British state, under the influence of a merchant lobby, picked a fight and imposed the drug on Chinese markets by force. One can argue, as many Chinese do, that the Qing were foolish to attempt to insulate their country from European influence. But it is a strange leap to argue that Chinese isolationism justified the conduct of the British or the other European powers that piled into China after Britannia had kicked the door open. One defence sometimes still aired is that the British were merely meeting a demand for the drug in China. By this rationale the Mexican military would today be justified in launching a bombardment of American border towns on the grounds that cocaine is popular in America and US prohibition is damaging the bottom line of its drug cartels. Some of the Qing aristocracy were partial to opium, say the apologists. Do they seriously believe that international relations should be established on the principle that nations with hypocritical rulers can legitimately be invaded? In the end all this desperate rationalization demonstrates our own continuing state of denial when it comes to facing up to our colonial history.

China was never colonized in the manner of India or parts of Africa. Yet for most Chinese this is a distinction without a real difference. The Chinese state was forced to hand over territory and trading rights at gunpoint. And the state was subjected to a series of punitive expeditions by European, Japanese, American and Russian forces, including the one that looted and burned down the Summer Palace in 1860. Field Marshal 'Everything's all Sir Garnet' Wolseley's description of that event in his memoirs makes it clear this was an attempt by the British army to terrorize the population. 'A gentle wind carried to Pekin dense clouds of smoke from this great conflagration, and covered its streets with a shower of burnt embers, which must have been to all classes silent evidences of our work of retribution. I am sure it was taken as an intimation of what might befall the city and all its palaces unless our terms of peace were at once accepted.' Wolseley added: 'The great, the essential aim of our policy was to make all China realize that we were immeasurably the stronger, the more powerful nation.'[29]

Other European nations were keen to teach the Chinese the same lesson. German troops were dispatched to China to protect

Western citizens and commercial interests of the Second Reich after the Boxer Rebellion in 1899. Kaiser Wilhelm II addressed soldiers in the port of Bremerhaven on the North Sea as they prepared to set sail:

> When you come upon the enemy, smite him. Pardon will not be given. Prisoners will not be taken. Whoever falls into your hands is forfeit. Once, a thousand years ago, the Huns under their King Attila made a name for themselves, one still potent in legend and tradition. May you in this way make the name German remembered in China for a thousand years so that no Chinaman will ever again dare to even squint at a German!

The German troops lived up to this vile exhortation. Though they arrived too late to suppress the undoubtedly murderous Boxers, they behaved with extreme brutality in the Chinese countryside around Beijing. And everyone in Europe knew it. The Kaiser's reference to Attila in his speech was what won German troops the nickname of 'Huns' in the First World War. The soldiers of other nations were rapacious too. In the post-Boxer chaos, a French novelist and adventurer called Pierre Loti broke into the Forbidden City. 'It is fun to open cupboards and chests every day to explore the marvels here. I left home with a single suitcase. I will return with a huge load of baggage,' he bragged in a letter to his wife.[30] One does not need to be a frothing Fen Qing to feel distaste at such scenes. Historians have a tendency to suck their teeth, shake their heads and point out that China 'turned her back on the world' during the Ming Dynasty when the emperor banned overseas expeditions. Yet one can imagine many ordinary Chinese, at the end of the traumatic nineteenth century, wishing that the nations of Europe had been equally disposed to mind their own business.

There is another vital element in Chinese nationalism that the common view misses, namely its close historical association with the political reform movement. Liang Qichao was the cynosure of the reformist Chinese intelligentsia in the late Qing era, and what radicalized Liang was China's defeat by the modernized Japanese military in the one-sided war of 1895. The defeat, wrote Liang, had awoken the Chinese people 'from the dream of four thousand years'.

He studied European political philosophers and came to the conclusion that the power of industrialized Western nations flowed from their political constitutions. These countries were powerful because they were democracies.

The constitutional monarchy that Liang advocated would create individual rights and involve the public in determining the fate of the nation, but it would also put national defence at the heart of political life. Liang's rival, the republican dissident Sun Yat Sen, also built his programme around nationalism, making it one of his 'Three Principles of the People'. The nationalist–democratic connections grew stronger as the years went by. The student protests and intellectual flowering known as the May Fourth movement was sparked in 1919 by widespread anger at the post-First World War Versailles Treaty, in which European powers determined to hand over Germany's Chinese territories in Shandong to Japan, rather than returning them to China. The driving force behind May Fourth, Chen Duxiu, described why nationalism and democracy were both necessary for national salvation. 'We have to follow the times, and nationalism has truly become the best means by which the Chinese can save themselves,' he argued. 'To use this doctrine, the Chinese must first understand what it means ... contemporary nationalisms refer to democratic nations, not nations of enslaved people.'[31]

That ideological cord linking nationalism and political reform is as strong today as ever. Nationalists tend to advocate not only a more assertive foreign policy, but political liberalization too. In 1999, after the protests outside the American embassy in Beijing, Wang Xiaodong, one of China's Neocomm authors, denounced the state-controlled news channels for failing to report that the Chinese government had agreed to pay for damage sustained by the Beijing embassy building in the protests. Wang said that China needed a media that told the truth and a government that sought popular consent before making such concessions. He added, in a direct challenge to the Party, that people should have a right to vote out political leaders who failed to defend national interests. More recently, anti-Japanese protestors in 2012 in Guangzhou carried a banner that read: 'Turn fury into power. Desire political reform.' The Communist Party might well fret about street nationalism getting out of hand and undermining China's economy, but what terrifies the cadres still more is the prospect of being swept away by the nationalists' pro-democratic tendencies.

One nationalist blogger, Li Chengpeng, wrote recently of how he became disillusioned with his own government when he learned that schools that collapsed in the 2008 Sichuan earthquake, killing hundreds of children, had been constructed to poor standards due to the corruption of local government officials. Li called for a new kind of patriotism, one that put political reform at home first. 'Patriotism is about constructing fewer extravagant offices for the bureaucrats and building more useful structures for farmers,' he said. 'Patriotism is about drinking less baijiu [a Chinese spirit] using public money. Patriotism is about allowing people to move freely in our country and letting our children study in the city where they wish to study. Patriotism is about speaking more truth. Patriotism is about dignity for the Chinese people.'[32]

This is not to argue that Chinese nationalism is some wholly benign force. But one must understand its progressive dimension. It is also essential to recognize that there is a lively debate in China about the right way for people to exhibit their patriotism. Historian Yuan Weishi came to prominence in 2006 when he wrote an essay for *Freezing Point*, a supplement of the state-controlled *China Youth Daily*, in which he criticized Chinese school history textbooks. In that essay Yuan advocated a progressive and open-minded patriotism. 'It is obvious that we must love our country,' he said. 'But there are two ways to love our country. One way is to inflame nationalistic passions ... In the selection and presentation of historical materials, we will only use those that favour China whether they are true or false. The other choice is this: we analyse everything rationally; if it is right, it is right and if it is wrong, it is wrong; calm, objective and wholly regard and handle all conflicts with the outside.'[33]

The Communist Party's control of the school history curriculum and the regime's constant references to China's 'century of humiliation' will, no doubt, make it harder to attain the maturity outlined by Yuan Weishi. So will the fact that the regime is incapable of facing up even to its own history. The twin twentieth-century disasters of the Great Leap Forward and the Cultural Revolution are glossed over in school textbooks because they were the work of the Party. Yet there is no reason to believe a more mature and tolerant patriotism will forever be beyond the reach of the Chinese people. And there is no reason why the Chinese outlook must always be shaped by historic 'resentments', any more than those European nations that also suffered so grievously in the fires of the nineteenth and twentieth centuries. Like Russia, China must navigate the transition out of totalitarian Communism. Like India, it must come terms with the legacy of colonial violence. China faces steep challenges, but it is a mistake to imagine these challenges are unique.

COLONIAL DREAMS

In the meantime, we should attempt some honest introspection of our own. The constant talk and imagery of China 'ruling the world' betrays a mental universe still crowded with gunboats and pith helmets. Chinese investments in Africa, viewed through this prism, become not mutually beneficial trade agreements between equal nations but a colonial-style resources grab, a repeat of the behaviour of Belgians in the Congo, the Germans in South West Africa, or the British in Kenya. While we talk about protecting the 'liberal democratic order' our colonial fixation suggests that what is really worrying us is the prospect that China will have the opportunity to throw its weight around on the global stage in the manner of European states 150 years ago.

The endless talk of China becoming a new 'superpower' is just as revealing and out-dated. There is no doubt that America is influential and powerful, especially so since the implosion of the Soviet Union, but it hardly enjoys untrammelled power. The military quagmires of Afghanistan and Iraq have exposed the limits of America's aspirations to reshape the world in its own image through military might alone. Even with its massive economy and dominant military the US does not 'rule the world'. And, more to the point, nor will China. Nor will any nation over the coming century. The entire concept is an illusion in an era of nuclear weapons and rising equality between nations. If higher living standards in China – and also India, Brazil and Turkey – will help to dispel that illusion, so much the better. Economics has changed the world too. Unlike the old Soviet Union and the US, China and America are interdependent.

China manufactures a large proportion of US imports and the Chinese help to fund Washington's trade deficit.

Our fixation on nebulous concepts such as hegemony is dangerous because it distracts attention from the real geopolitical challenges of the century. With the end of the Cold War no great ideological differences over the economic future remain between the most powerful nations. China's Communist Party is Communist in name only. All of the world's major powers have a common interest in a host of areas, from counter-terrorism, to preventing nuclear proliferation, to security of global sea-lanes, to ensuring the stability of world trade and the robustness of global finance.

The Economist argues that China's economic rise has already made the rich world 'worse off' because the country's appetite for natural resources has pushed up global oil prices, making petrol more expensive.[34] That's one, somewhat selfish, way of looking at things. Another, more constructive, framing of the issue would be to interpret the higher fossil fuel prices as a market signal for all economies to develop alternative, sustainable, forms of energy, which will reduce the world's dependence on finite and polluting hydrocarbon resources such as oil.

Above all else, the world's nations have a mutual interest in environmental sustainability and preventing runaway climate change. China might be the world's largest national producer of carbon dioxide emissions, but its emissions per capita are a seventh of the US output. Only 3 per cent of the Chinese population owns a car. The biosphere simply cannot cope with a world in which every Chinese has the energy inefficient lifestyle of a twenty-first-century American ('a big car, a big house and Big Macs for all', as Thomas Friedman has put it).[35] The 2009 Copenhagen talks failed, but the urgency of the need for the nations of the world to cooperate to cap emissions and to develop new forms of low-carbon energy production has only intensified.

Runaway climate change would spell mutually assured ruin across the planet. Crop yields would collapse as average temperatures crept up, low-lying cities would be inundated by rising sea levels and the world would see hundreds of millions of environmental refugees. China is probably even more vulnerable in the early stages of global warming than Europe and America, since it needs to feed a fifth of the world's population with less than 10 per cent of its arable land. The Middle Kingdom occupies a region firmly in a global 'arc of instability' liable to suffer acute water shortages by 2025.

In the context of such planetary-scale challenges the concept of 'ruling the world' feels irrelevant. Western alarmists and Chinese militant nationalists who talk up the inevitability of armed confrontation are two cheeks of the same wobbling posterior, each seeming to justify the other's existence. In an era when the major threat is environmental collapse, it threatens to be truly disastrous if international relations become framed as a game of chess, a zero-sum exercise in which one player must win and one must lose.

This is not to say that our governments can afford to be complacent about the behaviour of the regime in China. The US and Europe should understand they are dealing with an inherently unstable autocracy. It is conceivable that desperate leaders in Beijing might, one day, take up arms in the East or South China Seas in order to distract public attention from some domestic scandal. Alternatively, they might feel too weak to avoid a conflict, with chaotic events forcing their hand. There is plenty of scope for accidents to happen. A collision between Japanese and Chinese vessels in the East China Sea has already created one spark in recent years. Responsible nations have no choice but to treat this danger as a fact of life – and to try to head off a conflict early, or end it through negotiation if they cannot.

Yan Xuetong may be right that threats to the lives of Chinese workers abroad will trigger a Chinese military intervention abroad. Public pressure could demand it. That is not so unusual. Exactly the same political demands weigh on Western leaders. The goal of true statesmen should not be to frustrate that impulse, but rather to channel it through the world's existing multilateral institutions such as the United Nations. There is already a platform to build on: China has more troops and police (1,870 in 2012) deployed on United Nations peacekeeping missions than the US, Russia and the UK combined.

Our challenge over the coming decades will be to break out of the mental chains of paranoia and to end the counterproductive obsession with inappropriate concepts such as hegemony. Fretting about the aggregate size of China's economy is an invitation not to thought, but to thoughtless fear. Jealousy makes no sense. How many of us would willingly swap a wealthy life in a small economy for a poor life in a large economy?

If we treat China like an enemy it is liable to become one. The mentality of a zero-sum world will become a self-fulfilling prophecy. We need to accept the inevitability of greater international equality and messy multilateralism if the challenges facing the peoples of all nations are to be properly addressed, never mind solved. The world needs to be saved, not ruled.

CONCLUSION

Sideways a mountain range, vertically a peak.
Far-near, soaring-crouching, never the same.
There's no way to tell the true shape of Lushan,
when you're in the middle of the mountain.

All Chinese school children learn this short verse by the eleventh-century poet, Su Shi. The subject matter is the country's most achingly beautiful mountain, the cloud-enveloped Lu, in Jiangxi province. But it's also a poem that invites the reader to contemplate the importance of perspective in life. As the chapters in this book have shown, our own perspectives on China have often been dramatically skewed over the centuries.

Why? Why do we frequently end up playing a game of Chinese Whispers, hearing distorted tales about the place and its people? Could it be that we so often get China wrong because it is not really China we're thinking about, but ourselves?

PENSIONS FOR PROSTITUTES AND
TAXES ON LAWYERS

The Portuguese explorer Mendes Pinto described the sixteenth-century China he encountered in his memoirs. And it was a strange world indeed that he presented. Sketching the country's social welfare, Pinto conjured up images of pensions for aged prostitutes financed by a levy on younger whores. He wrote of homeless shelters paid for by a tax on unscrupulous lawyers and crooked judges.[1] It's not a world that any historian of China would recognize – and with good reason. What Pinto had written was not a factual description of the Ming era but a satire on his own native Lisbon society. Like Jonathan Swift in *Gulliver's Travels*, with his descriptions of the petty squabbles of Lilliput and Blefescu, Pinto wanted to use a fantastical far-off land to mock institutions and mores at home.

Few have been quite so brazenly mendacious as Pinto, but it's nevertheless clear that some of the biggest China enthusiasts of earlier eras were really preoccupied with moral reform in Europe. The Jesuits, whose reports provided the only window into China for most Europeans until the nineteenth century, relentlessly talked up the country's merits for this very reason. According to the Spanish friar and China traveller Domingo Navarrete: 'It is God's special providence that the Chinese don't know what is done in Christendom, for if they did there would be never a man among them but would spit in our faces.' The trope of Chinese virtue and Western sin was, for a time, taken immensely seriously. The German philosopher Gottfried Leibniz wished that the Chinese would send missionaries over to seventeenth-century Europe to instruct the West in the ways of Confucian enlightenment.

A backlash against this Sinophilia was inevitable. In the *Further Adventures of Robinson Crusoe* in 1719, Daniel Defoe had his fictional hero travel to China whereupon he encountered 'a barbarous nation of pagans, little better than savages'. Nor was China the shining example of efficient government that the Jesuits asserted: 'All the forces of their empire, though they were to bring two millions of men into the field together, would be able to do nothing but ruin the country and starve themselves.'[2] As the China scholar Jonathan Spence has noted, Defoe was denigrating China primarily in order to stick up for Britain.

The push and pull went on. Later in the eighteenth century, Voltaire's boundless love of all things Chinese went hand in hand with his anti-clerical agenda. By presenting priest-less China as the apotheosis of good government he was propagandizing for his own revolutionary programme for France. Similarly, when John Stuart Mill, in the following century, described China as a 'stationary' society he was hoping to make the flesh of the English creep over what would happen if they succumbed to illiberal Toryism.

The artificiality was glaring. Neither Leibniz nor Defoe nor Voltaire nor Mill ever went to China to see with their own eyes the nature of the country they were dismissing or venerating. And nor did they, one suspects, have any burning aspiration to do so, because their primary concern was not to bear witness to the flowery empire at the far end of the earth but to bring about change in their own society. The China of their imaginations was a kind of proxy battleground for the real, more important, war.

A pacifist British scholar called Goldsworthy Lowes Dickinson took this approach to its logical conclusion. In the aftermath of the 1901 Boxer Rebellion, when anti-Chinese sentiment in the West was at its height, Lowes Dickinson published a series of letters purporting to be from a Chinese visitor to the West called *Letters from John Chinaman*. The author acidly rejects the idea that Chinese civilization was inferior. Instead he presents a glowing image of a land where 'a man is born into precisely those relations in which he is to continue during the course of his life'. The Chinaman 'has both the instinct and the opportunity to appreciate the gifts of Nature, to cultivate manners, and to enter into human and disinterested relations with his fellows'. This was, of course, a utopian fantasy, not late nineteenth-century China, which was actually a pretty Hobbesian place to live, with the majority of the population enduring a brutish and short existence. Lowes Dickinson was, however, really launching an assault on what he saw as the debased morality and self-satisfaction of his own society. We might sympathize with his ends, but the fact is that he created a laughable caricature of China.

Even when foreign thinkers actually visited China and wrote under their own name, intellectual honesty was sometimes a casualty. In his 1920 lecture tour of the country, Bertrand Russell found a place that appealed to his pacifist convictions. 'If they are not goaded into militarism, they may produce a genuinely new civilization, better than any that we in the West have been able to create,' the philosopher suggested. Looking back, this was an odd observation because at the very time Russell was visiting, China was fragmenting into a patchwork of feuding warlord fiefdoms, with military commanders holding sway over huge territories of the dysfunctional new republic.

Russell went on: 'If the Chinese were to adopt the Western philosophy of life, they would, as soon as they had made themselves safe against foreign aggression, embark upon aggression on their own accounts ... They would exploit their material resources with a view to producing a few bloated plutocrats at home and millions dying of hunger abroad. Such are the results which the West achieves by the application of science.' This gives the game away. The philosopher, like Lowes Dickinson, while ostensibly speaking about the virtues of China, was really attacking the spiritual and moral shortcomings of his own native corner of the world.

WHAT WE TALK ABOUT WHEN WE TALK ABOUT CHINA

Our habit of using China to talk about home is stronger than ever. In 2012 a political attack advert created by the Republican Senate candidate for Michigan, Peter Hoekstra, was shown at half time during the televised Super Bowl. A young Chinese woman was pictured cycling down a causeway between two rice paddies. She stops, looks into the camera, and addresses Hoekstra's Democratic opponent Debbie Stabenow: 'Debbie spend so much American money, you borrow more and more from us. Your economy get very weak. Ours get very good. We take your jobs. Thank you Debbie "Spend It Now".'

Some American liberals pointed out that the setting of the advert – with conical hat-wearing rice planters toiling in the background – looked more like Vietnam than China. But perhaps they were missing the point. For the purpose of Hoekstra and his team was not to give a true representation of China. Their goal was to spread alarm about supposed government profligacy in America.

When the advert prompted a backlash for its racial stereotyping, in particular the fact that the Chinese woman spoke in broken English, Hoekstra tried to backtrack. His spokesman said: 'You have a Chinese girl speaking English, I want to hit on the education system, essentially. The fact that a Chinese girl is speaking English is a testament to how they can compete with us, when an American boy of the same age speaking Mandarin is absolutely insane, or unthinkable right now.'[3] What this (rather feeble) defence inadvertently hammered home is that the advert was really about America, not China.

Hoekstra's mistake, however, might have been that he wasn't subtle enough. Politicians on the right have become adept at using China as a covert weapon in their anti-state spending, pro small-government crusade. The Republican candidate in the 2012 US Presidential election, Mitt Romney, campaigned as an opponent of China, bashing Beijing for undervaluing its currency in order to poach American manufacturing jobs. Yet the former private equity baron also warned that China was becoming a better place to do business than America. 'When I heard the head of Coca-Cola say that the business environment in America is less hospitable than the business environment in China, I knew we had a problem,' he fretted at a fundraising meeting on the campaign trail.

In a similar vein, Kwasi Kwarteng, a politician in the UK Conservative Party, tells us that Britons suffer from a 'diminished work ethic' and must be prepared to work harder to compete successfully with China. He described how his eyes were opened to this inescapable reality on a trip around a Chinese factory. 'They have to do a certain job in an hour and if they do it in 58 minutes they get two free minutes in which they can sit down and talk to their friends,' recounted the seemingly admiring Kwarteng.[4]

The message resonates down from the top. At the 2012 Conservative Party conference David Cameron warned that the world was divided into countries, like China, that are 'on the rise', and countries like Britain that are 'on the slide'. The Prime Minister told delegates:

> What do the countries on the rise have in common? They are lean, fit, obsessed with enterprise, spending money on the future – on education, incredible infrastructure and technology. And what do the countries on the slide have in common? They're fat, sclerotic, over-regulated, spending money on unaffordable welfare systems, huge pension bills, unreformed public services. I sit in those European Council meetings where we talk endlessly about Greece while on the other side of the world, China is moving so fast it's creating a new economy the size of Greece every three months. I am not going to stand here as Prime Minister and allow this country to join the slide.[5]

Note what characterizes 'sliding' countries in the Prime Minister's mind: regulation of business, welfare spending, public services. The implied solution, therefore, to Britain's economic decline? Deregulate the private sector further, erode welfare provision and privatize public services. It's a message enthusiastically backed up by pundits and business executives who rarely miss an opportunity to tell us that Western nations must overhaul their economic model or find themselves trampled into the dust by low-tax Asian competitors.

One would never guess from the remarks of Romney that entrepreneurs in China find it so difficult to get loans from the country's state-controlled banks that they have been forced to seek capital from a burgeoning illegal lending market. Similarly, Kwasi Kwarteng seems oblivious to the growing number of illicit strikes in Chinese factories or the multiplying demands of workers across China's coastal factory belt for higher pay. Likewise David Cameron appears unaware that much of China's 'incredible infrastructure' lies unused and that this country 'on the rise' has pumped up an investment bubble of potentially disastrous proportions. One suspects that they care less about the reality of China than their own domestic vision for economic reform.

The same distortion is taking place when politicians and pundits laud Chinese educational institutions. Like the Jesuits before them, what these modern evangelists really seem to want is moral reform at home. Andreas Schleicher, the OECD statistician whom we met in the education chapter, remarked approvingly after a trip to China that, as he put it, the most impressive building in a poor town is likely to be a school. In the West, according to Schleicher that status would go to a shopping mall. 'You get an image [in China] of a society that is investing in its future, rather than in current consumption,' he said.[6]

What Schleicher failed, however, to mention was the fact that China still spends a smaller share of its GDP on education than any developed nation. Nor did he appear to notice that in the 2008 Sichuan earthquake, as we have seen, a series of schools collapsed crushing hundreds of pupils to death as they studied. These 'most impressive buildings' were made of substandard concrete because corrupt officials and builders had apparently compromised safety standards to cut their construction costs. Locals called them 'tofu buildings' because they crumbled under pressure like cubes of bean curd. Then again perhaps this is to miss the point, because Schleicher was not really talking about the Chinese education system so much as bemoaning what he regarded as the Western world's culture of decadent consumerism.

The habit of using China as a proxy battleground for domestic struggles is by no means the exclusive preserve of right-wingers and cultural conservatives. Progressives are just as liable to use the China spectre to push their own agenda. Recall the 2005 report by America's respected National Academy of Sciences, *The Gathering Storm*, which made quite an impact with its eye-catching warning that emerging economies, such as China, were catching up and, in some respects, overtaking America in their scientific research output. A follow-up report in 2010 was even more alarming, pointing out that China is now second in the world in its publication of biomedical research articles, having recently surpassed Japan, the United Kingdom, Germany, Italy, France, Canada and Spain. What these reports neglected to mention is that Chinese universities operate a bonus system whereby academics are rewarded based on their publication volumes, encouraging output at the expense of quality. It also glossed over the fact that, as we saw, the number of Chinese academic papers cited by other scientists is much less impressive than the publication rate. Why the omission? Again one suspects it's because the objective of the great and the good of American academia was not to perform a serious analysis of Chinese academic standards but to lobby for more public investment in the domestic science base. The authors spoke about China, but what they were really talking about was America.

The left sometimes brandish the China card too, although the policies they recommend in response to the competition from the East are the opposite of those on the right. Rather than smaller government, they want more state intervention. I recently had lunch with a former British trade unionist who lamented the inability of the government to approve long-term infrastructure projects. 'Say what you like about the Chinese government, but when Beijing says it wants something to be built, it gets built,' he told me, with a note of envy in his voice.

It's an increasingly familiar refrain. Charles Kupchan of the Council on Foreign Relations argues that: 'When up against [Chinese] state capitalism ... the Western democracies have little choice but to engage in strategic economic planning on an unprecedented scale. State-led investment in jobs, infrastructure, education and research will be required to restore economic competitiveness.'[7] Yet, as we

have seen, China's brand of state capitalism has resulted in dangerous economic distortions and waste. But that doesn't matter because
what Kupchan and my lunch companion are really concerned about
is securing more public infrastructure spending at home.

On and on it goes. Because China now has a space programme,
America, we're told, must invest in this sector too or get left behind,
stranded ignominiously on Earth. Dale Ketcham, Director of the
Spaceport Research & Technology Institute of the University of
Central Florida, cites the history of Admiral Zheng He's naval voyages in the Ming Dynasty to stress the need to keep spending on
space exploration:

> They went all over East Africa, India. They dominated the Indian
> Ocean. It was a stunning achievement, well before Columbus.
> And then they stopped. The Chinese sort of slipped into irrele-
> vance and weakness so when the colonial powers came they were
> easily dominated. There's a sense within the American mind-set
> that we've had our own grand fleets and had significant accom-
> plishments. If we stop exploring, if we pull back, there's a basic
> sense that that would indeed signal our decline.[8]

Who could fail to be swayed by such a traumatic image of America
not only falling behind China today but also sinking into the economic and moral stagnation of the Ming Dynasty?

PROJECTED ON A CHINESE SCREEN

Browsing this catalogue of hyperbolic fear and praise, one might be
tempted to conclude that the way we talk about China is utilitarian;
that the country is only ever used as a lever with which to gain domestic political advantage or lobby for public funds. Although that's
sometimes the case, there's also something more psychologically
complex taking place too. China looms so large in our imagination
not only because it's useful, but also because the country offers a
screen on to which we can project our dreams and nightmares.

First the dreams. The Jesuit missionaries of the sixteenth century
projected China as a country in which men like them were promoted as councillors to emperors, ignoring (or ignorant of) the fact

that the Confucian imperial exam system was, in truth, riven with corruption and nepotism. Physiocrats projected China as a state that subscribed to their economic theories on the transcendental value of land. That tradition continues today. The idolization of China's economy has reached fever pitch among business executives and pundits. Yet, as we have seen, the portrait they paint of a free-market wonderland is as divorced from reality as the Physiocrats' vision of China as a harmonious land governed by philosopher kings.

Many executives of Western multinationals today project China as a new capitalist Jerusalem, a land of eternally high GDP growth, the biggest untapped consumer market on the planet, the place where the state sees its function as to help the private sector to make money. Occasionally they will come up against an awkward fact that challenges this dream – reports of baby milk formula adulterated with a harmful chemical by a Chinese manufacturer, for instance, or a massive shopping mall that has been empty for eight years – but these are seen as tests of faith to be overcome. They cannot be permitted to interfere with the glorious vision.

Then there are the China nightmares. Montesquieu, in the seventeenth century, reviled China as a country where there reigned 'a spirit of servitude'. The Victorians projected China as a place where intellectual progress had come to a pathetic stop. What they were doing was imagining China as the very antithesis of everything they wanted their own nations to be: free, vigorous and expansive. One can see that same tendency in the work of Karl Wittfogel in the 1950s. As we have seen, this refugee from Nazi Germany presented ancient China as a despotism strikingly similar to a twentieth-century totalitarian state. Wittfogel, following a long tradition, glossed over the evidence and projected the nightmare.

China has been Caliban's mirror too. The most common nineteenth-century Western complaint about China was the country's overweening superiority complex. A British missionary, Donald Matheson, said that the cause of the Opium War had not been the Chinese state's resistance to the import of the stultifying drugs, but rather 'the arrogant assumption of supremacy over the monarchs and people of other countries claimed by the Emperor of China for himself and for his subjects'.[9] It wasn't just a British complaint. The sixth US president, John Quincy Adams, also placed the blame for the Opium War on 'the arrogant and insupportable pretensions of China, that she will hold commercial intercourse with the rest of mankind not upon terms of equal reciprocity, but upon the insulting and degrading forms of the relations between lord and vassal.' But it was Britain that took gravest offence. The prime minister, Lord Palmerston, bristled at Chinese 'assumptions of superiority' shortly before dispatching some gunboats to blast some sense into them.

All this talk of arrogance comes across like psychological projection in the sense described by Sigmund Freud – attributing one's own unacceptable impulses to another. For in a contest between China and Britain one might argue that Britannia had the more exalted sense of its own superiority. When Lord Macartney sailed to China to persuade the Qianlong emperor to open his kingdom to trade in 1792 it apparently came as an immense surprise to the British delegation that the mechanical contraptions, from clocks to telescopes, that were rolled out to impress the hosts did not lead to an instant acknowledgement from the Chinese of the Western nation's technological ascendancy.

When asked to kowtow before the Qianlong emperor, Macartney was affronted by presumption enshrined in the request and, seemingly oblivious to the irony, responded: 'I will get on one knee before my king and two before my God, but the notion of a gentleman prostrating himself before an Asiatic barbarian is preposterous.'

There's another kind of projection today. As we have seen, China is often presented as an aggressive and nationalistic monster, intent on taking over the world. Here is a short list that gives a flavour of the books about China that have been published over the past fifteen years: *The Coming Conflict with China*; *Hegemon: China's Plan to Dominate Asia and the World*; *The China Threat*; *Showdown: Why China wants war with the United States*; *Red Dragon Rising: Communist China's Military Threat to America*; *Beware the Dragon: China – 1,000 years of Bloodshed*. One would imagine from this flood of paranoia that China had some uniquely terrible history of colonial aggression. True, China has been no pacifist Shangri La through its history, but it wasn't the Middle Kingdom that sailed to the other side of the world in the nineteenth century, blasted its way in to another culture, and proceeded to carve up a distant empire into spheres of influence. That was us.

When our political leaders solemnly warn of China's 'new coloni-
alism' in Africa, when economists assert that Beijing wants to claim
its 'place in the sun', and when writers speak of the day when Beijing
'rules the world', isn't it them, rather than the 'historically minded'
Chinese, who are unable to escape the past? One might describe it
as an intellectual pathology. We keep getting swept up by the same
currents of thought, the same foggy dreams and fears, that have
always attended our encounters with China. Most of us aren't even
aware when we're mouthing some hoary old nonsense first spouted
by a Jesuit missionary five hundred years ago, or the paranoid fantasies of Victorian thriller writers, or even, on occasion, some tenet
of Maoism.

WHAT FATE HAS IMPOSED

We're so stubborn. As these pages have attempted to show, our view
of the Middle Kingdom over the centuries has been characterized by
an impressive immunity to the facts. Our old friend Montesquieu
in the eighteenth century described China as 'the place where the
customs of the country can never be changed'.[10] The American
sociologist, Gerrit Lansing, came to that very same conclusion in
1882: 'the Chinese have remained the same, generation after generation and century after century, content always to live and die in
the conditions that Fate has imposed upon them.'[11] Compare that
with the Shanghai advertising man, Carl Crow, in the 1930s, who
remarked, 'there is a permanence about the life and institutions of
China'.[12] Finally, in 2009 British author Martin Jacques described
how 'China has experienced huge turmoil, invasion and rupture but
somehow the lines of continuity have remained resilient, persistent
and ultimately predominant.'[13]

As we have seen, this four-hundred-year-old stereotype of stasis is
quite wrong. In the time of Montesquieu, China's spiritual life had
been revolutionized by the arrival of Buddhism from India, men had
been forced to wear their hair in a long pigtail by the country's new
Manchu overlords and the custom of female foot-binding was growing ever more popular among the gentry. When Lansing set pen to
paper, the introduction of new crops from the Americas had allowed
the population to triple in size, a cult led by an unhinged Christian

convert had set fire to much of the country and a 'self-strengthening' movement was gathering pace as the Qing rulers tried to modernize their military in order to deflect the incursions of predatory European powers. When Crow sat down to sketch the nation, the Chinese had overthrown their empire, outlawed the barbaric mutilation of girls' feet and cut off their demeaning pigtails. By 2009, when Jacques offered his view, China had been plunged into Communism and then a form of managed capitalism. Few nations have experienced a more profound and often agonizing cycle of social and institutional overhauls. Yet in our eyes China seems destined to remain a land frozen in time, a place, like my ancestral village of Jung Wo Lei in Guangdong, in which nothing ever changes.

The idea that an insatiable China is swallowing up the world's natural resources might seem like a fresh thought, prompted by the country's economic renaissance in recent decades. The Zambian economist Dambisa Moyo in 2012 asked: 'In a zero-sum world, what will happen if China wins the race for resources? Other countries seem to be asleep while China is making a concerted effort.'[14] The Spanish journalists Juan Pablo Cardenal and Heriberto Araujo, on the same subject of China's influence in the developing world, have written that 'we are facing a slow but steady conquest destined to change the lives of every one of us and which is most likely already laying the foundations for the new world order of the twenty-first century: a world under Chinese leadership'.[15]

In reality, this theme of Chinese resource imperialism has been around for many decades. In 1965 one political scientist warned that China's 'movement against the Indochinese peninsula and the Southeast Asian Extension islands is clearly directed toward the acquisition of the abundant minerals and agricultural wealth of these areas, and toward a commanding position in Asia, the Pacific, the Middle East, and Africa.'[16] Indeed, going further back, we find the theory that there are too many Chinese to be sustained by their land's native resources was put forward by Thomas Malthus in his 1798 *Essay on Population*. China, said the Anglican clergyman, was 'more populous in proportion to its means of subsistence than any other country in the world'.[17] This was why, according to Malthus, the Chinese people had been regularly culled by nature's famines. One might have hoped that the fact that China's population has quadrupled since Malthus's day would have discredited mechanistic theories of the interaction of resource supply and population growth, but it seems not.

We continue to nurse an ancient fear that a vast Chinese population will inevitably overspill its borders and invade the rest of the world. In the eighteenth century the French Jesuit missionary Joseph Premare warned in a letter home from Canton that: 'The country, however extensive and fertile it may be, is not sufficient to support its inhabitants. Four times as much territory would be necessary to place them at their ease.'[18] In a 1910 dystopian fantasy about China, Jack London imagines the immense Chinese nation 'spilling over the boundaries of her Empire ... just spilling over into the adjacent territories with all the certainty and terrifying slow momentum of a glacier'.[19] Such ideas were still popular in the 1960s. In that decade an American geographer, Preston James, was haunted by similar nightmares to London's fifty years earlier, warning that 'China is one of those unhappy countries doomed to choke on its own vast numbers.' James went on:

> If China is thrown into convulsions by the ultimate despair of millions of individuals, and if these individuals become aware of the geographic setting of their misery, what is likely to be their avenue of escape? Northwards, through Manchuria, into thinly-populated eastern Siberia? Southward, through southeast Asia, perhaps even into thinly-populated Australia? Westward, through Inner Asia, along the ancient routes of invasion, and even into Europe?[20]

A Chinese invasion seems ever imminent in our minds.

THE CHINESE MIND

Just as unshakeable down the centuries have been our preconceptions of the character and mores of the Chinese. American author Boyé Lafayette De Mente writes guidebooks for Western businessmen venturing into Asian markets, which have included such titles as *Asian Face Reading* and *Samurai Strategies*. In his 2009 publication, *The Chinese Mind*, De Mente described some 'traditional

Chinese ethics' that foreigners should be primed to expect: 'People [give] whatever answer they believe is right for the circumstance at hand – that will be the least likely to get them into trouble or simply inconvenience them in some way.'[21] In other words, steel yourself to encounter dishonesty. Are the Chinese always to be regarded as rather immoral?

Or perhaps not immoral, but rather adherents to fundamentally *different* moral values. Sir Martin Sorrell is the boss of the world's biggest advertising agency, WPP. In 2005 he wrote how 'we in the West tend to believe that our value system and beliefs are the same as theirs, that what we consider good or bad is the same for them. It is not necessarily so, and gaining a deeper understanding of the Chinese mind is exceedingly important.'[22] One can hear an echo, there, of Jack London, who a century earlier told us 'their thought-processes were radically dissimilar'. According to London: 'The Western mind penetrated the Chinese mind but a short distance when it found itself in a fathomless maze.'[23]

Again and again, the same themes keep returning. The idea of Chinese 'inscrutability' remains as popular as it did in the days of Rudyard Kipling. 'Thirty years ago, only its [China's] inscrutable leaders were recognized in the West,' remarked Angus Fraser of the BBC in 2010.[24] In 2012 Philip Stephens of the *Financial Times* saw the new president Xi Jinping offering 'a perfect definition of inscrutability'.[25]

Chinese child cruelty retains its grim fascination for us too. In the seventeenth century, Friar Domingo Navarrete described to his Western audience how he saw the parents of an unwanted baby girl watch the infant die and how 'her little feet and arms drawn up, her back upon hard stones in wet and mud ... she that had pierced my heart with her cries could make no slightest dent in the bowls of those tigers'.[26] Inspiration, perhaps, for the publishers of Amy Chua's memoir about how she terrorized her children in true Chinese style. In 2010 they thought up a perfect name to grab readers: *Battle Hymn of the Tiger Mother.*

It's almost as if we are afraid of relinquishing the fantasies and the stereotypes. Take the phrase that to many of us sums up the Chinese ability to think in centuries: 'It's too early to say.' This is supposedly how Zhou Enlai responded to Richard Nixon in 1972 when the

American president asked for the urbane Chinese premier's view on the ramifications of the French Revolution. This tale has now been debunked. The state archives in Beijing, and also the testimony of a US official, show that Zhou believed Nixon had been asking about the impact of the French student uprising of 1968, not the execution of King Louis XVI and the storming of the Bastille, when he made his Sphinx-like remark.[27] In other words, his answer related to the events of only four years ago. But the myth of the Chinese who think in centuries lives on because it fits our preconceptions so exquisitely.

Or consider: 'May you live in interesting times'. It is not a phrase known in China. And yet it is endlessly asserted to be a timeless piece of Chinese wisdom. Why? Is it because it fits with our vision of the Chinese enigma?

MODERN NOT ANCIENT

As we have seen, there is a tendency to assume that the Chinese are in thrall to their ancient history. But often it seems we are the ones who are obsessed with the country's past. Communist leaders are forever presented as modern-day emperors. The Gao Kao is seen as a continuation of the old imperial examination. Some even interpret the one-child policy as a kind of updated infanticide. Even contemporary political anger in China has to be framed by outsiders in terms of imperial times. 'Ethnic revolts and protests against corruption helped bring down plenty of Chinese dynasties in the past; maybe they will do so again in the near future,' suggests Ian Morris, a historian at Stanford University.[28] In 1776 America gloriously cast off the shackles of British imperialism through a unilateral declaration of independence. In 1789 France set out on a great revolution that swept away feudalism. Both were landmarks in global modernization, significant chapters in the book of human liberty. And China? All China can look forward to, apparently, is yet another peasants' revolt.

Corruption in China is, we assume, a manifestation of the traditional concept of 'guanxi', whereby a person is beholden to family networks. 'It goes back thousands of years and is based on traditional values of loyalty, accountability, and obligation,' proclaims

Bloomberg's *BusinessWeek* magazine.[29] Yet one struggles to under-stand what differentiates this from the family cronyism and kinship graft practised throughout the rest of the developing world (or indeed parts of the developed world). Is there really a specific Chinese form of corruption?

These are misleading ways to think about China because, far from living in the past, the country has been struggling to modernize for more than a century and a half. From the nineteenth-century self-strengthening movement, to the foundation of the republic in 1911, to the Great Leap Forward of the 1950s, right up to the state's immoderate investment in high-speed rail in recent years, China has been desperately trying to thrust itself into the modern world. As Wang Gungwu, a historian at Singapore University, puts it: 'The Chinese have tried to be modern, not too reluctantly but too often.' Wang also points out that nationalism, socialism, capitalism, liberalism and Communism – all the political and economic creeds that China has adopted over the past century – have come from the outside.[30] This calls into question our view of China as a place saturated with Confucian antipathy to foreign ideas. The country has, in fact, embraced Western utopian visions more fully than just about any other nation. As this book has argued, this undermines the increasingly popular suggestion that liberal democracy and political pluralism can never take root in China. If the Chinese can swap Confucianism for Communism why should they be incapable of swapping Communism for liberalism?

The nineteenth-century philosopher Herbert Spencer took Charles Darwin's theory of evolution and applied it to groups of humans, thus creating the modern theory of race and racial competition. Spencer also believed that culture was destiny. 'So long as the characters of the citizens remain unchanged,' he argued, 'there can be no substantial change in the political organization which has slowly evolved from them.'[31] We now reject Spencer's Social Darwinism, but his conception of fixed cultures and rigid political forms remains immensely popular, particularly when we talk of China.

We should, perhaps, think again. Chinese culture is not static, and never has been. Moreover its pace of change is accelerating in myriad ways. Attitudes to work, lifestyle, sexuality and diet are all evolving quickly. Most significantly of all, there are signs of a shift in how people feel about female babies. The old bias for sons is changing as parents realize that women can earn just as much as boys in a modern economy. If we approach China with the view that the country is locked into some kind of cultural prison we are liable to miss these transformations, or dismiss them as transient.

This prism of cultural determinism through which we are prone to analyse China is especially unhelpful because it implies the Chinese people are incapable of reforming the most unattractive parts of their society, such as the casual racism, the bigotry, and the cheap regard with which human life is often held. These same evils were once rife in Western societies, but they have been, at least partially, eroded by the natural elements of contact with the outside world and a generational evolution in attitudes. China can, and will, go down the same road of reform.

WHO LOST CHINA?

Chinese Whispers distract us from some of the most important things that are happening in the country. 'There will be slight opportunity for any such revolutionary ideas as Communism to gain a foothold in China,' concluded Carl Crow in 1937 in his stereotype-saturated book *The Chinese Are Like That*.[32] Concepts of class struggle, he informed readers, were quite alien to the Chinese, who could only conceive of the world in terms of extended family clans. Twelve years later, of course, Mao Zedong was proclaiming the foundation of a Communist republic from the great gatehouse overlooking Tiananmen Square.

Mao's victory prompted a 'Who lost China' debate in the US as Congressmen commenced a rancorous inquest into this strategic Cold War setback. Of course the framing of the debate said a lot. Washington imagined that it was in control of events, that China was somehow America's to 'lose' in the first place. But the debate was also telling because almost everyone involved was naïve about conditions in China or blinded by their own ideology.

The American military advisers had certainly overestimated the competence of Chiang Kai Shek's nationalists and underestimated the capabilities of the ruthless Communists. The 'Old China Hands' of the State Department had done better in some ways, accurately forecasting a Communist victory. Yet these self-styled experts, many of them scholars of Chinese culture, had also grossly exaggerated the domestic popularity of the rapacious and brutal Communist forces. And they were hoodwinked remarkably easily by Mao's presentation of himself as a moderate agrarian reformer. As for the Congressmen who heaped blame on the State Department for being Communist fellow travellers, they were more interested in stoking up an atmosphere of domestic threat than trying to learn any real lessons from what had taken place in China. One of the moving forces behind the debate was the notorious Wisconsin Senator Joseph McCarthy, who would go on to lead a hysterical and ugly witch hunt for Communist sleeper spies in American public life.

Britain has also had many Old China Hands, scholar-diplomats with an impressive knowledge of the Chinese language who present themselves to credulous politicians as holders of the secret to understanding the mysterious Chinese. Their record, alas, has been little better than that of their American counterparts. As we have seen, they advised London to stall on introducing representative government in colonial Hong Kong. They also badly misjudged the Tiananmen Square crisis in 1989. Chris Patten, the former Hong Kong Governor, recounts driving past the protesting crowds with Sir Alan Donald, the British ambassador to Beijing. 'Notice that the police are wearing brown plimsolls,' Sir Alan said. 'You don't wear plimsolls if you're going to stamp on people.' Patten recorded how the diplomat went on to explain to him that the confrontation between students and the regime was 'a sophisticated Chinese drama in which everyone knew their part and in which tradition and shared national ambition would help to secure an accommodation in which all would be able to save face'.[33] If only that had been true.

There are lessons for today's leaders here. They will make the same kind of mistakes in dealing with China if they keep giving credence to the stereotypes and myths outlined in this book. How should they respond if mass pro-democracy protests break out again in Chinese cities? How should outside powers react to a future diplomatic crisis between China and one of its neighbours? Should our universities continue to welcome Chinese students in significant numbers? Should Chinese firms be allowed to acquire European and American companies? How to cope with rampant computer hacking of

Western institutions which seems to be directed by the Chinese military? How to react to Beijing's threats to withhold investment from those nations whose leaders meet Tibet's Dalai Lama? There is no simple answer that one can give to these questions, but the response should be guided by a clear-sighted and objective view of the Chinese regime and the Chinese people, rather than the Whispers that are chronicled in these pages.

Snapshots of China can be fatally misleading. Consider some of the traps into which we fall. Chinese people are buying guides to Confucian thinking so we assume they are incorrigible Confucians. Some people in Chongqing are singing Cultural Revolution-era songs so they must be incorrigible Maoists. There are violent anti-Japanese protests in Chinese cities so China must be an angry neo-colonialist power. Yet another skyscraper has gone up in Shanghai so the Chinese are reinventing capitalism. Children study hard for exams so they live in a land of Tiger Mothers. Youngsters put in twelve-hour shifts at factories in Shenzhen so they must be a nation of workaholics.

We need to understand how China works as a society instead of drawing conclusions from a series of disconnected fragments. Take the economy. If one only focuses on the impressive GDP growth numbers, one misses the more important reality of wildly unbalanced economic development and exploding inequality. One also does not register the pivot back from an entrepreneur-led economy to state control in the 1990s and 2000s. A focus on economic projections alone can lead one to miss the fact that Chinese average incomes are still, even after three decades of spectacular growth, only less than a quarter of the levels of Europe and America. If one doesn't consider the threadbare social safety net, it is hard to understand why the Chinese feel the need to save such a large proportion of their incomes.

Take politics. If we conceive of the Chinese as a homogeneous mass we miss the growing social strains, the contempt that many city dwellers feel for migrant workers in their midst. If we don't grasp those dislocations it is no wonder we find the simultaneous enthusiasm for Mao and Confucius baffling. Too often we overlook the social context, namely a search by many Chinese people for old forms of community and consolation.

Take international relations. If we assume that the paranoid and sometimes belligerent Communist Party will remain in power forever because it has the full support of a grateful population, we naturally begin to fear a growing Chinese influence on the world. But if we understand the extreme fragility of the party's position and the disdain in which many people hold their leaders, we begin to feel differently about the prospects for international relations in the coming decades. The Party may not be in control for ever. If we obsess about China 'ruling the world' we miss the bigger truth that we are all far better off now that its 1.3 billion people are not locked in a North Korean-style economic jail.

Perspective is essential. In 2012 the Boston Consulting Group released a survey showing that 83 per cent of Chinese think their children's lives will be better than theirs. Only 28 per cent of Britons felt the same, along with 21 per cent of Americans and 13 per cent of Germans. We interpreted this as another sign of a changing of the guard of global power – more proof of how the Chinese will inherit the earth.[34] But consider the context in which Chinese respondents answered the question. In 1978 China was one of the poorest countries in the world. At the end of the Mao era the average calorific intake was just two-thirds of what it had been under the Qing Dynasty. Now China is approaching the status of a middle-income nation and almost the entire population can eat its fill. Is it any wonder middle-aged and elderly Chinese believe their children's lives will be better than theirs? I have seen that generational advance made flesh in the living conditions of my own family in Guangzhou, who, as we have seen, have graduated since 1986 from three sparse rooms in a decrepit housing block to a comfortable modern apartment.

A wide perspective is especially useful when it comes to interpreting contemporary Chinese nationalism, the phenomenon that causes us considerable alarm. The translator and historian Julia Lovell has described Chinese nationalists as trapped in an unstable combination of 'self pity and self-loathing'.[35] Yet this description omits one of the most significant dimensions of Chinese nationalism, namely the movement's historic connection with the champions of political reform. The Communist authorities are wary of the activities of the fanatical 'angry youth' because they fear anti-Japanese demonstrations could spill over into demands for regime change.

Of course we have to recognize that Chinese nationalism is a complex and unstable phenomenon, which can bolster the existing regime too. We tend to find it baffling that there still remains any respect for the Communist Party after it delivered such death and agony to the Chinese throughout the twentieth century. It is a rare Western television documentary on China that fails to show throngs of reverent domestic tourists paying their respects at Mao's birthplace in Shaoshan, Hunan province. Part of the explanation is that the Communists, despite all the suffering they caused in the twentieth century, are still seen as having helped to end the brutal Japanese occupation of the country in 1945. This sheds light on another misconception. Popular concerns over the integrity of China do not reflect a popular demand for authoritarian rule, as some of us tend to assume, but rather this association in the minds of many Chinese people between a breakdown in central authority and social misery.

This is why predictions from outsiders of the economic 'collapse' of China prompt such irritation on the part of many Chinese. To them it sounds like we are willing a catastrophe on the country. In Zhang Yimou's 2002 historical fantasy film *Hero* the character played by Jet Li allows the cruel Qin emperor to live for the sake of national unity, sacrificing his own life in the process. This ending inspired distaste among some Western critics who saw the film as an apologia for tyranny – propaganda for the Communist Party even.[36] Yet to a Chinese public, for whom national disunity is associated with great suffering, the ending made sense.

The predominant Chinese outlook is anti-imperialist for similar reasons. They associate that era, from the arrival of British gunboats off Guangdong in 1839 to the expulsion of Japanese forces in 1945, with chaos and death. To some extent, certainly, this popular resentment at a 'century of humiliation' is stoked by Communist Party propaganda. Then again, the economic statistics do suggest an epoch of misery. Between the middle of the nineteenth century and the middle of the twentieth century per capita incomes in Japan rose threefold, in Europe fourfold and the US eightfold. In China they fell.[37] Moreover, if we insist on believing that Communist propaganda created the nationalist sentiment in the first place we are deluding ourselves. The imprisoned democracy campaigner Liu Xiaobo is a controversial figure in China. Many were angry when he was awarded the Nobel Peace Prize in 2010, not because of Liu's calls for political reform, but because he once suggested that China might need three hundred years of colonial rule to enter the modern world. Liu's off-the-cuff remark in a 1988 interview has been seized upon and repeated ad nauseam by his ultra-nationalist enemies to blacken his name. The point is not to endorse that particular witch-hunt, but to emphasize that such propositions really do not go down well with ordinary Chinese.

The complexity of popular emotions towards national pride was encapsulated by the radical 1988 documentary, *River Elegy*. As we saw in the first chapter, the film's argument was iconoclastic in the same tradition as the anti-Confucian May Fourth Movement. It called for the Chinese to reject their stultifying traditional culture and open their minds to the outside world. The film's scathing attacks on China's old imperial rulers were widely interpreted as a disguised criticism of the Communist Party – and indeed this is very likely what the writers intended. Yet *River Elegy*'s message was framed in patriotic terms. This was possible because, in China, paradoxical though it seems to many of us, the rhetoric of casting off tradition is considered patriotic. Attacks on China's 'feudal' past are still part of the official narrative of the Communist Party. This explains why the authorities took so long to ban the film, even permitting it to be shown a second time on Chinese state television before finally bringing down the censorship axe.

Our habit of drawing parallels between the behaviour of China's present rulers and the dynastic emperors thus misses the point spec-tacularly. China's modern leaders define themselves against those old imperial times. Seeking to place today's Politburo in an unbroken line with the Qing and the Ming makes as much sense as describing François Hollande as a successor to Louis XVI, or Barack Obama as a descendant of King George III. That rupture with imperial rule is the foundation of modern Chinese politics.

We need to understand the Chinese sense of racial identity as an element of this framework too. Nineteenth-century reformers believed that China would only be strong when it was racially uni-fied. A sense of race was considered a pillar of modernization. And this belief persists. The democracy protestors in Tiananmen Square in 1989 sang 'Heirs to the Dragon', Hou Dejian's anthem of Chinese racial unity, not because they were foaming bigots, but because of the historic association in Chinese thought between those sentiments and democracy.

Modernization means nationalism. Nationalism means democracy. Racial unity means nationalism. National disunity means suffering and arbitrary government power. We need to understand these associations in modern Chinese thought to have a hope of understanding the country.

WALTZING BENEATH THE STREET LIGHTS

Another implicit lesson of Su Shi's great poem is the need for humility, to comprehend how little we know. Some Internet commentators were quick to ascribe a link between the death of Wang Yue, the poor little girl who was run over and ignored by pedestrians in 2010, and a deficient Chinese morality. On the ABC news website in America one analyst asserted: 'it is absolutely the true character of the Chinese to ignore the helpless, unless they are your own relatives, and even so, only if there is some kind of monetary gain or some kind of advantage that can be gained'. Another linked the incident to geopolitics saying: 'The Chinese are a disgusting race that unfortunately will be dominant in years to come. Once they become the most powerful nation on earth all real emotion and living as we know it will cease and the robotic, unfeeling idiocy of this incident will become even more common.' In a sign of how everything China gets linked together, one commentator remarked: 'Tainted dog food, lead paint in toys, tainted milk for infants. What can one expect from heartless individuals?'[38]

I discussed the Wang Yue incident with my family in China and they were as a horrified as anyone in the West. Why did people not help? Their assumption was that the passers-by must have assumed it was some sort of scam. This sounds implausible, but elaborate street cons are not unknown in China. In Beijing's fume-choked Deshengmen bus station a few years ago I walked past a man who was kowtowing in the middle of the pavement. Next to him was the skeletal corpse of an old woman, her body covered from the shoulders down with a white shroud. A sign on the ground next to them, written by the man, asked for money since he was too poor to pay for the burial of his mother. I watched from a distance. After a few minutes, the man and his mother both got up, wrapped up the sheet, picked up the sign, and went to try their luck panhandling somewhere else. Did the passers-by in the Wang Yue case mistakenly think that a similar con was taking place? Or, another theory in China, did they pass by because of a spate of publicized incidents where people who had gone to help accident victims found themselves falsely accused of causing the injury and forced by the cash-strapped hospital authorities to pay for the victims' medical costs? Only the individuals in question can know. But we should surely be careful about passing judgement on an entire society's morality based on a single incident – even if the Chinese themselves do so. In the middle of Lushan we should acknowledge that there are things we don't see.

My sense is that we cannot hope to comprehend this kind of affair without understanding the extreme strains within Chinese society. It is a life of food scares, choking pollution and rampant corruption. It is a country where getting sick can bankrupt you and ruin your family. In 2010 a viral email expressed popular despair at the cost of living:

> Can't afford to be born because a Caesarean costs RMB50,000 [£5,000/$8,000]; can't afford to study because schools cost at least RMB30,000; can't afford to live anywhere because each square metre is at least RMB20,000; can't afford to get sick because pharmaceutical profits are up at least 10-fold; can't afford to die because cremation costs at least RMB30,000.

A lack of faith in officialdom compounds this sense of insecurity. China is a country where the government routinely lies, where officials covered up the spread of a deadly flu virus in 2003 and where public health authorities connived in a commercial blood-donation practice that ended up infecting entire villages with HIV. It is a country that has still had no national reckoning for the social cannibalism that took place in the Mao era, when children were set against parents, students against teachers and when millions were

deliberately starved or worked to death. Indeed, the arbitrary decisions of the Communist Party continue to resonate in a chorus of
suffering. The one-child policy has effectively put a financial value
on young lives. An estimated twenty thousand children are kid-
napped each year by criminal gangs, which then sell the infants on
for adoption, prostitution, or slave labour.

Despite the improvements in living standards, in China tens of
millions still live in shabby and overcrowded homes. Wages are low
and prospects for many, even with the country's remarkable economic progress, remain poor. China is, in some ways, an emotionally
bottled-up land, where young people have been known to surrepti-
tiously crush packets of dried noodles on supermarket shelves as a
way of venting their frustration. And this is also a place in which the
wealthy, with their state-granted monopolies and access to cheap
loans from state-controlled banks, are getting wealthier still, a land
where the offspring of the well-connected seem to be able to break
the law with impunity.

The novelist Yu Hua summed up his sense of modern China:

So intense is the competition and so unbearable the pressure that,
for many Chinese, survival is like war itself. In this environment
the strong prey on the weak, people enrich themselves through
brute force and deception, and the meek and humble suffer while
the bold and unscrupulous flourish.[39]

That sounds very bleak. And it's an exaggeration. Amid all the
stress and anxiety there is a sense of possibility and opportunity. 'In
China anything can happen – good and bad,' my aunt once told me.
There is also joy in Chinese lives, particularly the older generation
who went through such agonies in the Mao era. When I close my eyes
and think of China, the strongest images are of my grandmother's
oldest friend performing the slow movements of Qi Gong exercise
on the concrete plaza outside her tower block in Hong Kong with
other pensioners as the sun rises. Or my great-uncle taking a morning stroll in the Yue Xiu Park in Guangdong. Or the elderly couple
playing badminton under an escalator in an underground station
in Shanghai at 8 p.m., when the rush of commuters has abated. Or
pensioners waltzing to the music of a ghetto blaster, beneath street

lights, on a little scrap of concrete at the side of Renmin Square in the same city. Their homes are far too small to practise their hobbies and there are few public leisure facilities, so they have to go into the open, to find some common ground, to enjoy simple pleasures. For this generation there exists a dignity and security now that was often missing in the earlier chapters of their lives.

Where is China waltzing to? It is not the purpose of this book to answer. This is not intended to take sides in the debate about whether China's economy is heading for a crash, or to speculate whether there will be a military confrontation between Beijing and Tokyo (although it does touch on those issues). It is, instead, a plea for us to change the prism through which we all too often look at China.

It is hard not to play Chinese Whispers when the Beijing regime and vested interests in our own countries are keen to promote them. Nevertheless there exists a route to a better understanding. First the Orientalist clichés need to be put aside. Let us shed our obsession with the 'exotic East', the 'patience of Asia', the 'Tiger Mothers', the 'inscrutability', 'the yellow peril', 'the Oriental cunning' and the 'superiority complex'. We should consider whether the people of such a diverse and complex place can ever be bound together by a crude conception such as 'Chineseness'. The bipolar thinking that seems to demand that China must be either hell or paradise should also be ditched.

We need to bring to an end the long tradition of positive or negative projection, whereby China is twisted into either the inverse image of a glorious West, or the shining model of the future that puts Europe and America to shame.

The Chinese, as a people, are neither superhuman, nor subhuman. Let Chinese society be understood in its proper context, as a predominantly poor nation still integrating itself into the world after decades of enforced seclusion. The key is for us to start thinking of the Chinese themselves not as some homogeneous and intimidating mass of humanity, but as individuals. Like the one hundred million hand-painted porcelain sunflower seeds that Ai Weiwei commissioned for his 2010 show in the Tate Modern art gallery in London, each one is unique. There are good and bad people amongst them, just as there are anywhere else. Some are corrupt, some upright.

Some are brutal, some compassionate. Some are greedy, some frugal. Some are mean, some generous. Some are racist, some are tolerant. Some are narrowly nationalist, some are voraciously cosmopolitan.

There is no unfathomable 'Chinese mind'. The Chinese people tend to respond to economic and social incentives in the same way as anyone else on the planet. The Chinese worked longer in the fields after the Maoist collective farms were broken up because they could realize a share of the benefits of their toil. Children often study insanely hard because education is one of the few routes of upward mobility in a rapidly calcifying society. Pervasive official corruption erodes civic mindedness, turning people in on themselves. And savage political repression breeds fear and a reluctance to speak out against injustice (until, of course, fear gives way to desperation). Beneath all the anxiety, the Chinese have the same aspirations for their children as any other parents. The Chinese are not 'special'. China is a diverse, endlessly fascinating place, but it is a fallacy to believe that it floats apart from the rest of world history.

Pushing through an 'irksome throng' in some Chinese city in 1920, William Somerset Maugham expressed an empathy gulf that he, probably the most successful writer of his day, could not bridge:

> You cannot tell what are the lives of those thousands who surge about you. Upon your own people sympathy and knowledge give you a hold: you can enter into their lives, at least imaginatively, and in a way really possesses them. By the effort of your fancy you can make them after a fashion part of yourself. But these [Chinese] are as strange to you as you are strange to them. You have no clue to their mystery. For their likeness to yourself in so much does not help you; it serves rather to emphasize their difference.[40]

The author was, at least, honest about his inability to get into the interior world of the Chinese. But it is time to move beyond that incomprehension. There really is no Chinese mystery waiting to be revealed. To understand, we need only listen to our own hearts.

NOTES

INTRODUCTION, PP. 1–8

1 The pinyin translation of the Cantonese for 'January first' is 'Yat yut yat yat'.

2 'China's rise named decade's most read news story', Reuters, 8 December 2009.

3 'China's appetite for work and wealth', Jeremy Paxman, BBC website, 23 January 2012.

4 'America's Top Parent', Elizabeth Kolbert, *The New Yorker*, 31 January 2011.

5 'Is this the Little Girl who Taught Compassion to China?', Peter Simpson, *Daily Mail*, 21 October 2011.

6 *Made in China*, Gok Wan, Channel 4, 7 March 2012.

7 *Mr China*, Tim Clissold (Robinson, London), 2004, p. 156.

8 *The Philosophy of History*, Georg Hegel (Cosimo, New York), 2007, p. 131.

9 Quoted in *The Western Representation of Modern China*, David Martinez-Robles, 2008.

10 *The return of Dr Fu Manchu*, Sax Rohmer, 1916, Chapter XXVIII.

11 *The Problem of China*, Bertrand Russell, Chapter 12.

12 *Riding the Iron Rooster*, Paul Theroux (Penguin, London), 1989, p. 169.

13 'The Chinago', Jack London, *Harper's Monthly Magazine*, July 1909.

14 *The Problem of China*, Russell, Chapter 12.

15 *A Journey Through the Chinese Empire*, Evariste Régis Huc, 1854, Vol. II, Chapter II.

16 *Memoirs 1950–1963*, George F. Kennan (Little, Brown, Boston), 1972, p. 56.

17 *The Spirit of the Laws*, Baron De Montesquieu, Book 16, Chapter 8.

18 *The Wealth of Nations*, Adam Smith, Book I, Chapter VIII.

19 Quoted in *The Chan's Great Continent*, Joseph Spence (Norton, New York), 1999, p. 23.

20 *China's Millions*, edited by J. Hudson Taylor, 1883.

21 *Mao Tse-Tung: Emperor of the Blue Ants*, George Paloczi-Horvath (Doubleday, New York), 1963, p. 1.

22 *When a Billion Chinese Jump*, Jonathan Watts (Faber and Faber, London), 2010, pp. 1–5.

23 *China: Triumph and Turmoil*, Niall Ferguson, Channel 4, 19 March 2012.

24 *Chinese Characteristics*, Arthur Henderson Smith, 1894.

25 *The Travels of Marco Polo*, Book Two, Chapter 1.

26 Quoted in Spence p. 38.

27 Interviewed by Steve Paikin, *The Agenda*, Canadian TV station TVO, 4 January 2011.

28 'Mao Plan to Use A-bomb Told', New York Times News Service, 23 February 1988.

CULTURE, PP. 19–51

1 'The Great Exhibition and the Little One', Charles Dickens and Richard Horne, *Household Words*, 5 July 1851.

2 *The Problem of China*, Bertrand Russell, 1922, Chapter 12.

3 *On China*, Henry Kissinger (Allen Lane, London), 2011, p. 5.

4 *History of China*, Jean-Baptiste Du Halde, 1738, Volume I.

5 *The Yellow Peril*, Jack London, 1904.

6 *The Real Chinaman*, Chester Holcombe, 1895, Introductory.

7 *Guns, Germs and Steel*, Jared Diamond (Vintage, London), 1998, p. 323.

8 *The Orphan of China*, Voltaire, 1755, Act V, Scene V, translation by William Fleming (E.R. DuMont, New York), 1901.

9 *A Journey Through The Chinese Empire*, Evariste Régis Huc, 1854, Volume 1, Preface.

10 Speech at Banquet in Honour of Chinese Embassy, Boston, Ralph Waldo Emerson, 1860.

11 *China*, John King Fairbank and Merle Goldman (Harvard University Press, Cambridge), 2006, p. 25.

12 Quoted in *The Opium War*, Julia Lovell (Picador, London), 2011, p. 4.

13 *Science and Civilization in China*, Joseph Needham, 1972, Volume 1, p. 88.

14 *The Chinese*, Jasper Becker (Oxford University Press, Oxford), 2000, p. 4.

15 *Chinese Thought*, Herrlee G. Creel (University of Chicago Press, Chicago), 1953, p. 1.

16 *The Analects*, Confucius, Book III, 5.

17 'Salient Features of Chinese Historical Thinking', Huang Cheun-Chieh, *Medieval History Journal*, 2004.

18 *Billions: Selling to the New Chinese Consumer*, Tom Doctoroff (Macmillan Palgrave, New York), 2005, p. 107.

19 'More than Half of Chinese can't Speak Mandarin', *Xinhua*, 7 March 2007.

20 *Struggling Giant*, Kerry Brown (Anthem Press, London), 2007, p. 13.

21 *China*, Fairbank and Goldman, p. 129.

22 *The Last Emperors*, Evelyn Rawski (University of California Press, California), 1998, p. 81.

23 *The Analects*, Book XIX, 17.

24 *The Analects*, Book XV, 13.

25 *The Sextants of Beijing*, Joanna Waley-Cohen (Norton, New York), 2000, p. 20.

26 *Islam in China*, Mi Shoujiang and You Jia, translation by Min Chang (China Intercontinental Press).

27 *A New History of Christianity in China*, Daniel H. Bays (Wiley-Blackwell, Oxford), 2012, p. 7.

28 *The Travels of Marco Polo*, Book 2, Chapter 2.

29 *The Penguin History of Modern China*, Jonathan Fenby (Penguin, London), 2009, p. 21.

30 According to Verity Wilson, quoted in 'Kublai Khan: China's favourite barbarian', BBC website, 9 October 2012.

31 *The Manchus*, Pamela Crossley (Blackwell, Oxford), 1997, p. 12.

32 *The Last Emperors*, Rawski, p. 6.

33 *The Sextants of Beijing*, Waley-Cohen, p. 15.

34 *The Penguin History of Modern China*, Fenby, p. 67.

35 *The New Democracy*, Mao Zedong, 1940.

36 'Debating the Cultural Revolution: Do We Only Know What We Believe?', Mobo Gao, *Critical Asian Studies*, 2001, No 34.

37 *The Ugly Chinaman*, Bo Yang (1985), author quoted in *Deathsong of the River*, Richard Bodman (Cornell, New York), 1991, p. 28.

38 *Wild Swans*, Jung Chang (HarperCollins, London), 1991, p. 5.

39 *Americanization, Westernization, Sinification, Modernization or Globalization of China?*, Yu Keping, 2001.

40 *To Live*, Yu Hua, translation Michael Berry (Anchor, New York), 2003, p. 249.

41 'Dialect Reinforces City's History and Culture', *Global Times*, 13 December 2011.

42 'Low-fat British Bird Roasts Peking Duck', *Daily Telegraph*, 9 June 2002.

43 *History of the World*, Andrew Marr, BBC One, Sunday 14 October 2012.

44 *China's New Confucianism*, Daniel Bell (Princeton University Press, Princeton), 2008.

45 'Finding Flaws in the National Character', interview with Jiang Rong, US National Public Radio, 26 May 2009.

46 'A Better Life? The Wants and Worries of China's Consumers', Economist Intelligence Unit, 2012.

47 This trinity may have been mistaken by Charles Dickens for what he described as 'three Chinese divinities of the Past, Present and the Future' in the Hyde Park Place gallery in 'The Great Exhibition and the Little One' (above).

48 'The Clash of Civilisations?', Samuel Huntingdon, Foreign Affairs, Summer 1993.

49 *On Liberty*, John Stuart Mill, 1859, Chapter 3.

50 'China and Western Technology in the Late Eighteenth Century', Joanna Waley-Cohen, *American Historical Review*, Vol. 98, No. 5, December 1993.

51 *The Times*, 10 September 1841, quoted in *The Opium War*, Lovell, p. 176.

52 Quoted in Lovell, 2011, p. 256.

53 *Chinese Characteristics*, Arthur Henderson Smith, 1890, Conclusion.

54 *The Three Principles of the People*, Sun Yat Sen, 1927.

55 'Beijing's Urban Makeover: the Hutong destruction', Open Democracy website, 11 June 2006.

RACE, PP. 52–75

1 'Chinese Immigration: a Sociological Study', Gerrit L. Lansing, *Popular Science Monthly*, April 1882.

2 *The Problem of China*, Bertrand Russell, p. 138.

3 *Nations and Nationalism since 1780*, Eric Hobsbawm (Cambridge University Press, Cambridge), 1992, p. 66.

4 'How China's Nationalism Was Shanghaied', Lucian Pye, *Australian Journal of Chinese Affairs*, No. 29, 1993, pp. 107–133.

5 *The Three Principles of the People*, Sun Yat Sen, translated by Frank Price, 1927.

6 'You'll never be Chinese', Mark Kitto, *Prospect*, 8 August 2012.

7 *Eugenics: A Reassessment*, Richard Lynn (Prager, Westport), 2001, p. 319.

8 'More than a category: Han Supremacism on the Chinese internet', James Liebold, *China Quarterly*, 2010.

9 *When China Rules the World*, Martin Jacques (Allen Lane, London), 2009, p. 271.

10 'Gm and Km allotypes in 74 Chinese populations: a hypothesis of the origin of the Chinese nation', T.M Zhao and T.D Lee, *Human Genetics*, 1989; and 'Genetic Structure of the Han Chinese Population Revealed by Genome-wide SNP Variation', Jieming Chen, Houfeng Zheng et al, *American Journal of Human Genetics*, Vol. 85, Issue 6, 2009.

11 'A Roman City in Ancient China', Homer Dubs, *Greece and Rome*, Volume 4, Issue 02, October 1957.

12 *The Discourse of Race in Modern China*, Frank Dikotter (Hurst, London), 1992.

13 *Joining the Modern World*, Wang Gungwu (World Scientific Publishing Company, Singapore), 2000, p. 4.

14 'Competing Narratives of Racial Unity in Republican China', James Liebold, *Modern China*, Vol. 43, No. 2, 2006.

15 *The People's Peking Man: Popular Science and Human Identity in Twentieth-Century China*, Sigrid Schmalzer (University of Chicago Press, Chicago), 2008.

16 '"Ethnic" children revealed as fakes in opening ceremony', *Daily Telegraph*, 18 September 2008.

17 'Peking Man and the Politics of Paleoanthropological Nationalism in China', Barry Sautman, *Journal of Asian Studies*, 60, 2001.

18 'Evidence that a West-East admixed population lived in the Tarim Basin as early as the early Bronze Age', Chunxiang Li, Hongjie Li, Yinqiu Cui et al, *BMC Biol*, 2010.

19 'Mystery of the Mummy's Chinese Travel Ban', *The Independent*, 5 February 2011.

20 *The Spirit of Chinese Politics*, Lucian Pye, (Harvard University Press, Cambridge) p. 56.

21 'The Melting Pot Generation', British Future, 11 December 2012.

22 'The Rise of Intermarriage', Pew Research Center, 16 February 2012.

23 *Sons of the Yellow Emperor*, Lynn Pan (Kodansha, New York), 1994, p. 129.

24 *Identity and Ethnic Relations in Southeast Asia*, Chee Kiong Tong (Springer, Dordrecht), 2010, p. 236.

25 'Big Trouble in Chocolate City', *Toronto Star*, 1 August 2009.

26 'Anti-black Racism in post-Mao China', *China Quarterly*, Volume 138, June 1994, pp. 413–37.

27 'Tinted prejudice in China', CNN, 24 June 2012.

28 'China's black pop idol does not expose her nation's racism', Malcolm Moore, Daily Telegraph blog, 5 November 2009.

29 Interview with author, 15 September 2012.

30 'China's Changing Views on Race', *New York Times*, 13 December 2009.

31 China Statistical Yearbook 2011.

32 'Obama's Half Brother Makes a Name for Himself in China', *Time*, 17 November 2009.

33 'Majority of Americans Say Racism Against Blacks Widespread', Gallup, 4 August 2008.

34 *The Monkey and the Dragon*, Linda Jaivin (The Text Publishing Company, Melbourne), 2001, p. 268.

POLITICS, PP. 76–104

1 'Call me if there's a revolution', Melissa Chan, Al Jazeera blog, 20 February 2011.

2 'Why the Chinese are not Inspired by Egypt', David Pilling, *Financial Times*, 16 February 2011.

3 Marx argued that economic forces, not ideas, were the motor of history.

4 *Philosophy of History*, Georg Wilhelm Friedrich Hegel, 1837.

5 *The Spirit of Laws*, Baron de Montesquieu, Book XVII.

6 *Politics*, Aristotle, Book 6, Chapter 7.

7 Quoted in Mark Kishlansky, *Sources of World History*, Vol. 1 (Harper-Collins, New York) 1995, pp. 269–73.

8 *Despotism in China*, Francois Quesnay, 1767.

9 *On a Chinese Screen*, William Somerset Maugham, p. 38.

10 *Analects*, Confucius, Book XII, 11.

11 *Asian Power and Politics*, Lucian Pye (Harvard University Press, Cambridge), 1985, pp. 182–214.

12 *The Third Wave*, Samuel Huntingdon (University of Oklahoma Press, Oklahoma), 1993, p. 307.

13 *The Abortive Revolution*, Lloyd Eastman (Harvard, Cambridge), 1974, pp. 179–180.

14 *China: Triumph and Turmoil*, Niall Ferguson, Channel 4, 12 March 2012.

15 'Real Meaning of the Rot at the Top of China', Daniel Bell, *Financial Times*, 23 April 2012.

16 *Oriental Despotism*, Karl Wittfogel (Yale University Press, New Haven), 1967, p. 141.

17 'Behind the "Modern" China', Robert Kagan, *Washington Post*, 23 March 2008.

18 *No One's World*, Charles Kupchan (Oxford University Press, Oxford), 2012, p. 11.

19 Jeremy Paxman, BBC *Newsnight*, 23 January 2012.

20 'On democracy', Han Han blog, 25 December 2011, translated on East South West North blog: http://www.zonaeuropa.com/weblog.htm.

21 'Daring Blogger Tests the Limits', Katherine Hille, *Financial Times*, 14 January 2010.

22 'Jackie Chan Says Chinese People Need to be "Controlled"', *Daily Telegraph*, 19 April 2009.

23 In fact Mao thought he was even more terrible. The Communist chairman said in reference to China's first emperor: 'He buried 460 scholars alive – we have buried 46,000 scholars alive. You [intellectuals] revile us for being Qin Shi Huangs. You are wrong. We have surpassed Qin Shi Huang a hundredfold.'

24 'China has banished Bo but not the "bad emperor"', *Financial Times*, 10 May 2012.

25 In 2012 the BBC produced a ten-part radio series in which the presenter tried to explain contemporary China through reference to its ancient past: *China, as History Is My Witness*, Carrie Gracie, BBC Radio 4, October 2012.

26 'The Next Emperor', *The Economist*, 21 October 2010.

27 'Review of Oriental Despotism', Joseph Needham, *Science and Society*, 1959, Volume XXIII, pp. 58–65.

28 Mao Zedong's July 1945 exchange with Huang Yanpei in Yan'an, quoted in *The China Story Yearbook 2012*, Geremie Barme, Australian Centre on China in the World.

29 'To believe that democracy was impossible and that the Party was the guardian of democracy,' as Orwell put it in 1984.

30 The International Institute for Urban Development in Beijing puts China's Gini coefficient at 0.438 in 2010. Under the Gini measure, perfect equality is 0 and perfect inequality is 1. World Bank data puts South Africa on 0.631, Colombia on 0.559 and the United States on 0.408.

31 Hurun Wealth Report 2012.

32 'China 2013', World Bank, 2012, p. 19.

33 *China in Ten Words*, Yu Hua (Pantheon, New York), 2011, p. 25.
34 'Where Wukan has led, Beijing will not follow', David Pilling, *Financial Times*, 8 February 2012.
35 '91% think new rich use government connections', *China Daily*, 9 February 2010.
36 'China's Billionaire People's Congress Makes Capitol Hill Look Like Pauper', Bloomberg News, 27 February, 2012.
37 'Hedging their bets', *The Economist*, 26 May 2012.
38 '2011 China Private Wealth Management White Paper', Hurun Research Institute and Bank of China, 29 October 2011.
39 Quoted in 'A Pop Idol Writer for China's New Generation', Louisa Lim, National Public Radio, 28 May 2009.
40 'Call me if there's a revolution', Melissa Chan, Al Jazeera blog, 20 February 2011.
41 Quoted in 'The Confusion of Being a Chinese Student in America', Helen Gao, *The Atlantic*, 12 December 2011.
42 'Behind the Great Firewall of China', Michael Anti, Ted Talks, June 2012.
43 'The revolution that wasn't', Charlie Custer, China Geeks blog, 20 February 2011.
44 Quoted in 'Text messages give a voice to Chinese', *Washington Post*, 29 July 2007.
45 'The Power of Youth', Yuan Yuan, *The Beijing Review*, 29 September 2011.
46 The 2010 Time 100, 29 April 2010.
47 Speech in Tokyo, Lee Kuan Yew, 10 November 1992.
48 *East and West*, Chris Patten (Macmillan, London), 1999, p. 26.
49 *Democracy is a good thing*, Yu Keping (Brookings, Washington), 2009.

EDUCATION, PP. 105–29

1 Quoted in *The Chan's Great Continent*, Jonathan Spence (Norton, New York) 1999, p. 38.
2 Quoted in *The Opium War*, Lovell, p. 55.
3 'Speech at Banquet in Honor of Chinese Embassy', Boston, Ralph Waldo Emerson, 1860.
4 *Desultory Notes on the Government and People of China*, Thomas Taylor Meadows (W.H Allen, London), 1847, p. 124.
5 'My Revolution for Culture in Classroom', Michael Gove, *Daily Telegraph*, 28 December 2010.

6 'Why Chinese Students Put Us to Shame', Sarah Gashi, *The Oxford Student*, 9 September 2011.

7 'Is China's Education System Keeping Up With Growing Superpower?', Jessica Hopper, ABC News, 16 November 2010.

8 'Rising above the gathering storm, revisited', *National Academy of Sciences*, 2010, p.46.

9 'Knowledge, networks and nations', The Royal Society, 2011.

10 'Get Ready for China's Domination of Science', Jonathan Adams, *New Scientist*, January 2010.

11 'China "to overtake US on science" in two years', BBC website, 28 March 2011.

12 'The World's Schoolmaster', *The Atlantic*, July/August 2011.

13 'China: The World's Cleverest Country?', BBC website, 9 May 2012.

14 *Britannia Unchained*, Kwasi Kwarteng et al (Palgrave Macmillan, London), 2012, p. 38.

15 'China's education system', Nicholas Kristof, *New York Times*, 15 January 2011.

16 *Battle Hymn of the Tiger Mother*, Amy Chua (Bloomsbury, London), 2010.

17 'The Competition that Really Matters', Center for American Progress & The Center for the Next Generation, August 2012.

18 'Doing Our Homework', Thomas Friedman, *New York Times*, 24 June 2004.

19 Barack Obama, speech at Campaign and Science Teaching and Mentoring Awards , 6 January 2010.

20 'The Discipline of a Chinese Mother', Allison Pearson, *Daily Telegraph*, 27 January 2012.

21 *The Thorny Gates of Learning in Sung China*, John W Chaffee (State University of New York Press, New York), 1995, p. XXII.

22 *The Last Emperors*, Evelyn Rawski (University of California Press, California), 1998, p. 81.

23 Quoted in *China in Ten Words*, Yu Hua, translation Allan Barr (Pantheon, New York), 2011, p. 119.

24 'Stay Rates of Foreign Doctorate Recipients from U.S. Universities, 2007', Michael G. Finn, Science Education Programs, Oak Ridge Institute for Science and Education, January 2010.

25 Defined by Shanghai 500 rankings.

26 Universitas 21 Rankings of National Higher Education Systems 2012.

27 'Knowledge, Networks and Nations', Royal Society, 2011, p. 25.

28 US Trademark and Patent Office, cited in 'Knowledge, networks and

nations', The Royal Society, 2011, p. 34.

29 Interview with author, 25 September 2012.

30 Editorial, *Acta Crystallogaphica* Section E, Vol. 55, Part 1, January 2010.

31 Interview with author, 16 February 2012.

32 Chinese Association for Science and Technology, 17 July 2009.

33 *The Diary of Ma Yan*, translated from French by Lisa Appignanesi (Harper Collins, New York), 2005.

34 *Capitalism with Chinese Characteristics*, Huang Yasheng (Cambridge University Press, New York) 2010, p. 245.

35 'England's "plummeting" PISA test scores between 2000 and 2009', John Jerrim, Department of Quantitative Social Science working paper, December 2011.

36 United Nations Human Development Report 2011 (data from 2006–2009).

37 Country note – China, Education at a Glance 2011, OECD.

38 *The Analects*, Confucius, Book II, 15.

39 *Demystifying the Chinese Economy*, Justin Yifu Lin (Cambridge University Press, Cambridge), 2012, p. XIV.

40 'The Education System that Pulled China Up May Now Be Holding it Back', Helen Gao, *The Atlantic*, 25 June 2012.

41 'Top Gao Kao Scorers Fail to Live up to Expectations', *China Daily*, 28 June 2010.

42 'Confessions of a Chinese Graduate', Eric Mu, *Danwei*, 2 September 2011.

43 Lunch with the FT, David Pilling, 21 April 2012.

44 'Open Doors', Institute of International Education, November 2011.

45 Hurun Wealth Report 2012.

46 'What more can we take away from the Chinese community?', Black Training and Enterprise Group, October 2010.

47 *Battle Hymn of the Tiger Mother*, Amy Chua, 2010, p. 86.

48 *The Diary of Ma Yan*, 12 September 2000, p.19.

49 'South Korea's Economic Reforms – a Recipe for Unhappiness', Ha-Joon Chang, *The Guardian*, 1 April 2012.

50 Country note – China, Education at a Glance 2011, OECD.

51 'Sputnik Scare, Update', Robert Samuelson, *Washington Post*, 26 May 2005.

52 'A Liberal Arts Education, Made in China', Eric Abrahamsem, *New York Times*, 3 July 2012.

53 *Factory Girls*, Leslie T. Chang (Picador, London) 2010, p.183–94.

WORK, PP. 130–65

1 'The Army of Canton in the High Sierra', Alexander Saxton, *Pacific Historical Review*, Vol. 35, 1966, pp. 141–52.

2 *Cornelius Cole: California Pioneer and United States Senator*, Catherine Coffin Phillips (Kessinger Publishing, US), 2005, p. 138.

3 Quoted in *An Essay on the Principle of Population*, Malthus, 1798.

4 Letter to James Oswald of Dunnikier, 1 November 1750 from *The Letters of David Hume*, edited by J.Y.T. Greig (Oxford University Press, Oxford) 1932, Vol. 1, p. 144.

5 *Barbarian Eye: Lord Napier in China*, Priscilla Napier (Brassey's, London), 2003, p. 88.

6 *Roughing It*, Mark Twain, 1872, Chapter LIV.

7 *Chinese Characteristics*, Arthur Henderson Smith, 1894.

8 *From Sea to Sea and other Sketches*, Rudyard Kipling, 1900, No. VII.

9 *The Chinese Are Like That*, Carl Crow (World Publishing, Cleveland), 1943, pp. 51–52.

10 *The Religion of China*, Max Weber (Free Press, New York), 1951, p. 231.

11 *The Yellow Peril*, Jack London, 1904.

12 Interview, *Daily Telegraph*, 15 September 2012.

13 *Civilization*, Niall Ferguson (Allen Lane, London), 2011, p. 284.

14 *The Good Earth*, Pearl S. Buck (Simon & Schuster, London) 1997, pp. 56–57.

15 'Glencore's Debt to China's Women', John Gapper, *Financial Times*, 27 April 2011.

16 'The Party of Work', David Brooks, *New York Times*, 8 November 2012.

17 *A Chinese Village*, Martin Yang (Columbia University Press, New York), 1945, p. 130.

18 *China Now*, Sheldon Weeks, 2 June 1977.

19 Jin Liqun, interview with Faisal Islam on Channel 4 News, 19 October 2011.

20 Interview with Joshua Cooper Ramo on 6 April 2004, quoted in 'The Beijing Consensus', Foreign Policy Centre, 2004, p. 67.

21 *China Shakes the World*, James Kynge (Weidenfeld & Nicolson, London), 2006, p. 73.

22 *The Chinese in Britain*, Gregor Benton and Edmund Gomez (Palgrave Macmillan, New York), 2008, pp. 29–68.

23 *The Penguin History of Modern China*, Jonathan Fenby (Penguin, London), 2008, p. 459.

24 'Rural Reforms and Agricultural Productivity Growth in China', Justin Yifu Lin, UCLA Working Paper no. 576, December 1989.

25 *Bad Samaritans*, Ha-Joon Chang (Random House, London), 2007, Chapter 9.

26 'Is China's Famed Work Ethic Fading?', Gallup poll, 25 January 2005.

27 Quoted in 'Working Titles', Leslie T. Chang, *New Yorker*, 6 February 2012.

28 'Why Do the Chinese Work So Hard?', Stevan Harrell, *Modern China*, Vol. 11, no. 2, 1985, pp 203–226.

29 'Rural Reforms and Agricultural Productivity Growth in China', Justin Yifu Lin, UCLA Working Paper no. 576, December 1989.

30 *Mao's Great Famine*, Frank Dikotter (Bloomsbury, London), 2011, p. 209.

31 *A Darwinian Perspective on Entrepreneurship*, Wei Shang-Jin and Zhang Xiaobo, September 2011.

32 *China Shakes the World*, James Kynge, 2006, p. 78.

33 'Chinese Indentured Labour in Peru', Lawrence Clayton, *History Today*, Vol. 30, Issue 6, 1980.

34 'Chinese Coolie Labour in Cuba', Evelyn Hu-Dehart, *Contributions in Black Studies*, Vol. 12, Article 5, 1994.

35 Letter to the Editor, *The Times*, June 5 1873.

36 *From Sea to Sea and other Sketches*, Rudyard Kipling, 1900, Chapter VII.

37 Quoted in *Sons of the Yellow Emperor*, Lynn Pan, 1990.

38 Quoted in *King Leopold's Ghost*, Adam Hochschild (Pan, London), 2006, p. 170.

39 *Indianapolis Times*, 28 February 1878.

40 'How Los Angeles Covered Up the Massacre of 17 Chinese', John Johnson Jr, *LA Weekly*, 10 March 2011.

41 *The Unparalleled Invasion*, Jack London, 1910.

42 *Sons of the Yellow Empire*, Lynn Pan (Kodansha, New York), 1994, p. 64.

43 *Becoming Americans*, Tricia Knoll (Coast to Coast Books, Portland), 1982, p. 28.

44 Quoted in 'Racism and Advertising in the late nineteenth century', James Chan, paper given at Association of Asian American Studies Joint Regional Conference, 25 March 1996.

45 *Mao's Great Famine*, Frank Dikotter (Bloomsbury, London), 2010.

46 Interview with Frank Dikotter, Asia Society's Asia Blog, 15 November 2011.

47 'How the US Lost Out on iPhone Work', *New York Times*, 21 January 2012.

48 'Foxconn Asks Employees to Sign Pledge Not to Commit Suicide', Bloomberg, 26 May 2010.

49 'Samsung Factory Exploiting Child Labour', China Labor Watch, 7 August 2012.

50 'Death from Overwork in China', China Labour Bulletin, 11 August 2006.

51 'In China, Human Costs are Built Into an iPad', *New York Times*, 25 January 2012.

52 'New Chinese Labor Contract Law', Institute for Global Labour and Human Rights, September 2007.

53 'The Voices of China's Workers', Leslie Chang, Ted Talks, June 2012.

54 'Foxconn Investigation Report', Fair Labor Association, 29 March 2012.

55 Interview with the author, 12 September 2012.

56 'The Greatest Ever Economic Challenge', Douglas McWilliams, Gresham College, 13 September 2012.

57 'Hard Graft can Make Britain Great Again', Dominic Raab, *Daily Telegraph*, 4 September 2012.

58 'Job Anxiety is Real – and It's Global', Sandra Polaski, Policy Brief, Carnegie Endowment for International Peace, 30 May 2004.

59 *China: Triumph and Turmoil*, Niall Ferguson, Channel 4, 12 March 2012.

60 From time-use surveys, cited in 'Cooking, Caring and Volunteering', Veerle Miranda, 2011, OECD Social, Employment and Migration Working Papers No.116, OECD Publishing.

61 Asian Productivity Organization Databook 2012.

62 Annual average hours worked in 2011 according to the Conference Board: Taiwan (2,174), Hong Kong (2,344), Singapore (2,287), UK (1,643), Germany (1,409), United States (1,705).

63 GDP per hour worked 2011 (in 1990 $) according to the Conference Board: Taiwan ($24.35), Hong Kong ($28.08), Singapore ($21.99), UK ($29.14), Germany ($30.71), United States ($39.96).

64 'Prison Slaves', Al Jazeera, 25 March 2012.

CAPITALISM, PP. 166–92

1 *The Religion of China*, Max Weber (The Free Press, New York), 1951, p. 104.

2 *Of the Rise and Progress of the Arts and Sciences*, David Hume, 1742.

3 *The Spirit of Chinese Capitalism*, S. Gordon Redding (De Gruyter, New York) 1993.

4 *Made in China: What Western Managers Can Learn from Trailblazing Chinese Entrepreneurs*, Donald Sull (Harvard, Boston), 2005.

5 'Beijing's Lessons for Central Banks, Stephen Roach, *Financial Times*, 5 March 2012.

6 Gary Becker blog, 10 October 2010.

7 'Fidelity's Bolton Cancels Retirement', Alex Frangos, *Wall Street Journal*, 26 November 2009.

8 Quoted in *The Gathering Storm Revisited*, National Academy of Sciences, 2011, p. 1.

9 'The Democratic Malaise', Charles Kupchan, *Foreign Affairs*, January/February 2012.

10 'The Future of Economic Convergence', Dani Rodrik, speech at Jackson Hole Symposium, August 2011.

11 'China's Superior Economic Model', Andy Stern, *Wall Street Journal*, 1 December 2011.

12 'The Threat to the Post-Mao Consensus', David Pilling, *Financial Times*, 21 March 2012.

13 *Winner Take All*, Dambisa Moyo (Allen Lane, London), 2012.

14 *Eclipse*, Arvind Subramanian (PIIE Press, Washington), 2011, p. 9.

15 Quoted in 'China Housing Bubble is "Over"', *Forbes*, 4 September 2012.

16 'China Could Lead the Fight for a Cooler Climate', Jonathon Porritt, *ChinaDialogue*, 13 November 2007.

17 'The Beijing Consensus', Joshua Cooper Ramo, The Foreign Policy Centre, 2004.

18 *What Does China Think?*, Mark Leonard, 2008, p. 134.

19 According to the IMF's October 2012 forecast US GDP in 2017 will be $19,745 billion. China's equivalent GDP will be $20,198 billion. Both figures in Purchasing Power Parity international dollar terms.

20 China 2030, World Bank, 2012.

21 World Bank data, Infant mortality rate (per 1,000 live births) was 52.8 in 1978 and 12.6 in 2011.

22 'China: the Road to Nowhere', *Financial Times*, 16 July 2012.

23 Calculations of the World Bank and Qu Hongbin of HSBC.

24 Figures from Ben Simpfendorfer of Silk Road Associates, a Hong Kong consultancy.

25 Global Financial Stability Report, International Monetary Fund, 2011, p. 40.

26 'US–China Economics and Security Review Commission', Report to Congress, November 2011.

27 Speaking at Ambrosetti Investment Forum, Italy, quoted in 'China's Revolution Risk', Ambrose Evans-Pritchard, Daily Telegraph blog, 10 September 2012.

28 *Red Capitalism*, Carl Walter and Fraser Howie (John Wiley & Sons, Singapore), 2010, p. 22.

29 Murong Xuecun, speech in Hong Kong, translated on Tea Leaf Nation website, 30 July 2012.

30 To take one example, CNN Fact Check argued on 23 October 2012: 'If China were to say it is no longer interested in buying U.S. debt, that could make it harder for the U.S. government to borrow the money it needs to operate.'

31 To put that in context, the government's low-income home construction target is for 36 million new units by 2015. Beijing could meet this almost twice over merely by requisitioning the country's existing empty homes.

32 China's National Audit Office put local government debt at RMB10.7 trillion in June 2011 but Victor Shih of Northwestern University estimates that the real figure is RMB15.4 trillion to RMB20.1 trillion.

33 'The Meaning of China's Slowdown', Barry Eichengreen, The Diplomat blogs, 31 July 2012.

34 'A Better Life? The Wants and Worries of China's Consumers', Economist Intelligence Unit, 2010

35 *The Travels of Marco Polo*, Book II, Chapter XVIII.

RULING THE WORLD, PP. 193–222

1 *From Sea to Sea and Other Sketches*, Rudyard Kipling, 1900, Book IX.

2 *The Story of a Soldier's Life*, Viscount Wolseley (The Book Supply Company, Toronto), Volume II, 1904, p. 2.

3 *Village Life in China*, Arthur Henderson Smith (Fleming H. Revell, New York), 1899, p. 53.

4 *The Hand of Fu Manchu*, Sax Rohmer, 1917, Chapter 20.

5 *On a Chinese Screen*, William Somerset Maugham (Vintage, London), 2000, p. 95.

6 *These from the Land of Sinim*, Robert Hart (Chapman & Hall, London), 1901, p. 52.

7 *China: Triumph and Turmoil*, Niall Ferguson, Channel 4, 12 March 2012.

8 'Behind the "Modern" China', Robert Kagan, *Washington Post*, 23 March 2008

9 *The Beijing Consensus*, Stefan Halper (Basic, New York), 2010.

10 'Niall Ferguson: Is US–China Economic Marriage on the Rocks?', interview with Nathan Gardels, Huffington Post, 27 July 2009.

11 *Losing Control*, Stephen King (Yale University Press, New Haven), 2011.

12 'In spite of the fact that we have no such fleet as we should have, we have conquered for ourselves a place in the sun', Kaiser Wilhelm II, Speech to the North German Regatta Association, 1901.

13 *China's Silent Army*, Juan Pablo Cardenal and Heriberto Araujo (Allen Lane, London), 2013, p. XVI.

14 In 2009/10 the China Development Bank and China Exim Bank lent more to developing world than World Bank.

15 'How China's Taking Over Africa and why the West Should be VERY Worried', Andrew Malone, *Daily Mail*, 18 July 2008.

16 'Inside the Sinosphere', Joel Kotkin, *Forbes*, 23 August 2011.

17 Opening address by Mao Zedong at the First Plenary Session of the Chinese People's Political Consultative Conference, 21 September 1949.

18 International Monetary Fund, gross domestic product per capita, 2012, current international dollar, adjusting for Purchasing Power Parity.

19 Boston Consulting Group, 18 October 2012.

20 'Austerity is Here to Stay', Martin Kettle, *The Guardian*, 14 November 2012.

21 'Valuing patents', *The Economist*, 5 January 2013.

22 'Looking to 2060: Long term global growth prospects', OECD, November 2012.

23 'Pushing China's Limits on Web, if not on paper', Edward Wong, *New York Times*, 6 November 2011.

24 'The World Economy: A Millennial Perspective', Angus Maddison, Organisation for Economic Co-operation and Development, 2006. In 2012 the OECD forecast that China's share of global GDP in 2060 will only be 28 per cent (Looking to 2060, OECD Economic Policy Papers No 3, 2012).

25 *The Dragon's Gift*, Deborah Brautigam (Oxford University Press, Oxford), 2011.

26 See *King Leopold's Ghost*, Adam Hochschild (Pan, London), 1998.

27 Quoted in 'Tears of Rage', Peter Hays Gries, *China Journal*, No. 46, July 2001, p. 30.

28 Willam Gladstone, speech in House of Commons, 8 April 1840.

29 *The Story of A Soldier's Life*, Viscount Wolseley (Charles Scribner's Sons, Fifth Avenue), 1904, pp. 74-83

30 Quoted in *The Chan's Great Continent*, Jonathan Spence (W.W. Norton, New York), 1999, p. 151.

31 Quoted in *From the Ruins of Empire*, Pankaj Mishra (Allen Lane, 2012), p. 183.

32 'Patriotism with Chinese Characteristics', Li Chengpeng, *New York Times*, 25 May 2012.

33 'Modernization and History Textbooks', Yuan Weishi, *China Youth Daily*, Freezing Point supplement, 11 January 2006.

34 'A game of catch-up', *The Economist*, 24 September 2011.

35 'China Needs its Own Dream', Thomas Friedman, *New York Times*, 2 October 2012.

CONCLUSION, PP. 223–49

1 *The Travels of Mendes Pinto*, edited and translated by Rebecca Catz (University of Chicago Press, Chicago), 1989, pp. 231–2.

2 *The Farther Adventures of Robinson Crusoe*, Daniel Defoe, 1719, Chapter XIII.

3 'Super Bowl Ads: Peter Hoekstra's Hits a Nerve', Tim Mak, *Politico*, 2 May 2012.

4 Comment is free interview, Kwasi Kwarteng, Guardian website, 17 September 2012.

5 Conference speech, David Cameron, Birmingham, 10 October 2012.

6 'China: The World's Cleverest Country?', Sean Coughlan, BBC website, 9 May 2012.

7 'The Democratic Malaise', Charles Kupchan, *Foreign Affairs*, January/February 2012, p. 67.

8 Interview on BBC Radio 4 *Today* programme, 27 September 2012.

9 Quoted in *The Opium War*, Julia Lovell (Picador, London), 2011, p. 27.

10 *The Spirit of the Laws*, Montesquieu, 1748, Book XIX.

11 'Chinese Immigration: a Sociological Study', Gerrit L. Lansing, *Popular Science Monthly*, April 1882.

12 *The Chinese Are Like That*, Carl Crow (World Publishing, Cleveland), 1943, p. VII.

13 *When China Rules the World*, Martin Jacques (Allen Lane, London), 2009, p. 197.

14 'Interview with Dambisa Moyo', Brian Bethune, *Maclean's*, 4 June 2012.

15 *China's Silent Army*, Juan Pablo Cardenal & Heriberto Araujo (Allen Lane, London), 2013, p. 4.

16 *A Geography of International Relations*, Albert Rose (University of Dayton Press, US), 1965, p. 385.

17 *An Essay on the Principles of Population*, Thomas Malthus, Book I, Chapter XI, 6th edition, 1826.

18 Quoted in *An Essay on the Principles of Population*, Thomas Malthus, Book I, Chapter XI, 6th edition, 1826.

19 *The Unparalleled Invasion*, Jack London, 1910.

20 Quoted in *The Idea of China*, Andrew March (David & Charles, Devon), 1974, p. 108.

21 *The Chinese Mind*, Boye Lafayette De Mente (Tuttle, Vermont), 2009, p. 38.

22 Foreword to *Billions: Selling to the New Chinese Consumer*, Tom Doctoroff (Palgrave Macmillan, New York), 2005.

23 *The Unparalleled Invasion*, Jack London, 1910.

24 'Eight Ways China is Changing Your World', Angus Fraser, BBC website, 15 October 2012.

25 'High-stakes Choices for China's Leaders', Philip Stephens, *Financial Times*, 11 October 2012.

26 *The Travels and Controversies of Friar Domingo Navarrete*, London, 1960, quoted in Spence p. 38.

27 'Zhou's Cryptic Caution Lost In Translation', Richard McGregor, *Financial Times*, 10 June 2011.

28 *Why the West Rules for Now*, Ian Morris (Profile, London), 2010, p. 587.

29 'You Say Guanxi, I Says Schmoozing', *Bloomberg BusinessWeek*, 18 November 2007.

30 *Joining the Modern World*, Wang Gungwu (World Scientific Publishing Company, Singapore), 2000, p. 6.

31 *The Study of Sociology*, Herbert Spencer, 1873.

32 Crow, p. 106

33 *East and West*, Patten, p. 17.

34 Global Consumer Sentiment Survey, Boston Consulting Group, 14 May 2012.

35 *The Opium War*, Julia Lovell, 2011, p. 360.

36 See review of J. Hoberman in *Village Voice*, 17 August, 2004.

37 'Chinese Economic Performance in the Long Run', Angus Maddison, OECD, 2007.

38 'YueYue, Chinese Toddler Run Over in Street and Ignored, Dies', ABC News, 20 October 2011.

39 *China in Ten Words*, Yu Hua (Pantheon, New York), 2011

40 *On a Chinese Screen*, William Somerset Maugham (Vintage, London), 2000, pp. 149–150.

INDEX

abortions, 145
Adams, John Quincy, 231
Africa: China and, 197–9, 208–9, 233;
  Chinese in, 64, 67; colonization scheme,
  148, 164; Communists and, 53–4
Africans, in China, 67–71
Ai Weiwei, 76–7, 205, 248
American Civil War, 30, 130, 151
ancestor worship, 48
animals, suffering of, 9
Apple, 155–6, 204–5
Aquino, Corazon, 66
Arab Spring, 76–7
architecture, 1, 47–8
Aristotle, 77
army, Chinese, 80, 208
'Asian values', 16, 97–8
astronomy, 33
Australia, 208, 235
authors, imprisoned, 206

ba ling hou ('after eighties generation'), 141–2
baby milk formula, 180, 231, 245
Bangladesh, 160
banks, 176, 178, 183, 228, 247
Becker, Gary, 167
Becker, Jasper, 22
Beijing: anti-African riots, 54; anti-American
  protests, 210–11, 217; bus station scam,
  245–6; cancer rates, 181; Chaoyang
  Park confrontation, 95; clampdown on
  foreigners, 56; expenditure per student,
  117–18; housing, 175; Hutong alleyways,
  51; lifestyles, 143; pro-democracy
  demonstrations, 76–7; property values,
  184; see also Tiananmen Square
'Beijing consensus', 170
Beijing Olympics, 43, 51, 62, 73, 75, 211
Beijing University, 128
Belgrade, Chinese embassy bombing, 210–11
Bethune, Norman, 61
bicycles, 3
birth rates, 189, 163
Bismarck, Otto von, 59

Blair, Tony, 97
Blue Funnel Line, 139, 153
Bo Guagua, 123
Bo Xilai, 82–3, 90–2, 123
Bo Yang, 37–8
Boer War, 152
Bolsheviks, 84
Bolton, Anthony, 168
'book lamp fields', 107
Boston, pesticide advertisement, 11
Boxer Rebellion, 50, 55–6, 216, 225
Brazil, 119, 219
Bremerhaven, 216
Brighton, Royal Pavilion, 14
Britain, see United Kingdom
Britannia Unchained, 159
Buck, Pearl, 134
Buddha, 27–8
Buddhism, 27–9, 31–2, 44–5, 233
Buffett, Warren, 197
bureaucracy, imperial, 80, 84
Burma, 200
Bush, George, 203
Business Week magazine, 238

Cameron, David, 227–8
cannons, 33
Canton, 10, 33, 107, 132, 195, 214, 235; see also
  Guangzhou
Canton Tower, 181
Cantonese, 2, 23, 41
'Cantopop', 73
cao ni ma ('grass mud horses'), 94
capitalism, Chinese, 166–92, 229–30; and
  Chinese culture, 166–7; and current
  account surplus, 182–3; and demographics,
  189–91; and dollar assets, 182–3, 185, 205;
  and domestic consumption, 186–7, 191;
  and financial sector reform, 190, 205; and
  investment boom, 173–6, 183–6, 228; and
  mercantilism, 182–3, 185, 188, 191; and
  property boom, 184–6; and state-owned
  enterprises, 177–8, 204–5
  and wage levels, 188–91

carbon emissions reduction, 200, 220
Carlson, Evans, 133
Carrefour, boycott of, 211
Carrhae, battle of, 57
cartography, 33
Chaffee, John, 112
Chan, Gloria, 98
Chan, Jackie, 82, 100
Chang, Leslie, 128, 157
Chaozhou, 24
Charles II, King, 114
Chen Duxiu, 35, 87, 217
Chen Shui Bian, 98
Chen Weiming, 128
Chen Yonggui, 137
Chengdu, 174, 210–1
Chenggong, 174
Chiang Kai Shek, 2, 49, 52, 98, 152, 199, 239
child cruelty, 236
childbirth, deaths in, 172
children's toys, 171
Chin, Randy, 65
China: books about, 232, 235–6; civil war, 2,
    195–6, 199; dependence on US, 219–20;
    GDP per capita, 202, 243; Japanese
    occupation, 59, 195; 'Middle Kingdom',
    22
China Can Say No, 199
China Investment Corporation, 137, 156
China Labour Bulletin, 155–6
China Labour Watch, 157
Chinatowns, 2, 9
Chinese character, 5–11
Chinese diaspora, 62–7, 198; and democracy,
    98–9; and work ethic, 135
Chinese Exclusion Act (1882), 99, 151–2
Chinese Industrial Co-operatives, 133
Chinese Whispers (the game), 17–18
Chinoiserie, 14, 34
Chongqing province, 90–1, 241
Christianity, 22, 30–1, 43–5
Christmas decorations, 171
Chu, Judy, 99
Chua, Amy, 6, 110–11, 124–5, 236
Churchill, Winston, 30
cigarette lighters, 171
cinema, 39–40, 73, 206
civil liberties, 178
Cixi, Dowager Empress, 34, 50, 86
climate change, 170, 220
    see also global warming
Clinton, Bill, 168

Clinton, Hillary, 197, 208
clocks, 232
clothing, 31–2, 35
coffee, 42
collectivization, 136–7, 140, 144–5, 249
Communist Party, 16–17, 220; apologists
    for, 102; and command economy, 84,
    181; and Confucianism, 36–7; corruption
    in, 91–2; and cultural homogeneity,
    48; and democracy, 76, 79–81, 86–7;
    and economy, 177–8, 181–2, 185, 191;
    and education, 115–16, 127; and famine
    of late 1950s, 95; foundation of, 87;
    and imperialism, 197; legitimacy and
    meritocracy, 79; and nationalism, 211,
    217–19, 242–3; and overseas education,
    123; protests against, 87–91; and race, 61–3,
    74; unpopularity of, 242–4
compass, invention of, 83, 109
Confucianism (Confucian values), 22–3,
    26–8, 37–8, 41–5, 238, 241; and capitalism,
    167; Communists and, 36–7; educational
    philosophy, 106, 110–12, 119, 126; and
    foreign religions, 30–1; and political
    arrangements, 78–9, 85; and work ethic,
    137
Confucius: Analects, 43, 51, 75, 78; Mao's
    hatred of, 37; temples dedicated to, 45
Confucius Institutes, 42–3, 206
Congo, 149, 209, 219
Conservative politicians, 159–60, 227–8
constitution, post-1949, 87
coolie (the word), 147
copyright piracy, 190
corruption, 22, 89–92, 101, 237–8, 246, 249;
    in Communist Party, 91–2; and economy,
    178–9; and education, 116, 118, 129, 228,
    231
Crimean War, 194
Crocker, Charles, 131
Crocker, Edwin, 130–1
Crow, Carl, 12, 15, 133, 233–4, 239
Cuba, 147–8
Cultural Revolution, 37, 43, 84, 90, 163, 218,
    241; and education, 112–13
culture, Chinese, 19–51, 238–9; 'culturalism',
    21–2; and developmental backwardness,
    166–7; and linguistic diversity, 23–4, 40–1,
    49–51; and religious diversity, 27–31, 44–6;
    Westernization of, 39–40
currency, common, 26
cyber crime, 12, 240–1

Daily Mail, 7, 198
Dalai Lama, 32, 48, 241
Dalian, 96
Daoguang, emperor, 214
Daqing, 136
Darwin, Charles, 115, 148, 238
Datong, 180
Dazhai, 136–7, 140, 154
Defoe, Daniel, 224
democracy, 8, 17, 43, 48, 76–104, 238; and
  Arab Spring, 76–7; and 'Asian values',
  97–8; 'Confucian democracy', 79; and
  cyberspace, 94–6; gradualist approach to,
  102, 104; and grass-roots campaigns, 96–7;
  and nationalism, 217–18; pro-democracy
  demonstrations, 16, 38, 72–3, 75–7, 93,
  101, 240; Sun Yat Sen and, 86; and village
  elections, 88
Deng Xiaoping, 3, 16–17, 170, 201, 210;
  economic reforms, 102, 140, 181–2; and
  one-child policy, 190–1; and Tiananmen
  Square protests, 16–17, 93, 101
diabetes, 42
dialectical materialism, 77
Diamond, Jared, 20
Diaoyu islands, 210, 213
Dickens, Charles, 19–20, 46
Dikotter, Frank, 58, 155
Donald, Sir Alan, 240
Dongguan, 73, 128, 173
Doubting Antiquity School, 35
Dragon Throne, 86
Dream of the Red Chamber, 177
drinking water, 172
Du Halde, Jean-Baptiste, 20
Dubs, Homer Hasenphlug, 57
Duncan, Arne, 6

East China Sea, 200, 210, 221
East India Company, 139
Eastman, Lloyd, 79
economic growth, 169–73, 202–5, 241
economic liberalization, 80–1, 102–3, 140–1
Economist, The, 83, 201, 220
education, Chinese, 17, 105–29, 188, 228,
  249; Communist Party and, 115–16,
  127; and Cultural Revolution, 112–13;
  higher education, 113–14, 119, 121, 128;
  imperial system, 111–12; inequalities in,
  117–18; overseas education, 122–3; PISA
  assessments, 109, 118–19; reform of, 127–9;
  university research, 115, 229; and Western

education, 108–11, 121, 127–9; *see also*
  examinations; universities, Chinese
Egypt, 25
Eight Banners, 26
Emerson, Ralph Waldo, 21, 107
emigration, 92, 149
energy efficiency, 169, 180, 190, 220
English language, 129, 226
environmental protection, 180–1, 185, 220–1
ethnic minorities, 57, 60, 62, 68, 74–5
eugenics, 56
European clone towns, 47, 173
eurozone debt crisis, 137, 201
evolution, and race, 58–9, 63–4
examinations: Gao Kao, 105–6, 119–21, 125,
  127–9, 237, 241; imperial system, 26, 31,
  34, 106–8, 111–12, 119–20, 127, 129, 231, 237
exchange rates, 182–3
expatriates, in China, 69

Facebook, 94
Fair Labor Association (FLA), 157
Fairbank, John King, 21
Falun Gong, 31, 93
famine, 95, 141, 155, 234
Fen Qing ('angry youth'), 211, 213, 216, 242
Feng Shui, 48–9
Ferguson, Niall, 12, 79, 134, 160, 196–7
filial piety, 37, 44, 79
Financial Times, 77, 134, 169, 236
First World War, 35
flu virus, 246
food and diet, 41–2, 242
food scandals, 179–80, 246
foot-binding, 38–9, 233–4
Forbidden City, 32, 82, 216
foreign policy, Chinese, 200–1, 207–10
Fortune Global 500 companies, 172
Foshan, 7
Foxconn, 155–6, 163
Freezing Point, 218
French Revolution, 237
Freud, Sigmund, 232
fu er dai ('second generation rich'), 142
Fujian province, 96
Fukuyama, Francis, 83

Galton, Sir Francis, 148, 164
Gao Xingjian, 206
Gathering Storm, The, 229
Genghis Khan, 21, 31
George III, King, 33, 244

German South West Africa, 209, 219
Germany, 43, 59, 62, 109, 115, 197, 204, 229;
    Chinese territories, 35, 217; Nazi Germany,
    80, 231; savings rate, 187
Gladstone, William Ewart, 214
global financial crisis, 176, 182, 186, 191
Global Language Monitor, 5
global warming, 12, 220–1; *see also* climate
    change
Gok Wan, 8
gongye hezuoshe ('gung ho'), 133
Goodnow, Frank, 103–4
Gove, Michael, 108, 110, 113
Great Depression, 151, 169
Great Exhibition, 19
Great Leap Forward, 84, 145, 154–5, 218, 238
Great Wall of China, 18, 26, 38, 84, 131
Greece, 160, 202, 227
Gu Jiegang, 61
Guangdong Museum of Art, 89
Guangdong province, 24, 47, 87, 163, 175,
    213, 234, 243, 247; emigration from,
    1–2; Japanese occupation, 2, 101, 212;
    pollution, 181
Guangming Daily, 211
Guangxu, emperor, 34, 86
Guangzhou, 16, 30, 140, 144, 177, 179, 213,
    217; author's family in, 3–4, 171–2, 175,
    184, 188, 242; child labour accusations, 155;
    grass-roots campaigns, 96–7; Huai Sheng
    mosque, 29; Muslims in, 67; pollution,
    181; Xiaobei district ('Chocolate City'),
    67–8; *see also* Canton
Guangzhou international airport, 67–8
guanxi (family connections), 129, 237
Guanyin (goddess), 45
gunpowder, invention of, 83, 109
Guo Fenglian, 137
Guo Jingming, 92–3
guo lao si (deaths from overwork), 156
gwei lo ('ghost man'), 72

Haier, 204
Hainan Island, 57, 82, 211
Haining City, 96
Hakka people, 65
Hallstatt, 47, 173
Hamre, John, 168
Han Chinese, 29, 31–32, 60, 62; cultural and
    genetic diversity, 57–8
Han Dynasty, 22, 26, 35
Han Han, 81–2, 92, 121

Hankou, 195
Hart, Sir Robert, 195
Harte, Bret, 9
Harvard Girl, 122, 124
health care, 172, 175–6, 188, 190, 246
Hebei province, 174
HEG Electronics, 155
Hegel, G. W. F., 8, 77–8, 85
Henan province, 179
Herder, Johann Gottfried von, 46
Hero, 243
HIV, and blood donations, 246
Hobsbawm, Eric, 53
Hochoy, Sir Solomon, 65
Hoekstra, Peter, 226
Holcombe, Chester, 20
Holt, Alfred, 139, 153
Hong Kong, 3, 23, 31, 167, 247; British
    seizure of, 214; Chungking Mansions,
    68; and 'Greater China', 13; Kipling's
    impressions of, 132, 148–9, 193; and
    mainland Chinese, 40–1; music industry,
    73; and political reform, 99–100, 240;
    racism in, 55, 68, 71–2; return to China,
    99–100, 164; seamen, 139–40; working
    hours, 159, 161
Hong Xiuquan, 30, 106–7
Hongwu, emperor, 84
Hou Dejian, 52–3, 75, 245
housing, 174–5
Hu Jintao, 87, 196, 201
hu kou registration system, 157
Hu Shi, 29
Hu Yaobang, 93
Huangpu River, 180
Hubei province, 105
Huc, Abbé, 10, 21, 35
Hui Muslims, 67, 117
Huie Kin, 154
human rights, 17, 48, 93–4, 97, 207
Human Rights Watch, 198, 209
Hume, David, 132, 167
Hunan province, 25, 71; Mao's birthplace,
    90, 243
Hundred Days Reform Movement, 86–7
Huntingdon, Samuel, 45, 79
Hurun Report, 122–3
Huxley, Thomas, 59
'hydraulic empire' hypothesis, 80, 84

Idle, Eric, 15
imperialism, Chinese, 197

income inequalities, 89–90
'indemnities', 195
Independent Chinese Pen Center, 206
India, 27, 29, 127, 137, 149, 201, 219, 233
Indian Mutiny, 194
Indianapolis Times, 150
Indians, 72, 137, 147
Indochina, 234
Indonesia, 66, 160
Industrial & Commercial Bank of China, 172
infant mortality, 172
'inscrutability', Chinese, 236
intelligence services, 80
Interlaken, 173
Internet, Chinese: and nationalism, 211–13; and political dissent, 94–7; and racism, 54, 71, 73, 75
iPhones, 155–6
Iran, 200, 209
'iron rice bowl', 188
irrigation works, 80, 84
Islam, 29–30, 44–5; *see also* Muslims

Jacques, Martin, 55–6, 169, 233–4
Jamaicans, 65
James, Preston, 235
Japan, 36, 115, 170, 208, 243; and Chinese nationalism, 59–60; disputes with China, 200–1, 210, 221; industrialization, 142, 187; Meiji Restoration, 50; and Qing China, 49–51; war crimes, 211–13; wars and invasions, 35, 50, 59, 195, 211–13, 216–17, 243
Japanese: anti-Japanese protests, 210–13, 217, 241–3; in China, 68; reputation for laziness, 142
jeans, 163, 171
Jet Li, 243
Jiang Fangzhou, 94
Jiang Rong, 43
Jiang Zemin, 25, 123
Jiangxi province, 116, 174, 223
Jiazhou Bay bridge, 174
Jin Dynasty, 26
Jin Liqun, 137, 156, 162
Jinggangshan University, 116
'John Chinaman', 11
Jung Wo Lei, 1–3, 17, 23, 172, 175, 234

Kagan, Robert, 81, 197
Kaiping, 2, 163

Kang Youwei, 85–6
Kangxi, emperor, 45
Kazakhstan, 200
Kearney, Denis, 150–2, 154
ken lao zu ('bite the old folks'), 141
Kennan, George, 10, 15
Kenya, 209, 219
kidnapping, 247
King, Stephen, 197
Kipling, Rudyard, 10, 132, 136, 148, 193–4, 196, 236
Kissinger, Henry, 20, 22, 97
Koizumi, Junichiro, 213
Korea, 34; *see also* North Korea; South Korea
Kotkin, Joel, 12, 198
kowtowing, 78, 232
Kristof, Nicholas, 110
Kuang Kuang's Diary, 122
Kublai Khan, 30, 192
Kupchan, Charles, 81, 168, 229–30
Kwarteng, Kwasi, 227–8
Kynge, James, 138, 146

labour: child labour, 155; coolie labour, 146–54, 165; forced labour, 78, 80, 140; slave labour, 26, 84, 247
labour laws, 156–7
Lamb, Charles, 41
land reform, 190
Landman, Margot, 108
languages and dialects, 23–4, 40–1, 49–51
Lansing, Gerrit, 53, 233
lao gai (prison camps), 164
Lazarus, Emma, 152
Lazy Mutha Fucka (LMF), 73
Lee, Bruce, 73
Lee Kuan Yew, 16, 97–8, 137
Leibniz, Gottfried Wilhelm, 14, 224
Lenin, V. I., 17, 48
Lenovo, 204
Leopold II, King, 149, 209
Leung Kwok Hung, 100
Li Chengpeng, 218
Li Jianli, 210, 212
Li Qiang, 157
Lian Si, Professor, 114
Liang Qichao, 86, 216–17
Lin, Justin Yifu, 15–16
Lin Zexu, 107, 214
Lincoln, Abraham, 51
Lignan Group, 177
Liqian, 57

literacy, 118, 127
Liu Mingfu, Colonel, 208
Liu Shaokum, 164
Liu Shaoqi, 36
Liu Xiaobo, 73, 93, 244
Liu Xiaoming, 166
Liu Yiting, 122, 124
Liverpool, 139–40, 153, 164
London, Jack, 10, 20, 133, 138, 152, 154, 235–6
London Missionary Society, 22
Los Angeles, lynching of Chinese, 151
Loti, Pierre, 216
Lou Jing, 54, 70, 72–3
Lou Ye, 206
Louis XIV, King, 45
Louis XV, King, 14
Louis XVI, King, 237, 244
Lovell, Julia, 242
Lowes Dickinson, Goldsworthy, 225–6
Lu Guanqiu, 178
Lu Xun, 36–7
Lushan, 246

Ma Yan, 116–17, 126
Macao, 147
McCarthy, Senator Joseph, 240
Macartney, Lord, 33, 46, 232
Malaysia, 66, 99, 113
male–female ratio, 145–6, 239
Malthus, Thomas, 234–5
Manchu script, 32
Manchuria, 32, 59, 136, 235
Manchus, 57, 60; and Qing Dynasty, 21, 32, 34, 60, 112, 233–4
Mandarin, 23, 41, 49, 206, 226
mandarins, 83, 106
manners, changing, 40
manufacturing: domestic, 162; global, 171; low-cost, 203–4
Mao Zedong, 2, 16, 52, 69, 196, 210; and Africa, 53–4; and autocracy, 80, 83–5; his birthplace, 90, 243; and Chinese superpower status, 199
and collectivization, 144; death of, 43, 182, 199; and economy, 181, 188, 199; and education, 112, 121; and language teaching, 49
'Little Red Book', 89–90, 136; nostalgia for, 89–90; personality cult, 84, 90; and race, 61–2; rejection of Confucianism, 36–7; and 'Who lost China?' debate, 239–41; and work ethic, 135–7, 140, 154, 165

marriage market, 145
marriages, mixed ethnicity, 71
Marx, Karl, 17, 77–8
Matheson, Donald, 231
Maugham, William Somerset, 78, 194, 249
May Fourth Movement, 35, 43, 87, 217, 244
Mazzini, Giuseppe, 59
Meadows, Thomas Taylor, 107
Mencius, 36, 85
Merkel, Angela, 213
Mexico, 127, 160, 164
Miao people, 57
middle classes, 80–1, 89, 94, 123
military capacity, Chinese, 200, 207–8
Mill, John Stuart, 46, 224
millionaires, 89, 92, 122
Ming Dynasty, 26, 29, 33, 78, 85, 216, 230, 244; dietary revolution, 41–2; isolationism, 49, 216
Mission Impossible, 40
missionaries, 7, 11–12, 22, 30, 33, 45–7, 78, 131–2, 194, 224, 230, 233
Mo Yan, 206
Mobo Gau, 37
Mongolia, 15, 57, 59, 174
Mongols, 21, 26, 30–2, 57
Montesquieu, 10, 22, 77–8, 85, 231, 233
Morecambe Bay cockle pickers, 158
Morris, Ian, 196, 237
Morrison, Robert, 22
Mount Lu, 223
Moyo, Dambisa, 169, 234
Mu, Eric, 121
Mubarak, Hosni, 76
Mugabe, Robert, 102
Muhammad, Prophet, 29
Mukai, Lieutenant Toshiaki, 212
Murong Xuecun, 179, 206
Muslims, 29, 32, 45, 48
  Hui Muslims, 67, 117
Mystery, 206

'naked officials', 92
Nanjing: anti-African riots, 54; Japanese occupation, 212
Napier, William, 132
Napoleon Bonaparte, 195
National Basketball Association, 39
National People's Congress, 91
nationalism, 35, 51, 210–19, 242–5; and political reform, 216–18, 242–3

Nationalist Party, 103
Navarrete, Friar Domingo, 14, 106, 224, 236
Ndesandjo, Mark Okoth Obama, 71
Needham, Joseph, 83–4
'Neocomms', 199–200, 207–8, 217
nepotism, *see* corruption
Nestorians, 30
New Culture Movement, 86
New Life Movement, 49
New Scientist, 109
New York Times, 110, 135, 155
Newton, Isaac, 114
Ng, Mee Ling, 98–9
Nigeria, 209
night schools, 128–9
Ningxia province, 117
Nisbet, Sarah, 108, 121
Nixon, Richard, 20, 203, 236–7
Noda, Lieutenant Tsuyoshi, 212
noodles, 247
North Korea, 69, 85, 200, 208, 242
nuclear weapons, 208, 220
numeracy, 127
Nye, Joseph, 205

Obama, Barack, 71, 111, 196, 244
Obama, Michelle, 71
obesity, 42
oil prices, 220
Old Summer Palace, 33
one-child policy, 17, 56, 74, 93, 126, 141, 145,
   163, 237, 247; and economy, 188–91
opium, 2, 46, 214–15, 231
Opium Wars, 2, 33–4, 46, 214–15, 231–2
'oracle bones', 25
Ordos, 174
Orwell, George, 134

Pakistan, 208
Palmerston, Lord, 232
Pan Chenguang, 114
Pan Wei, 82
Pan Yue, 181
Panama, 180
paper, invention of, 109
parenting, reform of, 124
patents, 115, 204
Patten, Chris, 99, 240
Paxman, Jeremy, 6, 81
Pearl River, 96
Peking duck, 42
'Peking Man', 63

Peking University, 113
Penang, 132
pensions, 188, 190
people smugglers (snakeheads), 158
'perankans', 66
Pereira, Galeote, 11
Peru, 147–8
Philippines, 66, 201
Physiocrats, 14
physiognomy, Chinese, 13
pigtails, 32, 150, 153, 233–4
Pinto, Mendes, 223–4
pinyin, 50
ploughshare, invention of, 83
police, 72, 80, 88
pollution, 173, 180–1, 190, 246
Polo, Marco, 13–14, 30, 192
pop music and culture, 73
population: growth in, 42, 145, 233–5; size of,
   11–13, 16–17; working, 163–4
pork, 41, 66
Porritt, Jonathon, 169, 180
Prato, 138, 146
Prémare, Joseph de, 131–2, 235
Premier League football, 40
printing, invention of, 83, 109
Programme for International Student
   Assessment (PISA), 109, 118–19
property boom, 184–6
Putin, Vladimir, 102, 200
Putonghua ('common speech'), 49
Pye, Lucian, 53, 64, 78

Qi Gong exercise, 247
Qianlong, emperor, 32–3, 46, 232
Qin Dynasty, 25–6, 49
Qin Shi Huang, emperor, 25–6, 83–5
Qing Dynasty, 32–4, 37, 45, 60–1, 85, 203,
   216, 233–4, 244; cultural isolation, 49–50;
   diet under, 242; education system, 112, 129
   end of, 1–2, 26, 35, 83, 104; and Japan,
   49–51; and Opium Wars, 214–15; racism
   under, 56, 58; and Taiping Rebellion, 30,
   106–7
Qingdao, 135, 174, 211
Quesnay, François, 78

race and racism, 8, 13, 52–75, 150–4, 238–9,
   244–5; and Communist nationalism, 61–3;
   in Hong Kong, 55, 68, 71–2; racial slurs,
   68; 'scientific' racism, 58–9, 63–4, 74, 238
racial diversity, 56–8

railway workers, 130–1, 138–9, 151
railways, Chinese, 97, 175, 193
Ranke, Leopold von, 46
rare earth metals, 200
Reagan, Roland, 197
Red Chinese Battle Plan, 196
Red Guards, 90, 113–14
reform movement, late imperial, 50, 85–7
religious diversity and tolerance, 27–31, 44–6
renminbi, 182–3; as global reserve currency, 169, 205
resource poverty, 209–10, 234
restaurants, 'red', 90
retirement homes, 44
Ricci, Matteo, 78
Rice, Condoleezza, 54, 71, 73
River Elegy, 38, 244
Rizal, José, 66
roads, 26, 162, 170–1, 175
Rohmer, Sax, 9, 194
Romney, Mitt, 227–8
Royal Society, 109, 114–15
Russell, Bertrand, 9–10, 20, 53, 225–6
Russell, Lord, 149
Russia, 80, 82, 84, 102, 200, 219

sailors, Chinese, 139–40, 153
Samsung, 155
San Francisco, 154
Sanskrit, 28
Sarkozy, Nicolas, 201
Saudi Arabia, 102
Sautman, Barry, 69–70
savings, 183, 187–8, 190
Schleicher, Andreas, 109–10, 118, 228
scholars, castration of, 84
science, 83–4, 115, 229
Second World War, 101, 139–40, 152–3, 212–13
self-censorship, 94, 206
selfishness, 81
Shaanxi province, 60
Shamian island, 179
Shandong province, 217
Shang Dynasty, 25, 35
Shanghai, 12, 34, 139, 180, 184, 213, 241; anti-African riots, 54
   Anting German Town, 173; Bund, 195; construction sites 134; expenditure per student, 117–18; femmes fatales, 32; French Concession, 48; housing, 175; language, 40–1; lifestyles, 143; pensioners in, 247–8;

pro-democracy demonstrations, 76–7
schoolchildren, 106, 109, 118; Thames Town, 47, 173; Waibaidu Bridge, 39; Xintiandi shopping district, 177, 187
Shanghai Cooperation Organisation, 200
Shanxi province, 136, 180
Shaoshan (Mao's birthplace), 90, 243
Sheffield, 3, 64, 146
Shen Wenrong, 178
Shenyang, 138
Shenzhen, 134, 155, 173, 241
Shenzhen Museum, 100–1
Shi Huang highway, 174
Shifang, 96
Shukman, David, 109
Si Ma Qian, 35, 84
Siberia, 235
Sichuan earthquake, 164, 180, 218, 228
Sichuan province, 42, 96, 174
Silk Road, 27, 63–4
Sin, Cardinal, 66
Singapore, 121, 132, 139, 167; and 'Greater China', 13; oppressive regime, 97, 99; working hours, 159, 161
'Sinicization', 58
slave trade, abolition of, 147
slimming products, 39
Slovakia, 113
Smith, Adam, 10
Smith, Arthur Henderson, 13, 47, 132, 163, 194
smugglers, 51; *see also* people smugglers
soft power, 205–7
Song Dynasty, 26, 38, 112
Song Jiaoren, 103
sorghum, 41
Sorrell, Sir Martin, 134, 236
South Africa, 152–3
South China Sea, 221
South Korea, 110, 126, 174, 187, 208
Southeast Asia Extension islands, 234
sovereign wealth funds, 137, 204
Soviet Union, 16, 82, 127–8, 136, 169, 219
space exploration, 230
Spence, Jonathan, 224
Spencer, Herbert, 59, 238
Sri Lanka, 164, 202
Stalin, Joseph, 85
state-owned enterprises, 177–8, 204–5
steel production, 171
Steinbeck, John, 152
sterilization, forced, 93

stirrup, invention of, 83
stock market, Chinese, 177
Su Shi, 223, 245
Sudan, 209
suicides, 155
Summer Palace, 33, 194, 215
Sun Liping, 89
Sun Yat Sen, 31, 35, 47, 49, 103; and provisional constitution, 86; and racial purity, 53, 56, 59–61, 74; 'Three Principles of the People', 51, 59, 217
superstitions, 48–9
Susman, Louis, 166
Swift, Jonathan, 223
Syria, 200

Tai Jing highway, 174
Taiping Rebellion, 30, 106–7
Taiwan, 15–16, 23; and democracy, 98; and 'Greater China', 13; military intervention in, 198; parenting reform, 124; and racial unity, 52–3; and work ethic, 141–2; working hours, 161
Taiyuan, 157
Tajikistan, 200
talent contests, 40, 54, 70
Tan Sitong, 45
Tang Dynasty, 26, 29, 41, 65
Taoism, 22–3, 28, 31, 45
Tarim mummies, 63–4
tea, 41–2
Tejero, Luis, 8
telescopes, 232
temples, 44–5
terracotta warriors, 26
textbooks, 58, 211, 213–14, 218
Thailand, 66, 160, 167
Thatcher, Margaret, 3
Theroux, Paul, 9
Tiananmen Square, 82–3, 239
Tiananmen Square protests, 16–17, 73, 75, 77, 88, 93–4, 101, 240, 245
Tianjin, 106
Tibet, 32, 48, 59, 62, 93, 211, 241
Tibetans, 57
Times, The, 46
Toishanese, 23–4
Tojo, General Hideki, 212
Tong Chee Kiong, 66
torture, 93
trade unions, ban on, 99, 156, 158, 168
'tributary system', 32–3

Trinidad and Tobago, 65
Turkey, 127
Twain, Mark, 132, 135, 147
Twitter, 94

Uighurs, 57, 62–3
ultrasound screening, 145
UN peacekeeping missions, 221
UN Security Council, 200
unemployment insurance, 188
Unhappy China, 199
United Kingdom: child labour, 142–3; Chinese in, 3, 64–5, 98–9, 152–3, 158; Chinese students in, 122, 124; economic productivity, 204; GDP per capita, 202, 243; property values, 184; racism, 69, 152–3; work ethic, 159–61
United States of America: attitudes to China, 134; Chinese in, 64–5, 98–9, 147, 149–54; Chinese students in, 122, 124; Chinese workers in, 130–1, 138–9; dependence on China, 219–20; economic decline, 172; financial assets, 183, 193; GDP per capita, 202, 243; military capacity, 208, 219; percentage of global output, 205; political advertising, 226–7; racism, 69–70, 75, 150–4; railroads, 130–1, 138–9; 'Who lost China?' debate, 239–40; work ethic, 159–61; see also Chinese Exclusion Act
universities, Chinese, 113–16, 128, 229
urbanization, 170, 186
Urumqi, 62
US Chamber of Commerce in China, 156
Uzbekistan, 200

vaccines, 172
Verbiest, Ferdinand, 33
Veriah, Harinder, 55, 72
Versailles Treaty, 217
Victoria, Queen, 196, 204
Vietnam, 201, 208, 226
Voltaire, 14, 21, 31, 107, 167, 224

Waley-Cohen, Joanna, 33, 46
Walter, Carl, 178
Wang Gungwu, 60, 238
Wang Jingxi, 136
Wang Lijun, 91
Wang Qianyuan, 211
Wang Xiaodong, 217
Wang Yang, 88

Wang Yue, 7, 245–6
wars of religion, 44
Washington consensus, 170
Washington Post, 47
Water Margin, 28
water resources, 169, 181, 221
Watts, Jonathan, 12
Weber, Max, 133, 166–7
wedding dresses, 39
Weeks, Sheldon, 137, 140–1
Wei Shangjin, Professor, 145–6
Weibo, 94–5
weights and measures, 26
welfare spending, 188, 227–8
Wen Hsiang, 195
Wen Jibao, 42, 87
Wenzhou, 97, 171
white goods, 171–2
Wilhelm II, Kaiser, 197, 216
Wittfogel, Karl, 80, 83–4, 231
Wolseley, Field Marshal Sir Garnet Joseph, 194, 215
women: shortage of, 145–6, 239; and work, 134, 144, 157
work, as punishment, 164
work ethic, Chinese, 130–65, 227–8; and challenge to the West, 159–65
    under Communists, 136–7, 140, 144–5, 154–5; and generational shifts, 141–4, 163–4; and income levels, 143, 157, 161–2, 164
    and internal migration, 146, 163; and 'middle-income trap', 162
    and piecework, 163; and productivity, 160–2; and strikes and protests, 138–40, 154, 157, 228; and work–life balance, 144
workers' conditions, 155–8
working hours, 159–63
working population, size of, 163–4
writing system, Chinese, 23, 26, 49–50
Wu language, 40–1
Wuhan, 54
Wukan protests, 87–90
Wusong, 34
Xi Jinping, 24–5, 123, 236
Xia Dynasty, 25, 35

Xiamen chemicals plant, 96
Xi'an, 26, 30, 210, 212
Xie Tingfeng, 73
Xing Wei College, 128
Xinjiang province, 29, 48, 57, 62–3
Xue Jinbo, 88

Yan Fu, 59
Yan Sun, 70
Yan Xuetong, 198–9, 207, 221
Yan'an, 135
Yang, Martin, 135
Yang Rui, Professor, 55, 115, 129
Yangzhou, 30
Yao Ming, 39
Yasukuni shrine, 213
Yellow Emperor, cult of, 24–5, 60, 63
Yellow River, 38, 51, 84
Yu Dan, 43
Yu Hua, 40, 90, 247
Yu Keping, 39, 102
Yuan Dynasty, 26, 29, 31
Yuan Shikai, 103–4
Yuan Weishi, 214, 218
Yunnan province, 29, 174

Zambia, 197–8, 209
Zau Chernggong, 2
Zau Gasam, 2, 50
Zeng Guofan, 30
Zhan Minxuan, Professor, 129
Zhang Xiaobo, 145–6
Zhang Yimou, 40, 206, 243
Zhao Jing (Michael Anti), 95
Zhao Xing, 144
Zhejiang province, 27, 96, 171
Zheng Guanying, 85–6
Zheng He, Admiral, 29, 49, 230
Zhou, Raymond, 72
Zhou Enlai, 74, 236–7
Zhou Qifeng, 123
Zhoukoudian, 63
Zhuang people, 57
Ziamen, 34
Zimbabwe, 200